The Year Ahead 2002

The Year Ahead 2002

Susan Miller

Creator of Astrology Zone ®

BARNES
&NOBLE
BOOKS
NEW YORK

This book is dedicated to the men and women who have worked so hard to help me in dozens of ways make AstrologyZone.com what it is today:

Kerry Eielson, Tom Warmbrodt, Joe Warmbrodt, Jenn Warmbrodt, Edward Rubinstein, Randall Crane, Dawna Shuman, Soozy Goldfarb Miller, Michael Pilla, and Anne Estes,

I am grateful for each, for their fine advice and good cheer, and most of all, for their unending faith in me and to my continuing endeavor, AstrologyZone.com.

I send my thanks and heartfelt appreciation to one and all.

Susan Miller

CONTENTS

A WARM HELLO FROM SUSAN MILLER

If you are reading this book, you are curious about the future. In my experience, curious people have a much more creative approach to their lives. They seem to do everything with special flair, and are prone to enjoy life more as a result. Creative people — and by that I mean those who are open to life's possibilities, not necessarily artists — tend to take an active role in shaping their lives.

You are exactly that kind of person, and this book has been written for you. In *The Year Ahead 2002*, we will delve into the cycles that will affect your sign in the twelve months to come. Knowing in advance which areas will be most affected by the trends in your sign can help you make the best of what the universe has to offer.

The Truth About Astrology

"Fate" does not play a role in astrology, although that's a common misconception. Astrology is the study of cycles, some of which bring happy, rewarding episodes and opportunities; others bring challenging conditions that force us to change. Ultimately, we have to take full responsibility for the outcome of our lives. Astrology is not a religion, nor does it try to replace traditional religion. In fact, your faith and deepest beliefs, your feelings about morals and ethics are reflected in the horoscope's ninth house.

1

Change, of course, is our only constant, for the planets are continually on the move. Some cycles repeat, while some are so rare that they are literally once in a lifetime occurrences. One thing is certain: on the day you were born, the ten heavenly bodies were in a formation never to be repeated in the sky, making your talents and qualities truly unique. The thing I love about astrology is that there are no "right" or "wrong" choices — only ones that are right for you. Astrology gives you control; how you use it and what results are, in large part, up to you.

Take Note of Special Dates

Many readers copy the dates I list into their personal calendars. It helps to know which dates favor what kinds of activities, when one should choose to initiate an endeavor, or when to hold back. It's also fun to see if opportunity comes knocking on the special dates I list. Life is a wonderful laboratory that continues to give us information. We have an infinite capacity to learn if we just pay attention to what we see. Astrology gives you a formal structure within which to assess all areas of your life.

When you read your report for *The Year Ahead 2002,* you will note that I put your present life in the context of where you've been as well as where you are likely to be headed. In order to understand the future, we need to look back from where we came. Because astrology's underpinnings are mathematics, we can go backwards or forwards in time, analyzing trends that occurred in the past to understand why we made certain decisions, and in planning for the future. Knowing which areas of our lives will be favored (or not) at certain points in the future makes it easier to prioritize in the present.

While we can't control everything in life, we can control a large part of it. We can at least craft a thoughtful response to those conditions we find difficult or challenging. The axiom is true that states that it is not what happens to us that matters, but how we react to those conditions. Numerous times I have seen events that could initially be labeled as "bad" but turn out to be true blessings in disguise. Studying astrology helps you see the value in *all* that happens and helps you generate innovative ideas about how to deal with life's challenges.

My Website, Astrology Zone

I love to delve deeply into life's possibilities — you probably already know that about me if you are familiar with my website, *Astrology Zone*. Writing for *Astrology Zone* each month is one of my life's great joys. In creating *Astrology Zone* back in December 1995, my goal was to write a report each month that would be highly detailed and easy to read, conversational in style. Happily, on the Internet and in new electronic mediums like eBooks, I have all the room I need to explain the planetary configurations — something that's not always possible with the traditional print media.

To supplement your copy of *The Year Ahead 2002*, pick up your free monthly horoscope reports from my web site, *Astrology Zone,* at www.astrologyzone.com. Each report would further explain the trends I forecast in your Overview.

In addition to your monthly report on my web site, browse the personality section called "Life and Love." In it are many fun and informative articles that should resonate with you and those you love. The site will also teach you about the various planets and their cycles. I write all my own material, so if you like what you read here, you will probably like my web site. All my articles on *Astrology Zone* are free of charge, and are updated regularly.

If you like what you read and want to stay in touch, please also sign up for my free mailing list. (Your email address will not be sold, as I believe cyber-privacy is very important.) You will receive free monthly newsletters that give you late breaking news, analysis on world events, a calendar of appearances and lectures on the astrology circuit, dates of book signings (I'm also an author; more on that later) and on important days to watch for every month.

One little hint: If you know your "rising sign" (also called the "ascendant"), read the forecasts for that as well as for your Sun sign (the sign that people are most familiar with). This will give you a more complete picture of what's going on in your life. Your rising sign is as relevant to who you are as your Sun sign. This is true on my site, in this book, or whenever you read any astrological material by any author. The rising sign is determined by the exact time, date and place of your birth. Don't worry if you don't know yours yet. You will still be put at an enormous advantage by reading your Sun sign in this book. If you would like to get your horoscope chart done to know your rising sign, there are many sites that offer this on the Internet. Some chart services are free, while others ask a small charge. I strongly recommend looking into it.

You may like to know something more about me. I am an accredited astrologer and a professional writer. As a contributing editor to *Self* magazine, I write on astrology every month for a national readership; I was also recently named a contributor to *Teen* magazine, to begin this

4

spring. My newest book, *Planets and Possibilities*, was just released by Warner Books (2001). Available in hardcover and paperback, my book can be found at any Barnes & Noble retail store or online at www.bn.com.

A Brief Bio: My Beginnings as An Astrologer

Looking back, the fact that I became a full-time, professional astrologer came as a surprise. Even though my mother was an astrologer and I showed an early interest in it, I was discouraged from pursuing a career in this field. Nobody in my family wanted me to learn astrology, least of all my mother. Nothing suggested I would choose this course — I majored in business in college and had other plans. I suppose what a friend once told me is true: "Astrology has a way of choosing you, rather than the other way around." That is exactly what happened to me.

My interest in the subject began in earnest when I was 14. As it would happen, my mother would teach me everything I know about the subject — but not until later. "A little knowledge is dangerous," she would warn, an admonishment I have heard more than once. "Why not let me answer any questions you have?" she would ask. Being an astrologer herself, she understood all too well the responsibility an astrologer has to her public to be accurate and to communicate clearly, lest there be a misunderstanding.

As a girl, my mother kept her knowledge of astrology to herself. She never told anyone all she knew, and she advised me to do the same. She never charged a fee to do charts for people. Instead, she kept her practice to reading charts of interested family members, always with astonishing accuracy. When my uncle was missing as a soldier in World War II (before I was born) she calculated the exact day and hour that my father would hear the good news that Uncle Peter was alive and well. It turned out she was exactly right, and her prediction seemed even more remarkable when my father learned that my uncle had been part of the Normandy invasion (the reason why the letters stopped for so long) and only he and one other soldier in his platoon survived.

From then on, my mother tells me, my father stopped teasing her about her interest in astrology. Growing up, I never once heard my father disparage my mother. He would just say that he didn't understand how astrology worked and that he had to admit, my mother certainly knew her craft. He acknowledged to me that it wasn't necessary to know why planes fly or precisely how penicillin works to enjoy the benefits. Bless his heart. He never ceased to amaze me.

When I was pressing my mother to teach me astrology at age 15, she said she felt that any understanding of the subject would require intensive learning. She said it would take twelve years of careful study just to grasp the basics and even then, she felt, I would only have scratched the surface. "Better to know nothing at all then just a little," she would say. She was right, of course, but you rarely understand your mother's wisdom when you are a teenager. Tell a teenager not to do something, and of course, that's what they will do!

Lots of Time to Read:
Early Years Were Spent in Hospitals

During that period of my life, I was very ill due to problems with a congenital defect to my leg. While recuperating, a process that took three years (one of which was spent in a hospital), I was completely immobile, had zero social life, and had plenty of time to think. Of course, I wanted answers. I particularly wanted to know if I would ever walk again, as a main nerve was severed in my left leg in a then-recent surgery. I had so many surgeries during my sophomore year of high school that I had to drop out. Virtually all my education was self-taught. I took all the state exams and SATs at home with a Board of Education monitor. I lost no time, and after skipping a few years of high school, I entered college at 16.

My mother, being the eternal optimist, kept telling me my ordeal was a gift, and that I would be grateful for having had the experience later in life. She said it was a valuable time of "character building." As wild as this sounded, she was right. It would take some time for me to understand this. My mother has had a profoundly positive effect on my view of life. I believe that all things happen for a reason, and that we can find goodness and miracles everywhere.

I did keep my promise to my mother to study astrology with her for twelve years, which today seems astounding. When you are 14 or 15, twelve years is about double your present life! It was the only way she would help me, and my thirst for learning was so strong, I figured, ok, I am up to this challenge. It is only now that I realize why she was so insistent that I take things slow and meditate on each point. It is easy to speed along when you begin astrology, but if you go too quickly you miss the nuances — which, in astrology as in life, distinguish white from black.

At the same time, I pursued degrees and got a job. My first profession was publishing. After working in magazines for a time, I decided I wanted to have my own business, and started a business of representing photographers, because I love photography. Over the course of ten years, I made many friends in the industry. When one of my client friends would go through a hard time, I would look at their horoscope and together we would generate some ideas about the various solutions that were open to them. My friends always encouraged me to write what I was saying, and I started a column with a very small magazine. Still, astrology was more a personal interest than a vocation.

Art director friends and other executives began adding my telephone number to their auto-dial functions of their phones and ringing me up whenever they needed help or advice. In June of 1992, due to an eclipse, I broke my femur (thigh bone) for the third time in my life (the same leg I had problems with earlier). The incident led to another year of recovery in bed, but turned out to be a very defining moment. I had no idea how far-reaching that point in time would turn out to be.

While I recuperated through another bout with my leg, I turned to writing about astrology while I remained in my photography business. After all, I had plenty of time to write, being bed-ridden! I was surprised that the magazine editors liked my style, and in no time I had a column for *McCall's* and a few months later *Self*. I never imagined I would ever be writing! About a year later, Time Warner urged me to take it further. They said, "Let's give you a place on our website." That was how *Astrology Zone* was born, and it changed everything. I got serious about astrology. It's been my love, work and life ever since.

Do You Want to Learn Astrology?

If you'd like to learn about how astrology works and don't

have an astrologist for a Mom as I did, I would be happy to teach you personally. You can take a free online class with me on the Barnes & Noble University web site. I teach an introductory class that lasts five weeks, with two lessons a week, and that requires no previous knowledge of the subject. The class encompasses eight lessons and five sublessons that you can easily print out for future reference, and even share with friends. There are lots of classes you can choose from on the Barnes & Noble site. (It is fun to look through them all!) Mine is under the section entitled "Life Improvement." Just go to: www.barnesandnobleuniversity.com

If you are very busy, remember, you don't have to "be" in a classroom at any given time. The lesson posts are held in a virtual classroom in cyberspace. You can pick up your lessons any time that is convenient to you. (Barnes & Noble will send you a note twice a week to let you know exactly when each lesson is posted. If you happen to be away on a trip, your lessons will be up all month, so you can still pick them up when you get back.) It's a very convenient way to learn. Turn on your computer and press print, staple the notes together and read them on the way to work in the morning! Do it on your own time.

If you have a question after reading your lesson or about anything you read in this book, you can post a note to me on the class bulletin board. I come by several times a week to read the students' messages, and all the students can read all the posts. The more you post, the more everyone gains. There are no tests, no grades, and there's no worry of being late. Any time you stop by is the right time. You'll have a chance to meet people with like interests. It's so much fun being stimulated by interesting conversation. If you feel you want to take a class again, just sign up again! It will always be free, and the material and methods of teaching vary!

Thank You, Dear Reader

Thank you for taking the time to order this book. I hope you enjoy your forecast. Please share with me any suggestions you have for how to make future books better.

Each year brings us a chance to gain greater wisdom, resolve and understanding, through experiences we have and people we encounter. Every day holds possibilities for new, meaningful relationships. We get to re-establish the old ties, and continue to learn from the people we know and love. We evolve, we mature, and no matter how old we are, we continue to grow. That is the gift we call life, and it is a very precious one, indeed.

I wish you the very best in the bright New Year ahead, dear reader! I also look forward to keeping in touch with you on the net! See you there!

Sincerely,
Susan Miller

2002 THE YEAR AHEAD:
A YEAR OF ACTION

2002 will be a kinder and gentler year than 2001. The planets that orbit on the very outer rim of our solar system — Pluto, Neptune, Uranus, Jupiter, and Saturn — will hold remarkably stable, upbeat placements in the heavens for most of the year. These planets are the most powerful planets in the sky, for in moving so very slowly through the constellations they stay in each sector long enough to yield influence. They impart their messages in a very deliberate, memorable way.

Typically, a new year yields a plethora of planetary aspects, some good, some not-so-good, all rolling toward us pell-mell. We digest the news they deliver as best as we can. This year is unusual in that it holds only one difficult configuration in late May — the third and final opposition of Saturn to Pluto. (The first two we've already had experience with.) Though tough, this aspect is outweighed by highly positive planetary energy. Undoubtedly, after you get through some rather tense periods in the first few months of the year, you'll enter an ideal environment for putting new endeavors in motion.

Of course, it's not only how the planets get along with each other that matters, but more importantly how they relate to each person's Sun sign. Even the most harmonious pattern in the sky can be challenging if one's planets get in the way of these big guys steamrolling around the zodiac. In either case, it is always an asset to have a friendly sky to shelter you from above. It's easier to handle bad news on a sunny day — it somehow feels better than getting it on a rainy day.

If you are prone to saying "someday" when it comes to your dreams, this is the year to stop wishing and start doing. It is time to get off the fence, especially in the second half of the year. If you get in touch with your true passion and learn to express it with conviction, you will be handsomely rewarded. It is a year to weigh the practical outcome of either staying where you are and doing more of the same, versus breaking out of your comfy egg to take fledgling steps toward something better. I'm sure what you have is just fine; it's just that there's so much more out there for you. You may be living within unnecessarily narrow perimeters. You've gotten used to your confines. It's time to break out of them!

Of the five outer planets in our solar system, only Jupiter will change constellations this year. All the other powerful outer planets will stay in the signs that they occupied last year. Each of us has hopefully gotten a grasp of what is expected by now, and can get on with the process of living. Energy that last year went to adapting can this year be used for taking the initiative. Jupiter's move into Leo will help you think beyond the borders of your present frame of mind, to venture into brand new territory.

As the year opens, Jupiter will still be in Cancer, to stay until July 31, 2002. Jupiter enjoys this placement, so this is a pleasant period — especially for the water and earth signs that have not had as much cosmic favor recently.

(Those signs are Cancer, Pisces, Scorpio, Taurus, Virgo and Capricorn.) This placement symbolizes the start of a new life. From this position, Jupiter encourages growth, particularly with finances, which could show a lift soon after the year begins. If the economy does bubble up, unfortunately any surge in prosperity seems to be short lived. Its underpinnings are not secure and may wobble soon after June 2003. Enjoy it while you have it!

The housing industry will be the healthiest sector in 2002, particularity in the first half of the year. Expect increased residential construction projects, and a generally heightened interest in buying or selling property. If you want to refinance your house, consider doing so early in 2002. After August 1, conditions appear to be less attractive.

The cocooning instinct we exhibited last year will deepen. Expect strong sales of home entertainment products, family games and video rentals, cooking and kitchen aids. Cabin fever will start to creep in by mid-year. Instead of being content to huddle at home, by the third quarter we'll want to get out and find a little fun with our loved ones. Attendance of Broadway shows should skyrocket by autumn (in Northern hemispheres), giving New York City the boost it needs. Fine restaurant dining will rebound too, and popular musicians should report record sales. Theme parks that experienced such a drop in traffic last year will see a resurgence, as families seek to enjoy a little time out together.

Children's programming will blossom, as will after-school programs. Teachers may finally be paid a bit more and enjoy the respect they richly deserve. International charities that aid the plight of unfortunate children, such as UNICEF, may report higher levels of giving. Leo is, after all, the sign that is the guardian of little ones everywhere.

This change of tone mid-year will be due to Jupiter's move into a bright, warm, enthusiastic Leo (a fire sign) on August 1. Leo teaches us to have fun, live it up, and celebrate our lives. It also encourages us to appreciate unique, artistic forms of self-expression, even if some of them seem a little over-the-top. Leo also likes to see things in their grandest, largest form. It is a strong, bold, gregarious sign that likes to be noticed. Fashion will celebrate with colorful looks. Adoration of and fascination with lifestyles of the rich and famous, which pundits predicted was over and done last September, are due to be back with a vengeance, providing fantasy escapism to millions. (This may make you groan to hear this, depending on which side of this issue you're on.)

If we lean too far into this trend, you may see a return to 80 s' yearning for flash and indulgence at a time when we can least afford the extravagance. Hopefully, we'll get all we need of luxury and black-tie tuxes. Having Jupiter in Leo can be generous to a fault — we don't want to wake up copper-penny-poor by the time Jupiter slides into more modest Virgo by mid-2003. Indulge when you can't resist, but do what you can to keep your feet on the ground.

With these key five planets congregating in fire and air signs — most of them in "mutable" or breezy, communicative and flexible placements — this year will be marked with creativity in fashion, theatre, music, dance, art and graphic design. A preponderance of the planets in fire signs, especially in the second half of the year, will bring a spirit of optimism and risk-taking. The mutability of the planets seems to encourage us not to try so hard to get it right from the start. Play, experiment, see what happens, then make course corrections to get things back on track. There will be no aura of judgment, no precise timetable for finished projects, or rigid expectations for what they will look like. What matters this year is that you start things anew.

Now let's discuss the one aspect alluded to earlier, the difficult 180-degree opposition of Saturn to Pluto. It really shouldn't be so bad. Since this is a continuation of the conflict that started in the middle of 2001, we all have some experience with it, and should have developed the necessary coping skills. We should also have the relief of knowing that this is the last time we'll have this difficult dynamic for another three decades.

This aspect will be felt mainly in the political arena. It is known to bring international conflicts to the surface. Indeed, whenever Saturn and Pluto clash, there is usually an uprising or conflict in the world. This was the case for the United States in September 2001, as it was in the early 1960s with Vietnam, and earlier in the years that led to World War II. (Saturn opposes Pluto every 29 years.) Once we get beyond May 25, 2002, Saturn and Pluto will go their separate ways. Thus, many of the tensions we have experienced and are still dealing with at the beginning of the year should recede in the second half of 2002.

On another score, Saturn will reach a superb angle to Neptune this year. This alone will bring us reason for inspiration and hope. The root of this extraordinary period goes back to 1989 when Saturn and Neptune first met in the sign of Capricorn. That was the beginning of a thirty-seven year cycle, of which we are now about a third of the way through. The next meeting of Saturn to Neptune in the same sign won't happen again until 2026.

Saturn restricts and limits time and resources, while Neptune inspires and adds vision to all it touches. Having an excess of Neptune's energy can lead us to become spacey and disorganized; having Saturn in excess leads to rigidity and fragility. This year there is far less danger of either. Instead of fighting for dominance, these two planets will bring their best qualities to the table and share them. There will be lightness, grace and balance. Saturn will offer stability, while Neptune, flexibility. While Saturn is practical and objective, Neptune can counter its coolness by introducing emotion and compassion. Where Saturn makes us focus on one thing at a time, Neptune suggests a wide range of possibilities. An equilibrium will be reached twice when these planets reach their strongest cooperation: on January 23 and April 1.

Amazingly, later in the year, on August 21 and December 16, Saturn will also support Uranus, the planet of surprise and innovation. Saturn and Uranus are also known to be opposite in method and approach. Saturn builds structure, while Uranus, the consummate iconoclast, smashes anything that it deems is outmoded or of little use. These two planets won't work at cross-purposes this year, but will work in tandem. Saturn will salvage what is useful from the past, and add a touch of practicality and stability to the swiftly moving technological or scientific changes that Uranus insists are necessary.

Uranus is now nearing the end of a monumental seven-year tour of Aquarius, a phase that ushered into the world the advent of the cell phone, video conferencing, the Internet and email. It brought innovations in telecommunications, television, cable, and the bio-sciences. Uranus will move into Pisces late next year but, as is the case with most major moves, Uranus will overlap both signs before fully committing to Pisces in November 2003.

Uranus' departure from Aquarius will mark the end of an era. At the same time, it will lay the seeds for a vastly different new phase in Pisces. The new era will emphasize spirituality, theology and philosophy, and may bring a return to traditional religions. (If not on a personal level, it certainly seems likely to engender a return to an interest in religion in general.)

It takes 84 years for Uranus to circle the Sun, and each time it moves into a new constellation is monumental. It affects everything in popular culture from the fashions we wear, the books we read and movies we see, to the world's political climate. In 2002, Uranus is still very much in Aquarius, so the emphasis remains on extending the frontiers of new technology. Humanitarian interests also fall under the domain of Uranus, so human rights and social issues will continue to dominate our public conversations. With Saturn supporting Uranus on August 21 and December 16, we may see some rather wonderful breakthroughs. In terms of technology, new inventions may well be so practical and useful that they instantly become part of our everyday lives. We will be introduced to things this year that we will marvel at ever having lived without.

Our biggest cosmic gift comes at the tail end of the year, when Jupiter contacts Pluto. This is one of the most heavenly of alignments. Whenever Jupiter and Pluto cooperate, success is close at hand. Jupiter symbolizes good fortune while Pluto symbolizes the powerful ability to transform energy from one form to another. When working together, Pluto will expand Jupiter's luck to a massive degree. Your two golden days for big initiations, especially those that are business oriented, will be October 27 and December 18, 2002

Five eclipses will shift to Gemini – Sagittarius, away from the recent emphasis on Cancer – Capricorn. As we near the end of 2002, on November 19, a single lunar eclipse will fall in late degrees of Taurus. (The following year will continue this trend of eclipses that emphasize Gemini – Sagittarius and Taurus – Scorpio simultaneously.) This November eclipse is the toughest one, as all the planets will be in fixed signs, and seem unable or unwilling to work with each other. This is a bull-headed aspect!

Eclipses do bring startling change. As we go through such dramatic events that make us feel like we are living in an opera, it's important to remember that these events keep us from becoming complacent and stagnant. Change makes us who we are. It is human nature to take things for granted; eclipses shake us, make us change, force us to reconsider our intentions and change direction, and return us to basic values.

Throughout 2002, you'll have many reasonable paths open to you if you look for them. Rather than lean back and expect everything to come to you, work this year to seek out your solutions. If you do, one option you turn up may be so pleasing you'll accept it the minute you see it. Finding all those possibilities may not be easy. The challenge is part of the fun. If you refuse passivity and look under every rock, you'll find a magnificent jewel of a solution.

I have saved some of the sweetest news for last. Venus and Mars, those delightful cosmic lovers, will engage in a sustained, enchanting flirtation in May that will last all year. By December they'll be completely in love and totally inseparable. At holiday time, we'll be given the gift of having this highly charged duo in the highly sexy sign of Scorpio, swimming in perfect syncopation in the sea of love. Their message for 2002 is one of hope and love. No matter what our circumstances, in the wide ocean of our dreams and within the depths of our deepest emotions, we can find that elusive, consistent, abiding love we long for. It is here on earth, the ultimate gift of the cosmos. Once we find that love, it will wrap us in the wings of angels and protect us from the harshest elements. That, my dear reader, may prove to be the finest news of all. I wish you the very best of all years.

ARIES

The Big Picture

Are you ready to dance, dear Aries? The music is playing, the stars are in the sky and a fragrant perfume scents the air. This happy state of affairs, which will reach a crescendo in the second half of 2002, is due to the entrance of Jupiter, giver of gifts and luck, into Leo, your house of true love. While you will have to wait a few months for this, it will be well worth it. You haven't seen a trend like this in the past ten years! This year will quite possibly be your best time to shine for the entire decade. Whether you are single and looking for a love mate, in love and hoping for commitment, or already "taken" and hoping to jazz things up a little, all Aries can benefit from this lovely influence.

For the first time in a long while, you'll be free to set your agenda. Not only that, for once, you'll be able to follow through with your plans in almost every area of life, without fear that an eclipse or some other planetary configuration will throw you off. While every year holds an upset or two, this year's sticky moments seem mild in comparison to those you've faced in the past.

The areas of your life that will show the most growth will be the softer, more personal realms. You will have a remarkable chance to make an upgrade in your domestic situation, and to travel near and far. You will also have an opportunity to make one or two new friends who will have quite a stimulating effect on you. Finally, and maybe most importantly (and now let's sound the trumpets!), you will have much greater chances of either finding new love or rekindling an established passion. Romance is a big theme. It is simply a magical year — one to remember, for sure!

Jupiter's position in a horoscope always gives us clues to those areas due for the greatest growth and happiness. This year, in 2002, Jupiter will occupy two key positions in your chart. As the year begins, this glittering planet will shine a golden lantern into your fourth house of home and family, and later, from August 1, 2002 for the next year, Jupiter will make your fifth house of true love burn brightly. This is fantastic news. Let's discuss both areas in greater detail, and take a look for what else is in store.

Love, Sweet Love

First, let's talk about your love life. As an Aries, this is almost always a number one priority! By mid-year, Jupiter, the planet of happiness and growth, will become fully ensconced in your fifth house of romance. Jupiter will reign in this enchanting house from August 1, 2002 to August 27, 2003 — nearly thirteen months! While you will have to wait a bit to feel this powerful effect as the year begins, when it comes, you'll feel it so strongly, you won't be able to imagine life without it! You have not had a visit from Cupid in more than a decade (since 1990–91 to be exact). By the time he comes with his fleet of little cherubs, it should be quite a welcome visit! I am sure you will enjoy your bubbling social life. What will be your favorite days for swooning love? July 24 gets my vote; the weekend prior, July 20, is a runner-up for the best date of the year for true love.

Most big trends happen not because of one big planetary configuration but because of a confluence of them. You have what it takes, Aries, to see a massive change in matters of the heart. Generally, the position of the ruling planet (in your case, Mars) always has significant bearing on what transpires in matters of the heart. In 2002, Mars' orbit will be unusually strong, moving surely and swiftly though the personal sectors of your solar chart. This was not the case in 2001. Mars dallied in Sagittarius and even went retrograde for a while. Neither of these things will happen in 2002. Then, when Mars finally got active last year, it remained in public parts of the chart, so your personal life was somewhat neglected. This year, Mars is all about those personal areas.

This January, Mars starts out in *your* sign (what more could you want!?) and moves purposefully through no fewer than eight signs! This will bring the variety you crave and a range of opportunities to your door. Last year, Mars moved through fewer constellations, pushing you to concentrate on a narrow agenda. (That may have been a good thing — you probably have some results to show for it.) This year will be more enjoyable. In 2002, Mars will end up in the house ruling physical intimacy, guaranteeing a sexy and glamorous year!

Venus adores her lover, your ruler Mars, and always likes to be near him. Last year, due to variations in their orbits, they were hardly ever together. This year, they will hardly ever be apart! I see you are laughing — it's true! March will be frothy and fun, due to Venus' presence in your sign. By May your mood is even *more* flirtatious, because after a brief separation Mars will have caught up with Venus again. With his arm around her, she'll glow with love. But the roots of this year's romantic tone are located at the very start, in January 2002, when Mars highlights Aries.

However, by the period from October 10 – November 22, 2002, when Venus begins to retrograde, you may wonder if your relationship has galloped along too quickly. If you determine this to be true, in the last quarter of the year you'll pull back a little, if only to think a little. If you are planning a wedding, try to avoid setting the date for this Venus retrograde period. It is never advisable to tie the knot during a Venus retrograde.

No matter what happens in October and November, by December Venus is back to her old self. Her position is so snuggly close to Mars, love will be simply remarkable. In that last month of 2002, Mars and Venus will dance in perfect step, whirling like Fred and Ginger in a love dance that just might take your breath away.

Lilliputians, the Joy of Life

If you want children or have children, this year will emphasize the pleasures of raising them. If you don't have a child but feel ready for parenthood, this is your year to move ahead. There are no longer any reasons to wait. The second half of 2002 simply glitters for all matters involving pregnancy, parenting and relationships with children of any age. Kids will bring joy and pride.

Should you have had any difficulties with conception, you can expect a breakthrough from the second half of 2002 through the beginning of 2003. Try to see a specialist soon. It would be wise to start early in the year, in January, while Mars is in your sign. Even if you are already seeing a fertility doctor, and feel some doubts, this would be a good time to seek a second opinion.

Adoption is also brilliantly favored. The related paperwork process, an aspect of adoption that discourages many couples, could be completed more swiftly than usual. Of course there will still be forms to fill out and interviews to go through, your mood will be upbeat nonetheless.

If you have children, but for any reason have lately found being a parent to be more responsibility than fun, this year will reverse all that. Kids are to be enjoyed! If you have had difficulty dealing with one child, perhaps a teenager, the problem may stem from your communication style. With Saturn in your third house (something we will discuss later in this report), you might try using a different approach. Be sure your heart comes through. Attitude, rather than words, may be at the core of your difficulties. If you are in the midst of a divorce, and have been torturing yourself over whether your kids are going to come through this period, relax. It looks like they will be supremely protected by a caring universe.

Career Takes a Back Seat To Pleasure

As an Aries, your career will always be important to you. Happily, your position and work environment should remain steady and could even become much more secure — a welcome change after the ups and downs of 2001. This year, however, your profession won't be the center of attention it was in the past. Instead, as we have been discussing, private pleasures will take center stage. Be glad for this development. This year will help you to find greater emotional balance, and allow you to experience the softer side of life.

Last year, in 2001, you hosted eclipses in two very sensitive areas of your horoscope, which created upheaval in your career environment (i.e., where you worked, who you worked for or the kind of work you did). There will be one more eclipse in this sector on June 24, a full moon eclipse that falls in this same lofty tenth house of professional acclaim. That eclipse will most affect those Aries born at the end of March, and will bring to fruition a situation that you have worked within for some time. The good news is, that eclipse is in a good angle to Uranus, planet of surprise, so perhaps an offer will come out of the blue. Mars will be well angled to Jupiter too, suggesting a high-level person, perhaps based at a distance or based at a university, could be quite willing to help you.

Watch Financials

In terms of finances, I should warn you about a difficult eclipse due in your house of earned income in late November, which could suddenly and dramatically change your source of income. The changes that occur will be based purely on the economy, not the quality of your work. Hopefully this will make room for an offer to earn more money. However, because this eclipse is cranky, it may not immediately bring the good news you want. Frankly, though, with all planets squared off, it doesn't seem you have many options at the time. A new job or source of income *will* show up eventually, but the timing is not clear. This eclipse seems to be bent on testing just how innovative and resourceful you can be; those who are willing to accept this mission will do well. After the whole episode is over, you may say, "At first I thought this was bad news, but in hindsight, they did me a big favor!"

Your most expensive months will be March, April, and December. While during these months you seem to be spending like mad, you will become pretty creative about increasing cash flow. Put on your thinking cap, dear Aries. Now that I have made you jumpy about that eclipse, here is the good news: You have a most magical week for getting a big raise. It comes earlier in the year, near June 2, and continues for the two weeks that follow the new moon June 10. Hooray!

Travel and Musing

After those eclipses shift to easier houses, you can expect a more secure and settled outlook. Your self-confidence should return, and you will feel more prepared to take a few risks. The 2002 eclipses will fall in the weaker, milder houses of the horoscope, houses far less likely to cause major problems.

Travel will have appeal. Is it time to buy that set of perfectly matched luggage, Aries? With so much activity in your third and ninth houses, with emphasis in Gemini and Sagittarius, much more travel is likely to be on your agenda. The end of April, the month of May, and mid-June should produce at least one outstanding outing. This year you may buy a car, too.

Expect Growth in Intellect, Creativity and Communication Skills

These same houses, the third and ninth, reflect your deepest attitudes and the workings of your intellect. They rule your guiding principals as well as your perspective on a whole range of subjects, including politics, religion, morality and ethics. You may view things a bit differently now, dear Aries. See what comes up in May, June and December.

Saturn's placement in your third house will work to help you think clearly and deeply all year. Your solar third house rules communication of all kinds, so you will learn to write, speak, research and edit your thoughts more effectively. If you are weak in any of these areas, you may want to take a few classes to brush up on them. While you are honing these skills, it seems to be necessary. For whatever reason, more seems to be at stake when getting your point across.

You'll have all kinds of opportunities to flex you newly expressive muscles. You may be asked to give an important speech, serve on a panel, judge a contest, or teach a group (even if you are not a teacher). No matter what your birthday, expect to get a good buzz from this stabilizing planet at some point during the year, for Saturn will be touching almost all bases at some point in 2002. Pluto, on the other hand, favors those Aries born April 4–7 the most. Support comes to those Aries through foreign people, and those based in publishing, academia and theological settings.

Saturn and Pluto have been in fierce opposition to one another, pushing and pulling at your beliefs and ideologies. At times, it's been hard to figure out *what* you really think, let alone express it! Issues seem so complex. These two planets have one more row on May 25, 2002, but they remain within very close range of each other for most of the first half of the year. The point of this opposition is to help you see things in shades of gray, and to push you to penetrate issue more deeply. If at times knowing where you stand seems a bit overwhelming, well, that's the whole point. You are maturing, and though it's not always comfortable, it's all that matters.

The tangible catalysts to your meditation about such deep issues is anyone's guess. A certain teacher may prod you on, or maybe a friend's rants about politics get your mind expanding into new places. You are forming new interests this year, and the books you read or the people you meet will make you grow. For sure, you will be rubbing shoulders with some pretty stimulating people. Though at times you may see your attitude shift ever so slightly, it will be months or even years before you see just how much your original position has changed. (Pluto brings massive change so gradually, you hardly see it happen.)

In the second half of the month, as Saturn moves out of Pluto's reach, Pluto sends a sensational vibration to Jupiter, planet of expansion, justice and happiness. This is sensational news for the world. Whenever these two planets get together, we experience success on a grand scale. Again, for you, the benefits seem both intellectual, creative and in areas of love and children. Simply fabulous dates to watch for are October 27 and December 18.

If you want to go back to school for a degree, the last quarter of the year would be a great time to do so. Why delay? Take out applications in the early part of the year so that you'll be ready. Your mind is hungry; give it proper fare. If money is a problem, voice your need. Someone wants to help you.

Friendship Brings Surprise and Stimulation

Now let's focus in on friendship and social groups. Who among us could live without the warm, cozy blanket that friends provide? For years, you have been hosting Uranus and Neptune in your eleventh house, the people portion of your chart. You have, no doubt, become accustomed to all the new faces that continually enter your life. Perhaps you have started to take for granted that you will always be this fortunate to meet so many new and interesting people. Not so! When Uranus makes the momentous exit from this house of your chart at the end of 2003, it will leave a space there for the first time in seven years. You will have come to depend on your friends and new contacts for surprise, a jolt of fun and entertainment. This will change radically at this time.

Before that happens, try to make an effort to join clubs and get yourself out there in the world. Make the most of your friends-favoring vibes. Go outside your industry or normal sphere to meet people. You may find that the folks you meet and the friends you make are younger than you, or quite unusual and unpredictable. (Of course, this is what draws you to them!) Those of you who were born from April 11 – 19 will benefit most from the position of Uranus this coming year. Lucky you, you are going to be around many new faces!

Days when friends are likely to amaze you with their support are August 21 and December 16. These are key dates for fabulous luck through friends and contacts. (This is true no matter when your birthday, Aries.)

Neptune also remains in your friendship house. The friends you make now could be involved in the arts in some way. They may be poetic, spiritual or especially sensitive souls who see beauty everywhere — and can help open your eyes to see it too. You may also join a club that helps you further your creativity or increases your knowledge of the cultural arts.

Volunteer for a Good Cause

Neptune also will ask you to consider the importance of giving something back. Getting involved in a humanitarian effort, volunteerism or a charity event would be a great way to use this positive cycle. You may also be involved in a community event, whether in real life or on the internet. Neptune only comes to this house once in a lifetime. Admittedly, once there, Neptune will stay for many years, in your case until early 2012. You have plenty of time to be transformed by this graceful planet.

Neptune gets enormous support from Saturn; this is a wildly wonderful development. If you are working on a creative project, Saturn will make sure you have the discipline to see it through. (We all know that creativity is like giving birth!) Dancers, composers, musicians, artists, photographers, novelists, poets and others in the arts will see a marked difference in their output. Others may find that friends ask them to take their artistic talents more seriously. Those of you who were born around March 27 – 31 will benefit the most. Circle January 23 and April 1 as magical for matters involving groups, friendship and humanitarian or creative efforts.

As if this isn't good enough, Neptune will not be working alone to encourage your creativity. In the second half of the year, you'll have Jupiter in Leo, as we discussed earlier. If you are paid for your ideas or designs, you may outdo yourself now. Get ready to raise the bar and set a new standard for the future. Even if you don't think of yourself as especially inspired, you may be surprised at what you turn out. Nascent interests and hobbies may prove to be so compelling, they consume your free time! Finding a new way to express yourself is the key here, so experiment and be playful, dear Aries.

Home Sweet Home

Your home life is also due for a big step forward. I mentioned at the beginning of this report, domestic improvements are as important a trend as romance will be in the coming year.

Last year got you thinking about your home life, asking yourself how you wanted to live, where, and possibly with whom. Yet you were at a disadvantage because eclipses buffeted your home and family sector, despite the presence of Jupiter, the planet that brings cosmic goodies. The fourth house, at the very bottom of your horoscope, acts as an anchor to all that you do. It describes your home, who lives there with you (if anyone), and the kind of environment you prefer. The full moon lunar eclipse that fell on December 30, 2001, may have brought some good news about your residence or family. As you read this, you may already be working out some plans related to that news.

There is no doubt that this is the year to try your hand at being Martha Stewart or Tim Allen. Home is where your heart will be! We spoke about how wonderful your love life will be, but first, you'll have to get your home life in order. Think of this year as your year to prepare your cozy nest for love. It doesn't matter how old you are, or what phase of life you are in.

Your best months in this time frame fall between March and July — with double stars on June and July, so watch for developments then. I adore July 3 and July 19 — fantastic days for home or family-related luck!

It will be important, however, to waste no time in these home-related matters. You will be benefiting from Jupiter's hospitality only until July 31, 2002. Once Jupiter leaves this fourth house, it won't be back until June 2013, twelve years from now. If you want to make changes, I urge you to jump on home-related projects during the first half of 2002, at which time you will be showered with luck.

Family support will be strong in the first half of 2002. If you need advice or even a loan, Mom or Dad will be there for you, helping you every step of the way. That is no small blessing!

While it is true that you already had opportunities to settle residential questions last year, from July through December 2001, Jupiter was not in a strong position. If you felt 2001 offered great promise but little reward, redouble your efforts now because, by George, you are going to see results. When Jupiter is strong — ready to leap over tall buildings in a single bound, there is nothing you can do but succeed.

If there is something you want to do — move, repair, renovate, decorate, change roommates, buy or sell property, do it now. If you are selling property or a house, for example, you will likely get your ideal price by mid-year, if not sooner. If you are buying land or a co-op, for example, you are likely to find something you like. Looking further down the road, once Saturn enters Cancer in June 2003 for a thirty-month stay, you will run into quite a difficult time selling or buying. Act now! You can use this trend in either a subtle or more obvious ways. You might want to buy a beautiful new house or condo, or if you are young, you may move into your very first apartment. Jupiter will make sure that your space be large, sunny, with spacious closets too! Most people find that they enjoy the space they find under Jupiter so much that they settle down and stay there for years.

If you already have an apartment or a house that you enjoy, now is the time to make some pretty or comfy upgrades. You may want to refresh your digs with new linens and other home-related accessories. This would be the time to give your apartment a fresh coat of paint, to make those long anticipated improvements and repairs. While you are at it, why not reorganize your closets, to make more space? It would also be an ideal time to build a home office, as Jupiter's presence suggests there's profit to be made in your residence. If that doesn't seem possible, think about doing more career-related entertaining. Invite your boss or client over. Home is where financial benefits are to be found.

If a home-related situation has been stressful (like dealing with an unruly landlord) be confidant that things will work to your favor. Just make sure to push for a settlement prior to mid-year!

Dreams tend to come true when you have Jupiter on your side. For instance, if you always hoped to own a set of antique silver flatware, you might be amazed to find a bargain price for a set at the flea market, or Grandma may decide to give you her extra set. (Remember: family support for you is exceptionally strong this year.) Consider renting a weekend cottage by the sea for a vacation in May, June or July. Or, if you can afford it, consider buying that second, weekend country house that you have mused about. When Jupiter visits, luck is with you, even if you think it would be an impossible dream!

Some Aries may have had concerns about an elderly parent's welfare. (This is not necessarily the case, but in case it is, I will address it here.) Jupiter's position in your house of home and family during the first half of the year suggests that your mother or father will enjoy golden vibrations. If one of your parents needs medical care, for example, it would behoove you to help them locate the right specialist during the first half of the year. If one parent needs a nursing home, set out to look at your options.

Go Back to Your Roots

I have one last suggestion for you, for a way to take advantage of these marvelous vibrations in the area of family. If you were adopted, and ever considered looking for your biological parents, the first half of the year would be the time to make a concerted effort to do so. If you are not adopted, but are curious about your family roots, set out to trace your family tree. You may be off on a new adventure!

Finally, you might find that in 2002, a long, drawn-out situation may be coming to a close. As odd as this might sound, the fourth house also marks what the ancients called "the end of all matters." If you find that you have reached a turning point in your private life, don't be fearful or sad to see something end. With that door closing, you are poised to embark on a new adventure and pioneer into new territory.

Soon you will be filled with passion and excitement. In a flash, you will sense correctly that all the conditions are right for you to shape your life. Make it the way you've always dreamed it could be. Back in 1996 – 1998, when Saturn was on your Sun, you learned some very hard life lessons and grew a lot in the process. Armed with that maturity, you are ready to put it to good use. You have so many important planets behind you — it is time to push, to experiment and to make some decisive moves. There is no holding you back, dear Aries.

Summary

After five years of cosmic challenges, you will welcome the change that your year ahead brings. Your love life will improve enormously. If you are single, you could finally meet your soul mate, and if attached, you can rekindle the funny, silly love you enjoyed so much when you had first met. In fact, just about every area of your life will open up for you. With Jupiter still in Cancer until July 2002, any real estate or residential decision will be blessed.

Due to the eclipses, what you do for a living, your job description, and / or your employer could have significantly changed recently. Now, your outlook looks more stable, although there is one more eclipse due in late June that could bring more change; it seems more likely to be beneficial. Financial changes seem positive for the most part, but watch the eclipse on November 20 for turbulence. Knowing this in advance, perhaps you can prepare for that eventuality, dear Aries. Saturn's move into Gemini is urging you to hone your writing and speaking skills, as they will be needed soon. Your attitudes may gradually shift and mature, as the cosmos encourages you to see things in greater depth and detail.

Much more travel and possibly a chance for higher education will become possible too, and all the while friendships and new associations will start to pop. Yet as said earlier, it is in love that you will see the biggest life changes. If you already are in love, you can have more fun, and even plan for a baby. If you have children, you can start to really enjoy them, now that the harder work of caring for them seems to be behind you.

Let go of the past, dear Aries. You are about to open the door on a whole new way of life — and it's a far better than the one you had before!

TAURUS

The Big Picture

The coming year is brimming with opportunity, dear Taurus. 2002 will finally allow you to pursue a number of new options instead of continuing to recycle the same old set of circumstances. If there were one perfect phrase to sum up the year ahead, it would be to say that it emphasizes decisive action over passivity.

You want a year that gives you room to experiment and grow, not one that teaches with tough challenge after tough challenge. (We have all had the unforgiving experience of being whacked hard for making a wrong turn.) Happily, you are entering precisely the kind of year we all want: big yet fair, busy but not frenetic. This year will allow you to push derailed areas of your life back on track.

2002 will also allow you to develop the private side of your life in a lyrical, spiritual way. There is a wonderful possibility that you will fall in love or grow much closer to the one you care for. It is a year that will allow you some diversions too, such as spontaneous, freewheeling travel or a hobby or fond new interest.

The surprises, twists and turns, ups and downs you've experienced in your career are due to continue, for sure, but with one big exception. There's stability and confidence underlying current professional changes. Perhaps this is because you have become accustomed to the new rules of the game and are coping better with them than in the past. It's also due to Saturn's hand in this, which we'll look at in some detail later.

In 2002, the ideas you discuss will have an unusually solid base, giving you the courage to plunge into new realms. Good, dear Taurus, for in a very real sense, your success in 2002 and beyond will be in direct proportion to your willingness to leave the past behind.

Money continues to be an area to watch with caution. Due to upcoming eclipses, one source of income may end, but if you play your cards right, you can turn this situation to your advantage. Losing a job can make you look for a better one. A major lunar eclipse in Taurus (highlighting late-May born Taurus) in late November will bring a relationship or endeavor to fruition, and clarify the road ahead.

Throughout this year ahead, your most impressive area of growth will occur in the personal side of your life. I see the strong possibility for a breathless romance if you are single, or willingness on your behalf to enter deeper waters in the sea of love. You are not usually moved emotionally — but then again, this is no ordinary year. There are positive planetary patterns related to pregnancy / children, too, and more time to devote to family members, such as a beloved parent or special sibling. And with property and home-related matters glowing in the second half, with a little effort you will be able to make your home so cozy that you may never want to leave it. Are you excited yet, dear Taurus? You should be!

Career Continues to Bring Kaleidoscopic Change

You have been on a remarkable journey over the recent years, one that has taken you over very diverse terrain. When Uranus, the planet of radical and unexpected change, entered your professional sector in 1995 for the first time in your life, you were given no choice but to accept the shifts hurled at you for the next seven years.

While everyone, everywhere, was destined to feel some of the changes wrought by these planets in the ensuing year (partly because they were in Aquarius–the sign, among other things, of the common man), you were touched more directly than most. Sooner or later, it became abundantly clear that standing still would not be an option.

This year, Taurus born at the end of their sign, from May 12 – 19 will most feel this pushing and prodding by Uranus. If that is you, Uranus seems especially bent on teaching you the value of adaptability and innovation. If your birthday falls prior to May 12, chances are you have already been buzzed by Uranus' unusual insights, and have had your opportunity to "get with the program". Although all Taurus will feel this planet's influence again in 2002, those earlier-born Taurus have, for the most part, finished their "tour of duty". For them, this year's affects will be buffered.

No matter when your birthday falls, if you ever wondered whether you are capable of continually reinventing yourself, at least professionally, the answer is a resounding yes! Some of you have already made that clear, while others will, quite soon. There is nothing to fear. As we said earlier, who wants to live through a re-run of last year?

There is no doubt that your sign was chosen to be at the forefront of the evolving technological revolution. While you might say incredulously, "Me? Why, I can't even run my vacuum cleaner, let alone my VCR!" Remember this: The universe, in its infinite wisdom, knows that a fixed sign like Taurus positioned in the vanguard guarantees careful oversight of such changes. Not only will Taurus objectively assess the emerging technologies for their practical use, but Taurus can also be counted on to preserve all that is valuable from the past. Thus, with *you* at the helm, the world gets the best of both worlds, past and present. If all proposals have to pass through your vigorous and somewhat skeptical filter, we are guaranteed the bottom-line truth fairly quickly: Will this fly? Does this have practical application? Do people want this? Will it make money?

The winds of change that started to breeze gently through your career in 1995 have subsequently picked up speed. By now they are blowing with tropical strength. Rather than see this as scary, you've come to view these influences as necessary, long overdue, and possibly even refreshing. Right you are! Two planets, Uranus and Neptune, sitting like beacons at the very top of your solar horoscope, are responsible for the forces gathering here. Now you are getting a grip on how to harness this enormous natural energy that will remain present in the years to come.

Uranus' main job is to sweep away those established structures that have outlived their usefulness and replace them with more relevant systems. You have probably noticed that most of the surprises in your life are centered on your profession.

Big outer planets have been pulling energy toward your professional (tenth house) sector like huge balls of gravity, sucking in everything and anything like a giant vortex. While at times this can be rattling — certainly a bit *too* stimulating, it can be enlightening and exciting. All this change has kept you very alert.

Three years after Uranus first entered Aquarius in 1995, something new came along. That new factor was Neptune's graceful and at times baffling influence in this same tenth house of career status. Neptune moves even more slowly than Uranus, and has no plans to leave this sector until early 2012. This dreamy, inspired planet has already begun to instill you with its wisdom. You have loosened up considerably when it comes to assessing change, and have acquired a new and wonderful playfulness and willingness to experiment.

As the planet of vision, Neptune has been busy teaching you the value of foresight. Since its entry here, you have a tendency to look farther down the road than you would previously have been inclined. You have begun to ask yourself a variety of hypothetical, "what if?" questions. As a Taurus, you typically avoid this kind of pondering. You feel much more comfortable focusing on the here and now, with all that you can taste and touch. You like being a producer, not idea-generator. Nevertheless, for whatever reason, you are being called on to pick up conceptual, creative and even forecasting skills.

This year, for those born between April 27 – 30, Neptune will be in a challenging angle to your Sun. You may have some difficulty judging the difference between what is real from what's just Memorex. Figuring out which deals have potential, which colleagues will stand by you, and who is telling you the truth could be tricky. Those

Taurus who feel temporarily stymied within a career environment of smoke and mirrors should slow down a bit, just as you would when driving along a highway suddenly blanketed by fog. Don't let this fuzzy atmosphere stop you from contributing your ideas — just consider them more carefully. Judging by your chart, the world is depending on you to provide them!

Will You Become the Media's Darling?

In 2002, Neptune's position at the very top of your horoscope, now due to get awesome support from Saturn, suggests your profile in the community may be rising. You may be asked to take on a much more public role in your company, neighborhood, city or at the world at large. It is common for people with Neptune on the mid-heaven points to be singled out by mass media. You may find yourself being interviewed on TV or being eased into the role of master strategist, planner or spokesperson. Get ready to meet the press, dear Taurus!

Alternatively, you may start to do well in the entertainment field, whether you'll be working with music, dance, as an actor, or in one of the many visual arts. With powerful planets positioned at the top of your chart, nothing is out of the question.

A Landmark Period For Setting a Career Course

Together, Neptune and Uranus are asking you to remain on the cutting edge of your specialty. You are expected now to become a master chess player, adept at predicting the consequences (both the long and short term) of your every move.

If at times, all this seems to be too much to handle, consider this: Neptune and Uranus won't be in your tenth house of professional dignity forever. When these planets move on to other houses, the career tensions you are feeling will end, and the warm spotlight that is shining on you now will dim. You may yearn for this period once it's gone, Taurus — stresses and all.

These are the most important career years of your life. Because the orbits of Uranus and Neptune are very slow, the cycles you are experiencing come but once in a lifetime. When you think of the importance of this period in this wider context, you see the magnitude of the opportunities before you. This is your time to shape the future. The ground is rich, and the possibilities enormous! Nothing worth having is ever won easily.

While it is natural to look forward, take a moment to look back to see how far you have come, and how well you've adapted. Although the process is not over, you are doing well! None of this has been easy, of course. Taurus is a sign that would rather leave things well enough alone, and opt for the tried and true. In the old days, it would have taken a complete breakdown of the system, bordering on chaos, before the typical Taurus would have been motivated to tinker with anything. Yet this is not the case any more, thanks to these big-guy planets and their orbits. You've come a long way.

Money Remains Tight... but Not for Long

In terms of finances, last year was tough. Although you aren't out of the woods yet, there are signs that things will improve. This year brings one difficult financial aspect, the third and final meeting of Saturn opposed to Pluto.

These planets fall in the two houses of your horoscope that rule money. This is a very rare configuration. When Saturn and Pluto dance, they meet three times before spinning off into very different directions. You experienced the first two meetings in August and November 2001. At that time, you built the skills necessary to deal with this configuration. It should be easier now. These planets' last stand will occur on May 25, 2002.

Let's look at how this has been playing out. All along, Saturn has been limiting your income in its tour of your second house of possessions and resources. Saturn's presence here suggests your employer is tight-fisted. Even if you changed jobs, it is unlikely you found a better situation. That can be frustrating, because, as the song goes, you work hard for the money — even when it's not enough.

Still, Saturn has been teaching you to spend, save and invest more wisely. Many people report that they earn more money during a Saturn transit, but agree that they had to work harder than ever to get it. You have never been one to shirk responsibility. Now you will learn to marshal and exploit your assets and resources, including your time, energy and talent. Saturn creates limits that make you focus on your strengths. You may now become aware of new skills (or new ways to use old skills) with enormous market value.

As if this wouldn't be enough to deal with, Pluto is in your eighth house, in a pushy, 180-degree opposition to Saturn. Whatever financial and professional issues you faced last year continue into the first half of 2002. If, for example, you have sought venture capital for a business idea, it appears that investors have offered harsh terms without much room to negotiate. This climate continues, and won't improve much for six months. (After that, it will.)

Problems with credit or a tax question were no more easily resolved — and continue to be sticky at the beginning of 2002. This has not been the time to go though probate about an inheritance, as the wheels of justice would have proceeded slowly (at best), or the will could have been contested (at worst). We often don't have any say in the timing of such events. You may just have to go with the flow.

The toughest factors at play would influence the division of property in a divorce or business. Pluto's presence suggests you've had to deal with passionate emotions on both sides; neither appeared to want to give an inch. If this describes a situation you can relate to, it would be better to let things slide until the second half of the year. Wait to settle the dispute until after Saturn and Pluto finish arguing.

Should anything reach critical mass around that May date, just vow to remain as practical and objective as possible. Even if the options could never be described as ideal, you'll probably have to choose one course of action. And you know what? Maybe that's not so bad — at least you can move on with your life.

Ah, that's life, dear Taurus. We are all in the same boat. Everyone, no matter what his or her sign, is feeling Saturn opposed to Pluto in some area of life. The good thing is, as noted, you have already experienced this aspect twice, in August and November 2001. Once you face this aspect again in late May 2002, Saturn and Pluto will have begun to separate, not to meet again for twenty-nine years. Although your attention to financial matters won't disappear altogether (Saturn is not due to exit your financial sector until June 2003), things will ease up. Few circumstances could be as intense as they have been lately.

Still, there is good news in the second half of the year! Pluto and Jupiter will team up on two sensational days of the year, and when they do (and this is a *very* rare aspect), success will follow. Dear Taurus, use them for any financial dealing!

Here are your five-star days for issues related to money, property, and even family support: October 27 and December 18. Mark them with a gold star!

Eclipses in 2002: Highlighting Finance

On top of that, from 1998 through early 2000 you endured the constant pounding of several difficult career eclipses in Aquarius and Leo. This made any solid, long-term planning nearly impossible. Every time you forged a map for your future, something unexpected came out of the blue to render it unfeasible. Those eclipses fell on the key angles of your chart, which is *not* the case in 2002.

No matter what you experienced, the episodes proved to be valuable because they taught you flexibility — usually a hard-won lesson for a Taurus. You still seem to be a little shell shocked from those years. Again, all I can say, 2002 will be different.

In 2002, there seems to be a change in your source of income or in your overall financial situation (represented by the second and eighth houses). Before you stand on your chair and scream "Oh no! I knew it! I am heading to the poor house!" Hold on. These eclipses can be blessings, because they can get you out of an unprofitable situation and into a far better one! Eclipses always make us reinvent ourselves, and these will be no exception.

Eclipses often bring random, outside forces to the fore, such as conditions operating within your industry, on the economy, or with company politics. These are conditions over which we don't have any control. As often as such effects are stressful, just as often they can prove to bring positive news. (For example, rather than fall victim to company politics, you might find that you have become the boss's pet!)

Watch for career and money news on or near the dates of the eclipses May 26, June 10, and December 4. Your key date for outstanding financial progress will be June 10.

If this year you should lose a big client or even become "downsized" at your job, know that this is due purely to economic factors and has nothing to do with the quality of your work. I know this is not much comfort in times like these, but it is very important. (To be clear, this is only a remote possibility, not a given.) As long as your reputation is intact, you have something powerful to offer in the marketplace.

By now, you are becoming more adept at maneuvering into new areas, and have swifter reactions. This could be the whole point of this cosmic episode: to encourage nimble resourcefulness.

Saturn Will Steady the Boat

As you navigate through 2002, keep in mind that every day will bring you closer to attaining greater professional stability. Uranus and Neptune will be getting surprisingly strong support from Saturn (second house to tenth house). That, dear Taurus, is headline news! You have not had help like this in ages. It will color your professional picture a brighter hue in 2002. It's news you can cheer about.

Neptune often gets a bad rap. It is often thought to be a planet that is lovely to look at, but that lacks substance. This won't be true this year, however, as Saturn will send a very stabilizing ray to your career and money sector all year. For proof, look to positive events on your two superb career dates: January 23 and April 1.

In the second half of the year, Saturn will also send kiss-kiss vibrations to Uranus, the idiosyncratic planet that tends to bring news and opportunity out of the blue. Thanks to this influence, your future will be every bit as stable as what you leave behind. That bears repeating: Wherever you are heading is every bit as stable as whatever you are leaving behind. (Are you feeling better, Taurus? Yes? Yes!)

Mark down two landmark days for surprisingly strong career progress thanks to this Saturn – Uranus configuration. They are: August 21 and December 16.

That August 21 date is interesting, as it falls near the full moon in your fame sector at 29 degrees, the critical degree of completion. Many significant events should be crystallizing for you by then — it's certainly a time to watch. (Don't go on vacation at that time; there's too much going on at the office!)

If you feel that you are in the wrong job, in the wrong industry, and want to make a complete career switch, get ready for change. Uranus will give you the impetus to cut your ties to the past, to pursue bigger and better things.

There is an equal possibility that you will find yourself at exactly the right place at the right time. You could be in for a major coup. Whatever unfolds in 2002 could be quite thrilling, and it won't take much work to get to where you need to go. Indeed, no matter which circumstance you find yourself in, you can make things work. Indeed, you can't lose.

Your Personal Life Will Shine —
Home and Family Get Biggest Boost

Now for some *very* big news! Maestro, can we have a drum roll, please?

Jupiter is about to shower your home and family life with cosmic luck, making 2002 a banner year to advance home-related projects. In quite a spectacular cosmic fashion, you will be able to create the home you always wanted. All domestic endeavors will blossom. If you need a new house or apartment, to buy or lease, you are in luck. The position of Jupiter always points to the areas due for the greatest expansion, and from August 1, 2002 to August 27, 2003, your fourth house of home will glitter brilliantly.

If you need to buy, sell, lease, make renovations or repairs, refresh or renew, redecorate or construct an addition, wait until mid-year (August and beyond) to begin. Indeed, so special is this trend, it represents your most fortunate period in over a decade to settle domestic matters. If you've not been able to sell your house, you will likely get your asking price, or if you've been frustrated with the process of buying a house, options will appeal to you in the second half of 2002.

Even small changes will perk you up, like getting that new area rug for the living room, that pretty set of everyday dishes or a few fluffy new towels to replace your old ones. (If you live with others, they will feel the same sensational morale boost. Your marvelous aspects will rub off on them!)

If you have had tension with your father (or possibly your mother), a roommate, or landlord, you will be able to reach a meeting of the minds in 2002. You would have to be the one to offer the olive branch, but if you do, you would be pleasantly surprised with the response. If you have been concerned about the welfare of a parent, the arrival of Jupiter to this house on August 1 should bring good news. They are protected in some way, and the circumstances surrounding them should take a turn for the better.

Those Taurus who have had strong, positive relationships with their mother or father should jump on the chance to spend a little extra time with her or him. It is also possible that your parent will want to help you in some appreciable way this year. If you need help (even financial help), go to Mom and Dad in the second half of 2002.

This year, you may want to learn more about your family heritage. Pursuing an interest in genealogy will send you off on a new adventure! Investigate things on the Internet to get started.

The last bit of news in this arena is certainly positive. Jupiter, the planet of good fortune, will brighten your fourth house. This is a key area of your chart, as it serves as the foundation of all that you do. It is thought to be the area that comforts you and allows you to refresh and restore your spirit. You've not had many good aspects to this house in recent years, so Jupiter's placement will be very welcome! It should revive your self-confidence and optimism!

Travel

Travel should be quite delicious in the first half of the year, right up to July 31, 2002. And while your trips may not take you far, what they lack in distance they make up in fun. Business trips should prove to be profitable. Early to mid-July looks glorious, so plan your vacation for that time!

If you want to buy a car, the first half of 2002 would be the perfect time to do so. However, avoid buying anything during the two Mercury retrograde periods, January 18 to February 8, and May 15 to June 8. Your car should bring you much pleasure and convenience. If you need one, there is no reason not to go shopping soon.

Mark the Date!

One of your most outstanding moments of the year will come on July 19 and 20, when the Sun and Venus, respectively, embrace lucky Jupiter. We only get a handful of jewels like this per year, so when they arrive, we need to use them! Be sure to have something special in mind to do on that day.

Not only are these dates ideal for travel, but for anything home or property-related, for signing agreements, and for enjoying your relationship with family.

Sensational Love!

If you have read this far, you've been very patient. I hope you will feel it has been rewarded when I reveal the very best of what I have to tell you about: your wonderful romantic aspects.

All year, Mars will be streaking rapidly through the private sectors in the lower half of your chart. Your personal life is due for the largest leaps forward and brings you your most impressive gains.

It has long been rumored in astrological circles that Mars, the planet of driving energy and focus, is always happiest when he is near his cosmic lover, graceful Venus. Because Mars rules your solar relationship sector, and

Venus is the ruling planet of Taurus, the placements of these two mythological lovers are often reliable indicators of one's romantic outlook.

Last year, Venus and Mars were hardly ever together. Mars was too busy riling up your eighth house financial sector (giving you little time to think about anything besides money) and Venus was busy going along her own orbit, with people to see, and places to go. Thus, last year might have been OK, but a little dull. This all changes now.

In 2002, Venus and Mars are intent to make up for lost time. In fact, they will be together almost all year — if they're not hand-in-hand, they will have a reunion to look forward to. Both planets will be very happy. La-de-da! This is going to be one hot romantic year, Taurus!

The cosmos is cooking up something special by the middle of February, just in time to create a memorable Valentine's Day.

The whole second half of February will be terrific — you'll have good vibes straight into early March. Romantic, creative and compassionate Neptune and fun-loving Venus will be in what astrologers call "mutual reception". This term indicates an elegant synergistic (and possibly even psychic) support from each planet to the other. This exchange is so powerful, it strengthens the energies of both planets in the process. What is so remarkable about this aspect is that Neptune, often called "the higher octave" of Venus, works to bring the love of Venus to a much more intense level. At this time, Venus will be not only loving but willing to make sacrifices in the name of love; her beloved, Mars, is going to be one happy planet. Thus, by the end of the first quarter of the year, these two beautiful planets may leave you breathless, when "as above in the heavens, so too, below on earth" you find the kind of love you were beginning to think existed only in dreams.

The whole second half of February is terrific, punctuated by a full moon in your house of true love on February 28. So far, so good!

Mars moves into Taurus in March, making it a key month on many levels. Remarkably, Venus and Mars have a turn at being in "mutual reception" as well — very rare, which gives you another, even *more* powerful chance at love. Oh, Taurus!

By April, Venus moves into *your* sign of Taurus, and remains there until April 26. In a wonderful twist of fate, there is a full moon the next day, April 27, in your house of commitment, a moon that will coax you to make a decision about your closest attachment. How is that for timing, dear Taurus? What will happen is up to you and how you feel. There is no reason to rush. Many other significant developments are in store.

June 3 arrives next, a gold star day for making commitments or pursuing anything dear to your heart. It will be your wonder day, when Venus kisses good-fortune Jupiter. *Wow!* Circle this one in red!

By September, Mars will move in to turn up the volume in your love sector. Your very best period will fall in the first half of the month. Later in the month, Mercury, the ruler of your fifth house of true love, goes retrograde.

If you are unsure about your attachment, you will put on the brakes now. Give yourself some space to breathe and some time to consider your next steps. If you are not really committed to anyone special, you may go back to a previous lover to see if you should patch things up. Or, you may ask a present lover to revisit an old problem for a new and better solution.

Suddenly, the last few months of the year mark a temporary setback in matters of love. October and November seem to find you clouded with doubt, and these months represent your only romantically problematic months in the whole of 2002. Venus will be retrograde, not only does it not bode well for furthering romance, because Venus is your ruler, this aspect tends to pull things apart. Everything you counted on happening will suddenly be put on a hold. You don't see this coming, and you understandably will be upset. Still, these two months could allow you the necessary time and space to consider what you are doing. If love is real it can withstand this temporary stall.

The period from October through November 19 would not be a good time to get engaged or married. It would be best to use this period to meditate about your next move. (Note that Venus is retrograde from October 11 to November 19, but I strongly recommend you keep at arm's length distance from the start of this period; don't be slow to act. After November 19, you can act immediately.)

November is not an easy month for another reason: a lunar eclipse in Taurus. This will most affect bulls born on or near May 18. Career is on your mind, as are relationships. The real message of this full moon lunar eclipse is a call to return to your core, to consider what *you* want, and to make adjustments if you've ventured too far afield of your deepest wishes.

Miraculously, just as you are about to give up on being able to control the course of true love, Mars comes to the rescue. The red planet sets off a fireworks display in your chart in December that you'll long remember. Just in time to enjoy the holidays! Magically, this is the time of the year we all associate with joy and sparkling, sweeping romance. That's just what's in store for you.

At that time, Mars embraces Venus and begins a slow and beautiful dance of love so magnificent, it is breathtaking in its power and majesty. It is not one you are ever likely to forget. Rarely have astrologers seen anything quite like this before. Remarkably, these two cosmic lovers choose to meet in your seventh house of commitment, and they stay within tiny mathematical steps, together, within a few degrees, for the *whole* month! Watch out!

Many astrologers feel that hosting Venus in the seventh house, in Scorpio, has a full moon effect. That is, this placement enlarges emotions to a tender and warm peak of excitement and fulfillment. That's what you have in December 2002! To say you have an adventuresome year ahead for romance is putting it mildly! Oh Taurus, I am so happy for you!

Summary

The overriding message of 2002 is that this is not the year to dream. It's the year to put dreams into action. It is a year to talk less and do more. As the zodiac's producer, that should please you, dear Taurus!

While your career will continue to be volcanic from time to time, the liquid atmosphere that such seismic activity creates will allow you to uncover opportunities, and to maneuver to the spot that will allow you to shine. Money seems to be the only sticking point. You may have to accept that employers are not feeling generous right now. Yet even *that* will work to your benefit. The very fact that no one seems to be offering you a fat salary on a silver platter will free you to take a job you love, rather than one that simply pays well. Work is to be enjoyed, not endured!

Travel is exhilarating in the first half of the year — especially July, so try to vacation. Later, in the second half, your home life will improve so much you won't want to step outside the door. Profit is associated with your home, too. I see the possibility to make a killing in real estate or to create a lucrative home-based business. If you have been concerned about a parent, Jupiter will serve as fantastic protection to your mother or father. Spend more time with your parents this year, Taurus.

Being the romantic that I know you to be, I am sure that the fantastic love-related aspects due in 2002 will please you most of all. Having the fifth house so filled with energy, as yours will be, bodes well for having a baby or enjoying the children you have now. Your creativity is about to soar. Dear Taurus, if you could sell your star power this year, you'd have a line at the door! Kisses to you!

GEMINI

The Big Picture

The coming year will be like two mini years rolled into one — much in the way last year was. The first half will be very similar to a year ago, which — considering the massive changes you have experienced — may be comforting. Then things get even better. You'll notice a vast improvement on every level during the second half of the year. By then, Saturn will have stopped arguing with Pluto, and Jupiter will have had a chance to deliver some delicious cosmic goodies.

As you get deeper into 2002 the outer big-guy planets (Pluto, Uranus, Neptune, Jupiter and Saturn) will wake up to the fact that you might need their help. Like cumbersome, mammoth marbles thundering their way along the floor of the night sky, each will roll into its position. The net effect will be like being given a chessboard with all your pieces in exactly the right places. Chess is not an easy game — you seem to have the power to ace it if you keep your wits about you.

The main heavy-duty planets (those which remain in a sign for years at a time) will stay in predominantly fire and air signs, elements that relate well to your air-sign Sun, throughout the second half of the year. Pluto will be in Sagittarius (fire), Uranus and Neptune in Aquarius (air),

Saturn in Gemini (air) and later, Jupiter in Leo (fire). Dear Gemini, what more compassionate environment could you possibly imagine? It is as if all your relatives are surrounding you, with their arms around you, patting you on the back. Having these planets in such compatible placements will help you move forward. There is no doubt that life has become hard lately. It should be good to know it won't *always* be an uphill battle.

Saturn, the taskmaster planet, has been in your sign since last year and continues to travel across Gemini throughout 2002 and into 2003. If you view seriously the new responsibilities that Saturn brings, you stand to benefit a great deal. Saturn cycles always coincide with periods of enormous personal achievement and growth. The lessons you learn will be substantial and lasting, and by the end of this cycle in June 2003, you'll feel polished and seasoned. While Saturn never brings rewards *during* its tour of duty, you can count on a payoff a few months after its departure in June 2003. Yes, you'll have to wait a while to see that reward, but rest assured. It is there for you!

Three eclipses this year will fall in Gemini and in your opposite sign, Sagittarius, and will clarify the nature of your closest romantic and business relationships. Those eclipses will arrive on May 26, June 10, and December 4. At those dates you may advance discussions on ideas or issues that surfaced around the Solar eclipse in Sagittarius on December 14, 2001. These 2002 eclipses will work in tandem with Saturn to help you define your goals and a new sense of self.

Financially, in the year ahead, you're golden. So important is this current trend that, truly, the experiences you have and decisions you make in the first six months of 2002 could set the stage for a whole decade of profit and security. The long-term picture should be clear by the middle of the summer. July will be simply remarkable! Let's step back and look at the larger picture. Try to view these planetary configurations and the bumps they bring as growing pangs, necessary to give form to your new life. You won't necessarily have to give up all of the past. If you feel that some of those parts are working well, keep 'em. The eclipses will systematically test the strength and viability of every area of your life, and will encourage you to choose which areas to concentrate on, which areas have the greatest potential for growth and happiness.

Standing on the threshold of 2002, it may be hard to imagine such vital changes underfoot, but I promise, they are there and they are exciting! You may soon wonder why you were so apprehensive about giving up your old life!

That was your at-a-glace overview, now let's get into the nitty gritty of your year ahead!

A Look at Last Year

The past helps create context for the present and future, so let's start with a look at 2001. Last year was a year to remember. You had two of the most powerful planets in the solar system — those which give form and structure to our lives — in your very own sign. As you began 2001, you hosted Jupiter, the planet of good fortune and happiness. A little later, at about the time Jupiter was packing his bags, Saturn, the taskmaster planet, arrived for a lengthy, two and a half year stay. Talk about contrasts!

Having Jupiter in your sign was a little like having your favorite uncle as a house guest. It is wonderful to have someone around who loves you, who continually surprises you with chocolates and other gifts, and who always makes sure there is always a little money on the table should you need it. That's what Jupiter's company feels like. With Jupiter in your first house last year, you felt free to come and go at will, whether to travel, attend social events, or to just to browse in shops. Life was joyous. This favorite uncle encouraged you to think big and bold, and infused your life with a sense of manifest destiny.

When Saturn replaced Jupiter you suddenly found yourself hosting a military sergeant. From then on you found yourself in Saturn's boot camp, up at dawn to do a hundred push-ups and jog around the reservoir. Instead of nibbling chocolates, you consumed military rations and read warnings about the perils of junk food. There were to be no more free gifts. Saturn refuses to give rewards that you don't earn the old fashioned way. Whenever you left the house, you were expected to leave contact information and abide by a curfew. Instead of presenting you with social events to enjoy, drill sergeant Saturn reminded you that there would be no TV until all the work is done. Your big dreams had to be viewed much more pragmatically, and trimmed down to fit a new reality.

Although Saturn gets a bad rap, it shouldn't. Though hard-won, Saturn's rewards are considerable and appreciable. You generate them yourself, without help, in a much more focused, concentrated, and even driven way than you would the gifts of, say, Jupiter. Frankly, Saturn's gifts make those of other planets pale by comparison! Jupiter delivers the initial opportunity for a deal and cause for celebration when the deal is struck; Saturn shows you precisely how to see things through, step by step. Saturn stands by you (or should I say, over you) as you labor through the process of reaching a goal, and makes sure you do it right. What you produce under a

Saturn rule is the best it can be. While you may wish Saturn would just leave, in hindsight you'll admit gratitude. You never knew you were capable of turning out such excellence.

In addition, Saturn teaches you patience, endurance, self-discipline, responsibility, practicality and prudence. Later, when you finally accomplish your dreams, the feeling will be mighty sweet. Your work garners the respect of everyone around you — VIPS, competitors and loved ones included. Saturn helps you realize your visions.

A Long Term Goal on the Agenda

At the beginning of 2002, you are again being asked to commit to a long-term goal, though you may have done so last year. It will involve a decision about which you care deeply and anticipate with great joy. Yet even those happy occasions require some serious reflection and focused of energy. That's exactly why you still need Saturn — to help you make the transition.

You might, for example, be planning to get married, to have a baby or to take on the care of an elderly relative who desperately needs you. Alternatively, you may choose to buy your first house or to launch an exciting new business venture. These types of decisions, those with far-reaching implications, are the hallmarks of a Saturn visit. As you see, it can represent the fulfillment of a long-term goal!

It might be wise to bear in mind that Saturn's orbit always takes two-and-a-half years, and Saturn comes by in this manner once every 29 years. That's why you don't have too much experience with these cycles. As you see, Saturn's visits will happen only two or three times in your lifetime, and for that reason are very valuable! As you enter 2001, you are nearly at the halfway point of this particular Saturn cycle. Having had about a year's experience with this taskmaster planet, the good thing about 2002 is that you have already begun to develop a familiarity with how this planet works, and can make the most of the rest of its visit.

The Value of Saturn's Tests

When Saturn entered Gemini in April 2001, the conditions in your work environment and personal life suddenly and without warning became constricting. Saturn began taking away the pillars of support you depended on for so long. As each support was taken away, one by one, you came to rely on your own abilities, beliefs and motivations. This is a common consequence of a Saturn visit. It is meant to foster independence and test your resolve.

Saturn expects a slow and deliberate effort, and will force you to follow rules and pay your dues. You may be involved in an apprenticeship in a new field, eager to learn the ropes. In some way, you are about to prepare for a new role. All these methods are Saturn's way of helping you establish a solid foundation and recognize your strength and determination. Indeed, once you are done with Saturn, you will realize that you have crossed a milestone, and that you have entered a whole new phase of existence.

While there is some degree of uncertainty and insecurity inherent in the process of testing your own strengths for the first time, you need to trust yourself and move forward. Saturn will teach you to deal with ambiguity.

Under this influence, you'll learn to make decisions in the light of incomplete information. As a Gemini, you prefer to analyze every fact you get your hands on, but now you may have no choice but to rely on your wits and intuition. You will called on to make an assortment of practical, no-nonsense decisions without a great deal of back-up. While it may feel like you are flying by the seat of your pants, there's nothing you can do about it. Sometimes there is no other way. The train is leaving, dear Gemini, and if you want to be on it, you'll have to be decisive.

Finally, keep this in mind: In times of ease, we learn nothing of great consequence. It is during Saturn cycles that we deal with the very essence of our lives, what they are about. In the process we come to know ourselves very well. Indeed, our most impressive contributions usually coincide with Saturn cycles. So as you see, this tough-guy planet will allow you to see yourself in your finest hour.

Then and Now:
From the Early 70's to 2002

If you are old enough, think back to the last time Saturn visited your sign, from June 1971 through January 1974. You probably made at least one conscious, monumental decision during that period. We usually have some say in which area we tackle under Saturn. If you look around your life today, you can probably see some issues similar to those present during that earlier period. Someone or something you are dealing with now relates directly to a decision you made at that time.

Saturn will cover a lot of ground in 2002, directly touching the degrees of almost all Gemini birthdays. The only members of the sign who will be exempt from this taskmaster planet's most direct, demanding rays are those Twins with early-Gemini birth dates, in May. Those Gemini have already completed the core part of Saturn's training.

Best Methods of Dealing with Saturn's Tests

It must be clear by now that your shoulders are about to bear yet more responsibility, if that is not already the case. If you learn to carry your duties squarely and with grace, you will have an easier time than if you resist or complain.

It is common to feel alone as you go through such a period. Saturn's influence can be quite isolating. Still, this may merely be your perception; if you need help, ask for it. Friends, family and professional peers are there for advice and moral support. Later, after you are done with Saturn's character-building program, it will be your turn to be more compassionate of others' needs. For now, learn to ask for help when you need it. Admitting vulnerability and learning to rely on others is one of the lessons you'll learn in this period. Still, there is a balance here, as Saturn wants to see you stand on your own two feet.

As you search for answers, you may discover that the world runs on its own timetable and that it simply does not jibe with yours. If you can't maneuver things to happen when you want them to, I certainly sympathize, dear Gemini. But don't give up. Saturn wants you to be patient and resourceful. It may throw a few roadblocks in your path to success, just to see what you'll do. You'll become quite adept in getting around those obstacles while retaining your principles. Luckily, you're a flexible Gemini. If there is any talent you were blessed with, it's the ability to come up with solid contingency plans!

There is another plus to a Saturn transit. While we are

battling the forces before us, we have no energy to be anything but the truest version of ourselves, both to ourselves and to the outside world. There is not enough extra energy to put on airs, or to be pretentious. It is at those times of stress that we come face to face with the person we truly are.

You need to develop deep roots to survive life's storms, dear Gemini. The deeper the roots, the taller the tree. You are in the process of building that foundation now.

What you need as you enter 2002 is a bright vision of hope. You want a promise that there is something more to life. You want proof that it is worth fighting for. Paradise lies just beyond the wilderness, dear Gemini, but it *is* there, and you *can* reach it. If at times you get a bit weary, remind yourself that the universe will not turn its back on you — it is there to help and support you. Nature does not create a tree and then forget to nourish it. Your dreams for happiness exist — your job is to fill them.

Love, Life and Relationships

First we'll look at the role of the eclipses on your identity and established relationships.

For the first time in ten years, the eclipses, those great ignitions of change in our lives, are back in Gemini and its polar sign of Sagittarius. It is once again time to reinvent yourself. This was evident almost a year ago in April 2001 when Saturn finally settled into Gemini. The eclipses will be working in tandem with Saturn to help you reach new heights, and to reach more evolved stage of maturity.

Add this all up, and it appears that some rather important change is underway. Eventually, you will see your old life fade into the background as your new moves in. You are one of the few signs that sees the powerful value in change — quite an asset now! Should you be tempted to return to the "good old days", consider that they may not have been so great, after all. You are replacing those years with something far more durable and relevant to your future.

Your identity is undergoing a vast transformation. No doubt, you'll need a little time to get used to this these transitions. Just as a man whose lost 100 pounds needs to adjust to his new image in the mirror (even though it is far better than before), you will need to get used to your new life. How you see yourself and how others are seeing you is radically shifting, and that will have an impact on your closest, most intimate relationships.

An eclipse can provide that which a relationship needs to survive. It can create a true sense of purpose in both partners, and strengthen their will to stay together. Sometimes, in order to make things work, a relationship needs an ultimatum, a competitor, or some other surprise that acts as a catalyst and energizes the alliance. Eclipses often reveal hidden truths by changing the dynamics surrounding a relationship, and bring to the surface events that are often quite out of anyone's control. For instance, suppose you are a man who has dated a special woman for three years, quite happily, but marriage has not yet been discussed. Then, suddenly your lady is given the opportunity to manage the Singapore office. She decides that not only does she want the job, she wants you to follow her to Asia as her husband. If you say no, she says that's it. In an instance such as this, out of either party's control, the lovely relationship comes to an end. Eclipses are wild cards that require life decisions.

Eclipses push us into circumstances that we would not

ordinarily look for. It is in rising to such occasions that we grow and develop. Eclipses always come in pairs, as a new moon and full moon, and the partnering eclipse falls in your seventh house of committed relationships. If you can secure the foundation you and your partner have built over time, you will come away with something of real value. However, if your partner is not as committed to the alliance as you are or vice versa, your relationship will end. What the eclipses won't tolerate is living in long-term limbo, where you pass like ships in the night, not interacting, just existing on the same plane. Though not an easy transition, it will be for the better.

In all cases, the eclipses will ask you to clarify what you have (or don't have). With that knowledge, you'll have no choice but to move toward a more honest, forthright relationship. It is equally possible you will feel a rekindling of passionate feelings the likes of which you have not felt for a long time. That would be a delightful outcome — and it's certainly very possible here.

These eclipses are set to occur in mutable signs. There will be a lot of room for talking, negotiating, stretching, growing, pushing and pulling. With such freedom of movement, no relationship issue is set in stone, and there's no reason to suffer in silence. Eclipses urge us to speak up, fix it or move on.

Some Twins will feel the effects of the eclipses in their business relationships. This is because your seventh house rules any committed collaborations, not just romantic ones. Pluto is thought to be one of the most powerful planets in our solar system. It is positioned on the very outer edge and takes the longest time to circle the Sun. Pluto's position in your seventh house makes it clear that others hold the keys to your future right now. Your relationships with people won't necessarily be clear cut, though. One minute you may be saying to your partner "I need space!" and the next minute, "No, I don't! Don't leave me!" This is typical behavior under Pluto's complex presence. You are seeing the benefits and drawbacks of closeness versus independence. Suffice it to say that you have quite a powerful relationship in your life, and if you can sustain it, so much the better. You'll begin to know where you stand this year, dear Gemini.

Your Best Months for Pure Romance

March 28 holds a tender and romantic full moon in your house of new love, true love. Circle it and the days around it for a romantic episode you'll long remember. Expect Father Neptune to bring his golden net down over you and your lover, to carry you off to his sea of love.

Later, it would be hard to beat the gorgeous, warming rays from mid-April through the first three weeks of May. Mars, that exciting mythological lover of the midnight skies, will embrace his favorite, Venus, and twirl her in a dance of love across a sky twinkling as brightly as diamonds. It will leave you breathless. These two planets will dance in the constellation of Gemini, a graceful, rare development — especially when you consider how hard it is for Mars and Venus to schedule time together in the first place. To have these planets reunite in your sign will be lucky for you, indeed. (Last year Venus and Mars were never together — this year, their passion for each other is so strong, no one can pull them apart for long!) Mercury is retrograde during part of this period, May 15 – June 8, so an old lover may enter the picture, or you may be of two minds about a current attachment (as exciting as it is.)

We already discussed the eclipses in Gemini and

Sagittarius. May brings one such eclipse to your relationship sector on May 26, which is Memorial Day in the United States. This lunar eclipse coincides with the only very difficult planetary aspect during this period, Saturn's opposition to Pluto on May 25. This creates *very* potent planetary energy, and everyone, everywhere will feel its effects. Saturn and Pluto are powerful planets. One is passionate and even obsessive (Pluto) while the other is more detached and practical (Saturn). Combining the two is a little like soaking burning coals in ice water. This weekend in May will be fraught with deep and turbulent emotions, so be careful. One of you might make a play for control of the relationship — it's not clear who's doing the maneuvering! Either way, some rather interesting revelations will come out of discussions you have at that time. Try not to shout. This configuration will most touch those Gemini born in the middle of their signs, near June 7.

More powerful romantic vibrations come in October, thanks to an absolutely remarkably strong new moon in your fifth house of love on October 6.

Shortly thereafter the mood changes dramatically. Venus begins to dally in retrograde (October 10 – November 21). This is not a good omen for the setting up of long-term romance or for untangling difficulties in a present relationship. When Venus is retrograde is not an auspicious time for weddings, either.

Happily, this saga has a good ending. Mars, sensing something is wrong, dashes over to this part of the sky to see what's troubling Venus, and arrives by mid-October. This comedy of love really begins to improve by the end of November. But wait! In case you thought that was it, there's more! Amazingly, love reaches a sweet crescendo near the December 4 solar (new moon) eclipse in

Sagittarius in your relationship sector, in perfect angle to both Jupiter and Pluto. Finally, the curtain comes down on 2002 with everything just as you like it. You're in a relationship that is sexy and fun, but also responsible and caring. Whew! After many twists and turns, your romantic episode works out perfectly in the end. All's well that ends well, no?

Career Progress is Better Than Expected

As you begin the year, Mars is set to put your career reputation in lights! Indeed, the first half of January may be a banner time for establishing yourself, dear Gemini, and you'll have the Red Planet to thank. (Just so you know, Mars was helping you in the final days of December 2001. As you begin the year, you may still be basking in the glow of events that occurred then.)

The two weeks following March 13 will trigger more outstanding career opportunities. In fact, the second half of March holds so much promise, you should be prepared to drop everything for meetings, interviews and professional presentations. This period has so much potential, it would be a crime to waste.

If you are self-employed, or if you have a responsible position at work, know that Mars will grant you special favor from the second half of April through May. This should prove to be one of your most critical times of the year to engage in any strenuous, concerted efforts. Start a new job, launch a new product or get funding for an innovative idea. You name it! The force is with you!

Finally, the Harvest Moon on September 21 will bring another key moment for upbeat news about your ever-rising career status. At this point, you'll reach a finale on past projects. The thundering applause for your work could make you blush!

Finances are Phenomenal March through July

You financial picture for 2001 is even brighter than your career prospects, if that is possible. Thanks to the Jupiter's position, you have some of the *best* financial aspects of any sign. At the start of 2002 you are probably entering a whole new financial cycle. The income you generate at the beginning of the year could represent a potent new revenue stream that will continue to bring rich profit in the decade to come. Think big and do not, under any circumstances, do not sell yourself short!

Last year, due to the presence of eclipses in your financial sectors, you may have lost or opted out of a major source of income. If so, and you have had difficulty finding a new one, redouble your efforts. Be sure to seek opportunities in a variety of places. With your chart, you could hit it big, but you have to roll up your sleeves and show the universe your intentions. While it is true that Jupiter was in your financial house for part of last year, you did not have much luck. Jupiter's orbit was weak, and its ability to be of service was dimmed. This year, this planet is moving in a much more robust cycle from March though July 2002 — that adds up to *five* incredibly lucky months! In fact, financial reward is one of your strongest themes of 2002. Abundant finances will probably cushion some of the other changes in your life. Having a little extra money always helps! If you felt disappointed by wimpy profits in 2001 despite your golden aspects, keep your spirits up. You are about to strike gold!

In the middle of this period, on June 24, comes the

lunar eclipse in your eighth house of credit and taxes. This will bring a deal, negotiation or a future loan or grant to the fore. Luckily, you still have Jupiter guarding your other financial house. Even though an ending or settlement is indicated, you have help elsewhere in your chart to protect all your interests.

One of your best dates within the abovementioned period would be July 10, when a new moon hits your second house of earned income. That moon sends a kiss to Jupiter, so you really will be fortunate. You'll have two weeks of strong energy following that day. Don't blow this wonderful opportunity!

Watch also July 19 and 20, when Jupiter sends kisses to the Sun and to your ruler, Mercury, respectively. These are five star days for financial news you won't soon forget!

There are two very important dates in the second half of the year, due to a stunning collaboration between Jupiter and Pluto: October 27 (a Sunday, but operative in the days leading up to it) and December 18, 2002. Both days are five star days, but the October date is best, for both planets are operating at a higher power. December 18 is interesting in that it coincides with the full moon in Gemini the following day, signifying that a matter of major, long-range importance is reaching a final round. In both cases, an intermediary (partner, agent, collaborator) is present. See what you can do to whip up in a meeting on those days!

It is clear that any bounty in 2002 will be money you earn, not money you win or are given. That's great news. You're getting rewarded for all the work driving you this year. No one can say you don't deserve it!

Communication

After August, your innate ability to communicate force-fully and eloquently will be valued by just about everyone. If you ever wanted to write a book or screenplay, contribute an important magazine article, create a web-site, teach a group, or lecture on a beloved topic, this is your year! It appears that your luck will be generated through an agent. If you don't have one, find one. Just remember: Your luck starts mid-year.

Those of you who are in sales should find success, as will those working in public relations, publishing, tourism, shipping or transportation, software develop-ment, telecommunications, marketing, computers, the Internet, teaching or library research.

Dates to watch are January 23, April 1, August 21, December 16, all five stars dates for pursuing advance-ments in these areas.

Travel

While it seems unlikely you are going to travel as much as you did in 2001, any journeys you undertake this year will be just as refreshing. Your trips will occur more spontaneously now too, especially from August on. That probably sounds like your cup of tea. You generally don't like making plans too far in advance. Why not plan a vaca-tion for August? The new moon on August 8 will trigger two weeks of opportunity for adventure.

There are two dates set to be exceptions to this year's rule, the "short distance is more fun in 2002" rule. When Saturn and Uranus conspire, longer-distance travel would be a big success, for pleasure and also for business. Circle August 21 and December 16.

Health and Fitness

Do you want to be slimmer and fit? One nice side effect of Saturn's visit is encouragement to lose weight healthfully. (Remember, Saturn always likes to see things done slow and steady.) If you've put on a few pounds, you now have the best opportunity in over a decade to slim down.

It will be important to eat right. Avoid burning the candle at both ends. Saturn is also exerting an influence on your vitality and looks, and wants to see you take a disciplined approach to your health. If you do, by the end of the year you will have mended your ways, well on your way to a healthier, stronger and fitter you.

While Jupiter expands all that it touches (including your hips), Saturn constricts all it comes in contact with. This is why you can expect to get back to your best, fighting weight. See your doctor for advice on how to begin. Then, if you can afford it, join a gym or take lessons on your favorite sport. Find an exercise buddy, or have a consultation with a coach, trainer, exercise instructor, or nutritionist.

One last piece of advice: Saturn is currently taxing your calcium reserves, so watch that you get enough of this mineral in your diet. Saturn's position in Gemini could give you problems with your hands, wrist and fingers, so take frequent breaks if you work on a computer. (This is recommended to ward off carpel tunnel problems.) Saturn's position could also bring difficulty breathing. It would be a good idea to take up aerobics and other cardiovascular exercises that would help increase your lung capacity. At the same time, renounce destructive habits that may harm your lungs long term. There's no such thing as a casual or social smoker. If you smoke at a party once a month, you smoke. You need to quit. If you suspect the air quality in your area to be detrimental to your health, see a doctor about measures to keep yourself healthy. Teeth may need attention too, so be sure to see a dentist if you haven't in a while.

As you see, you have quite a full year ahead! Luckily, you're the master juggler, Twin. If anyone can fit two years into one, it's you!

Summary

There is no doubt that you find yourself with a full plate this year. Many planetary indicators suggest massive change is underway. Last year you had Jupiter, the giver of gifts, in your sign. Life was big, bright and beautiful. Opportunity was strong, and your plans for the future impressive. Now, with Saturn, the taskmaster planet, in Jupiter's place as the dominant planetary influence on your chart, you're in for a change. The contrast between the two must be sharp. Saturn is coaxing you to scale down your ideas to make sure they have a chance of being approved. Saturn is, after all, a very conservative planet and will always encourage you to lower your risk.

While having had Jupiter in Gemini (mid-2000 to mid-2001) marked a fantastically joyful period, you have to admit Jupiter made you a bit soft. When you recently realized you had to fend for yourself and possibly even flex your survival skills, you were probably a bit horrified to find yourself rusty and out of shape. Now all that will be corrected. Saturn will help you get back to fighting form.

You will likely commit to one big goal during this period. It is an exciting one, for it will form a foundation for the future. Keep in mind that Saturn cycles always coincide with enormous personal growth. Once you do lift off, Saturn will see you succeed beyond your greatest expectations. Should you get knocked over, just get up again and keep on going. What we regret when we are old and wrinkled is not what we did, but what we failed to do. No one can ever fault you for trying.

Let's look elsewhere in your chart. Financial success should be remarkably strong in the first half of the year. Your reputation and career status climb in January, and then again in April and May. Other critical moments include a bright spot in September at the Harvest Moon. In the second half, you're given many chances to travel here and there, especially on frequent getaways of short distance. Making contact with siblings should brighten your spirit.

Romance has its usual ups and downs and a few surprising developments. April and May find Cupid and his little angles surrounding you. These are your most enchanting months of the year! And despite a cliffhanger or two in the latter part of the year, you'll manage to land sunny-side-up. Well done!

By time the glittery ball falls on Times Square in New York City to mark the end of 2002, you will look back at all the personal growth, and all you've achieved on so many levels and exclaim, "Wow! Did I do all that? That's a *lot!*" You'll have every reason to be proud, dear Gemini!

CANCER

The Big Picture

This should be a landmark year, Cancer. While each year holds certain opportunities, the ones you get this year are ideal — far better than anything you've seen in recent memory. In fact, during the first half of 2002, you have an extra bit of good fortune. Jupiter, planet of happiness and growth, names you "celestial favorite" as it continues to move through your sign in a once-in-twelve-year visit. Your luck should extend far beyond the normal confines. (Jupiter usually has an effect on one house at a time.) This planet's influence can be felt in several areas at once, including career, romance, money and health. Name your desires, Cancer! The universe is listening!

Furthermore, at some point each year, the outer heavy-hitters such as Saturn, Uranus, Neptune or Pluto (the planets that really set up the major themes of our lives) throw a spanner in the works with disruptive aspects. These tough challenges are sent down to sharpen our life skills and improve our character development. They pull our energy away from other areas of our lives with their demand for immediate and consistent attention. This year is remarkable. None of these planets is going to challenge your Cancer Sun. They'll be too busy creating mischief with other signs of the zodiac and will leave you alone for all of 2002! Granted, none of the four planets named has plans to go out of its way to help you, either. Without them pestering your life, you won't need the others' help anyway! And you still definitely have an edge with Jupiter, the fifth big-guy planet and arguably the most important one, on your side. More than any other planet, Jupiter has the power to protect you. Jupiter should also give you lucky breakthroughs and happy coincidences if you show the universe your passion and focus.

There is one hard aspect that will touch everyone: the third and final opposition of Saturn and Pluto. By the time these two end their long-standing argument on May 25, 2002 (something we'll discuss in detail later), the outer planets will be aligned in a highly compatible way. The beauty of their symmetry in 2002 is simply astonishing. Be thankful for this. It is a rare cosmic gift. By mid-year there will be no hard aspects due for any of us. With the year's sunny prospects and few of the usual obstacles and distractions, you'll be able to make real progress. You will be free to follow your own agenda, without pressure, unfazed by events happening elsewhere. At the end of 2002, expect to have a great deal to show for your efforts.

This year emphasizes action. You may be nudged a bit by the cosmos to get going. If so, good! It means the universe won't let you procrastinate any longer. It is time to work on those big dreams! You have an outstanding chance to find true happiness now, dear Cancer, but you will have to show the universe that you are determined. If you've spent the past few years standing on the sidelines, get ready to play ball. You may not have had a shot at the right opportunity (or the courage for change) in the past, but the coming year will provide you with the incentive and support you need. This will be your year, dear Cancer! No one could be more deserving!

Jupiter in Cancer

Jupiter is the largest planet in our solar system. Floating as a huge yellow-brown marble in space, Jupiter is so big that if you took all the other planets (excluding the Sun, which is technically a star) and bunched them all together, Jupiter would be bigger than all of them combined. This is an astronomical fact, and is the reason the ancients associated Jupiter with massive good fortune. Through eons of empirical research, going back to at least 2,500 B.C., this has proven to be true. Now, in 2002, this massive planet favors you.

Jupiter has been in your sign since July 2001; you're halfway through this trend. You may be thinking to yourself, "Well, last year didn't seem to be *that* good!" You are probably right. There were factors that prevented you from reaping the full potential of this generous planet. Jupiter's power was hampered by eclipses and other planetary forces last year. By early November, Jupiter, weary and in desperate need of rest, gave up and went to sleep. No doubt, Jupiter was murmuring to himself, as he nodded off: "I'll work on helping Cancer in 2002, when I'm more refreshed."

As January begins, Jupiter will still be fast asleep in retrograde. Hold tight. It is due to wake up with a boom on March 1, 2002. That's your big moment, Cancer. From that point on, everything should start to click into place. Once Jupiter wakes up, this mighty planet will be operating at full throttle through July, for a period of *five* months!

For the entire time, you may feel like a kid who's won a toy store contest, invited to pile as many gifts into your shopping cart as you can before the buzzer rings. You'll have to work fast! That's true for you. You have five months to gather all you can, to take advantage of all that's available to you. If your goals are big, you'll have to work in a very highly organized manner in order to reach them by the end of July. You will be able to put your hands on quite a bit of booty if you remain focused on your goal and your deadline.

It is a very potent time, rich with potential for rewards that could extend into the future for ten years or more. You will have to get yourself "out there." There is no doubt that you can have the help of influential people, but they need to get to know you exist and understand what you're after before they can be of any service. Few of us are able to do things alone. You have a naturally reserved nature, and leading a high-profile existence does not feel comfortable. Well, you're going to have to get used to it; visibility is essential now. Jupiter will give you confidence — more than you've had in ages. Just forge ahead, Cancer. The force is with you.

One of the dangers of this period is that you could become complacent — Jupiter's golden vibrations have been known to have that effect. You can't afford to give into it. How can you be in the right place at the right time if you're home napping? Be prepared to push yourself forward. This is no time to sit on your laurels, no matter how tempting. You must fight against lethargy.

Jupiter will teach you to think on a much broader scale than ever. You may look back and wonder why you never considered working on a tapestry this large before. International or long-distance travel may very well be part of the picture as you extend the edges of your parameter. You will become acquainted with more high-level people this year as well, and develop a welcome ease when dealing with them.

It is essential that you sow the seeds. Later, the year after Jupiter's departure, those seeds will sprout. While not every one of your projects, relationships and endeavors will blossom, many more than usual will. Because you are in such a golden cycle, your odds of success will skyrocket. That is why I am pressing you to concentrate while Jupiter bathes you in his consistently rich, golden light. Remember, you won't enjoy Jupiter's favor like this for another twelve years!

You'll be busy in July. Besides being the last month to reap Jupiter's rewards, July holds a promising new moon on the tenth, which — in the two weeks that follow — should usher in some of the best news of the year. Then, one of your very best days of the year will come on July 1 9, plus or minus three days when Jupiter teams up with the mighty Sun! That's news, sure to help you make a huge leap forward. Remember — in order to see the benefits of these days, you will have to roll up your sleeves and set things in motion. The universe must know your intentions!

While we are on the subject of sparkling days, mark down October 2 7 and December 1 8 as powerful and quite unique. Whenever Jupiter and Pluto are at work success is around the corner.

Your career will be a major trend in 2002. Jupiter is the ancient ruler of your solar tenth house of profession and recognition. But your good fortune won't stop there — Jupiter will be helping you in many more areas, including love, health and money. Later in this report, I will point them out to you, and let you know what to expect.

Expect Your Coffers to be Full in 2002

On its silent orbit through space, Jupiter will eventually reach its second destination, the constellation of Leo, where it will stay from August 1 until August 27, 2003 — thirteen glorious months! In this house, this mighty planet will expand your opportunities in a way that will increase your income and cash flow. In the second half of 2002, you'll find that people are willing to pay a great deal of money for your services. This is no time to sell yourself short, no matter what your circumstances, dear Cancer. Keep in mind that the money coming to you is money you will earn; it will not come from prize-winnings, divorce settlements or tax refunds. No, this is cash you will earn.

This year Jupiter will send a superb beam to Pluto on October 27 and December 18, two more truly phenomenal days for upbeat news regarding salary negotiations, financial deals and lucky breaks. These are five-star dates, the likes of which we only get a handful. Look upon them as precious and special, and use them wisely!

You may find yourself spending more money than usual this year. The good news is you'll be able to afford to. There's no reason to be concerned! Now may be a good time to make acquisitions you wanted to but couldn't make in the past. Congratulations, Cancer! It must feel good to be able to get the things you've long wished for.

Your most expensive months of 2002 will occur in the second half of July and the month of August. Down the road in the later half of 2003, I am so sorry to report that there is a possibility that your income may dip. It is not clear why this happens. Nevertheless, you may want to save a portion of your newfound stash of earned income.

Now let's examine the area of your chart ruling your eighth house of joint resources, taxes, commissions, credit, and settlements. Over the past several years, since as far back as 1995, you hosted unpredictable Uranus and confusing Neptune in this financial house. Their influence probably lowered your chances for any stable financial management. To make matters more difficult, you had a number of tough eclipses in this financial sector in 1998 – 2000, and the fall-out from those years may still be present. Every time you tried to surmount these obstacles, you found yourself sliding down the slippery slope of financial stability.

Being a financially conservative sign, this was especially hard to deal with. You need to feel that your accounts are in good standing, that you have enough money for a nest egg. You also want the security of knowing your future needs won't necessitate that you dig into your returns. This year could give you satisfaction on this front, and even reverse some of the unexpected difficulties you encountered financially in the last few years. You don't have to suffer forever, Cancer. This year will give you the chance to take a big step forward. If credit or taxes have been problematic (which may not have been your fault to begin with), you're in for an upswing. Once Uranus leaves this house in late 2003, things will get even better. There are so many reasons to believe you are on the way to a better place!

In this regard, there are a number of five-star dates to cheer about. Here they are, with an explanation of how to best make use of them: On January 23 and April 1, offer practical, innovative ideas to your boss. They may be richly rewarded. Saturn will be in perfect angle to Neptune, the planet of vision and creativity; their influence is having a charming effect on you. Neptune's role in these dates also suggests that if you are involved with creative or artistic ideas, you will see gratifying results.

On August 21 and December 16, you may benefit from a lucky financial break that comes out of the blue. Stabilizing Saturn will be in perfect angle to surprising Uranus, so press ahead!

The four dates just mentioned should be quite extraordinary. Do circle them on your calendar!

Career Stability Creates Balance

In a year that emphasizes money over promotion and career recognition, it looks like you'll choose to make progress where you are now rather than chasing after new positions and titles. You'll feel appreciated and rewarded. Judging by your chart, this is somewhat new. Let's look closely at your career prospects.

One of the best periods of the year for moving ahead professionally will be from January 18 through February 28 when Mars lights up your tenth house of career. Unfortunately, a Mercury retrograde phase will mar this period, rendering it unfavorable to new proposals or job offers. (As you see, in astrology, we often have to allow for conflicting influences.) Mercury will be retrograde from January 18 to February 8. It is fine to do research and have meetings before that time, but your most vital initiations, including acceptance of a new job, would be best made in February rather than January.

There is an exception to the rule of not taking a new position when Mercury is retrograde. If you should get an offer from an employer who you know from your past, such an offer would be safe. Should you get an offer from anyone you knew some time ago, consider it carefully. It could have value. Only under such circumstances would I advise accepting a new job under weakened Mercury.

Even with such restrictions, a new job is not a long shot. Mercury retrograde periods urge us to reconsider the past, and either develop the relationship or seek closure and move on.

After February, your next big professional moment will occur in the two weeks that follow the new moon April 1 2. Expect the unexpected, dear Cancer, all of it wonderful!

More possibilities will come your way during the first week of July, especially near July 2. The new moon on July 1 0, just a week later, should be gratifying not only for burgeoning career developments, but also for progress in your personal life.

A culmination to your professional situation appears to be brewing at the full moon in your career sector on October 2 1. That moon is making a respectful nod to Saturn, so whatever occurs, the results will be exceptionally stabilizing.

If you are starting a business, wait to do so when Jupiter returns to direct motion. Jupiter governs profits (among other things), and you'd certainly want them favored! Schedule the official start date for sometime between March 1 and December 4. (The incorporation date--the date when you receive your government approval to begin — is the official birth of a business.)

Again, be sure to avoid those Mercury retrograde periods, January 1 8 to February 8, May 1 5 to June 8, and September 1 4 to October 6. (Should you need these dates in a pinch, they are listed on my website for years into the future; go to "Current Trends" at *Astrology Zone*, (www.astrologyzone.com) where you can also read your monthly forecasts.)

Radiant Health

Jupiter should have a fabulously healing, rejuvenating influence on your mind, body and spirit. With just a little effort, you could look like a million dollars: vibrant, alive and gorgeous. The only drawback to having Jupiter in your sign is the tendency to put on a few unwanted pounds. Don't freak out! You can avoid this if you are careful about what you eat and serious about exercising each day. Why not join a gym if you don't already belong to one? If you do have a membership in a health club, use it every day! Preventative measures like working out regularly and eating well are much easier than going on a diet to lose weight!

If you are usually in a time-crunch, try exercising to video tapes at home in the morning before you go to work. There are lots of excellent new ones to choose from. If you hit the gym at dawn, you won't have any excuses for not going — excuses seem to accumulate throughout the day! (Yes, you'll have to get up earlier. So what? You'll be full of energy in 2002.) Research shows that people who work out in the morning exercise more consistently than those who exercise in the evenings, and see better results in weight maintenance. Most people find that last-minute delays, meetings, and fatigue are more likely at the end of the day. People name these as the number one reasons for not working out. Have a plan! With Jupiter in your sign in the first six months of the year, those pounds could show up without notice.

In terms of health, should you need any surgery or medical treatments this year, make sure you schedule them for the first six months of 2002, when Jupiter, the great healer, works on your behalf. Pluto is still in your sixth house of health prevention, and is well angled to the other planets. This means that Pluto will lend you awesome regenerative powers. You may not need Pluto's help now or ever, but it sure is comforting to know it is there. You are about to surprise everyone with your astounding ability to rebound. Two dates that may go down in the annals of your personal history as wonder days for health would be the days around October 27 and December 18.

Avoid Mercury retrograde periods for any health procedures: January 18 to February 8, May 15 to June 8 and September 14 to October 6.

Also, you might not want to have an operation at a full moon, as most people bleed a little bit more at those times. It is not wise to operate whenever Mars is transiting a sign — for more information, please check my web site, *Astrology Zone* (www.astrologyzone.com).

Readers have been asking about cosmetic surgery. Dear Cancer, I doubt you need plastic surgery, but if you insist, please avoid Venus retrograde periods. Venus is the planet of beauty and rules over these types of operations. Of course, you should avoid Mercury retrograde periods as well, and they are noted above. Venus will retrograde October 10 – November 21, 2002.

There are two eclipses due in 2002 that could reveal a health or dental issue that needs attention. Those eclipses will fall on May 26 and December 4.

Productivity in Private: Saturn's Domain

Saturn, the teacher planet, will remain in Gemini throughout 2002, in the position it's held since April of last year, your twelfth house. With Saturn in this house, chances are you are nearing the end of an important cycle. To best make use of Saturn's position (which will be quite friendly to Pluto, Neptune and Uranus), try to clear up details on lagging projects that need to be completed. Saturn's entrance in your sign in June 2003 heralds a very vital new era. You won't want to be weighed down by any left-overs from your past. 2002 is your ideal year to clear the decks.

Saturn's position this year is one of the best possible for sustained concentration and focus on important projects, such as writing a book, composing a piece of music, completing a thesis for a degree, designing a web site or mapping out a strategy for a new business. Be confident that you will be able to do a thorough, detailed and organized job this year.

Work for Excellence in Mind, Body and Spirit

The eclipses in Gemini and Sagittarius this year and next will work in tandem with Saturn to help you analyze your lifestyle. You will look hard at your path to the future, and will make the changes you deem necessary. These eclipses are touching houses that are considered "cadent", easier places to host eclipses than others. They should have a mild effect. In 2002, the eclipses may force you to move forward on psychological and health matters, and will show you which skills you need to do your job well. If ever there was a year to act instead of talk, this is it. Even enforced changes will be beneficial. You will not be able to procrastinate any longer.

The moon is your ruler, so the lunar eclipses touch you in a more personal way than other signs. Harness the energy of these lunar events by taking steps not to be physically healthy, but to find greater peace of mind. Saturn's present position in the twelfth house is an ideal placement for off-loading long-buried hurts, whether to a friend, family member, professional coach or psychiatrist. If you know you have a few self-destructive habits (and who doesn't have at least one?) well, dear Crab, this is the year to get rid of them.

Jupiter is also urging you to travel more than usual, especially during the first half of the year when your chart glitters so brightly. Even Venus and Mars will be at work for you. A quick escape would refresh your spirit in ways you can't even fathom. Try to come up with a destination, if only for a long weekend. If you can, go to a place near water. Your best periods for any kind of travel would be during the first two weeks of January, from May 28 – July 13, and August 29 – October 15.

Saturn's Opposition to Pluto: A Difficult Aspect

Last year the world experienced a very rare configuration, Saturn verses Pluto, on August 5 and again on November 2. These two planets will continue their long-standing argument on May 25, 2002. After that, they finally part and orbit in separate directions, not to meet again for 29 years. For you, during each meeting of this confrontation, both planets were (and will be) eyeing one another from the houses that rule your mental and physical health. Saturn will be a stern teacher; he wants you to follow the rules. When it comes to health, if you've been fudging nutrition or burning the candle at both ends, Saturn will whack you until you get with a healthier program.

Home is Where the Little Crab's Heart Is

A Cancer in an unhappy home is a very unhappy crab

indeed. This will not be a major year for residential concerns, but should you have to move, you do have a strong planetary boost from the Red Planet. From mid-October through November 2002, Mars will be in a great position to help you lead a more comfortable home life. Aim to settle domestic concerns at that time. It should be a breeze.

During the same period, a new moon on October 6 should bring plenty of news — expect it either on that date or in the two weeks that follow. This is true whether you want to move, buy or sell a house or condo, refinance, refurbish, redecorate, or repair. It's also an ideal dynamic for settling roommate and family concerns — despite Mars' presence and its tendency to spark confrontations. Everything will come out in the open. You'll be in a better position to find a solution and move forward.

Earlier in the year, on June 2 or on or near August 8, you may have a major breakthrough. Both dates are exceptionally lucky!

You have good vibrations even if all you plan to do is buy some pretty new things for your home; do so from August 7 to September 7 when Venus glides through your home sector. That would be a perfect time to hire a decorator, paint your apartment, buy a new piece of furniture, or just perk things up a bit. The last part of the year truly does seem to be packed with opportunities to make your home just the way you like it.

Romance Improves in 2002

This should be a much steadier year for romance than 2001. Last year, many Cancers did have the good fortune to find a soul mate. Jupiter's position gave you and the friends of your sign an amazing edge. However, as you enter 2002, if you are still not dating anyone special, get out and show your face to the world in the first seven months of 2002, your most golden period. May through July will bring some of your most enchanting meetings and magical encounters. It is finally your year to discover true love, for keeps. While new moons and eclipses can tell us a lot about the nature of your love life, the position of the sexy planet Mars and his beloved mythological lover, Venus, could be better indications of whether to expect any cosmic high-voltage between you and someone special. Last year Mars' and Venus' schedules kept them painfully apart, but this year they are together so often, the electricity generated could power the light bulbs of a whole nation! Best of all, these two planets will favor *you*, dear Cancer, over all the signs!

Are you ready for this? From May 20 to June 13, Venus will glide in Cancer. Your magnetism will be intense. This would be a terrific time to spend a little money on yourself for spa treatments and some new clothes.

At almost the same time, Mars comes by to jazz up your social life on its tour of Cancer from May 28 to July 13. During the last week in May, these two flirtatious planets will be close enough to kiss. You haven't seen anything like this before, dear Cancer! Va-Voom! They light up the midnight sky!

One of your first special days for love arrives on June 2, when happy-go-lucky Jupiter is attracted to kiss-me Venus, and both slip away to dance in the constellation of Cancer. This is a lovely day, and your lover (or mate, who really *is* your lover) may bring you a luxurious surprise.

We already mentioned the importance of the new moon on July 10, and its power to bring you happy news.

Remember, that new moon is in your sign. It sets the scene for two weeks of cosmic luck — and love. You may also recall that we talked about the momentous meeting of Jupiter and the Sun on July 19 in your sign. That date should have a marvelously energizing effect on your social life. As you can see, June and July are sure to be banner months for love! Summer, sweet summer!

Recent eclipses forced attached Cancers to sort out certain issues with their partners. Eclipses in one's own birth sign and in one's opposite sign (in your case, Capricorn) mark turning points in relationships. If a relationship is strong, it makes it through the period intact. If there is work to be done, that becomes very clear. If your love was strong you may have moved to a commitment or decided to have children. During the second half of 2000 and throughout 2001, you may have already experienced this first-hand.

There will still be one more eclipse in Capricorn before the wheel of the horoscope rotates to eclipses in Gemini – Sagittarius and Taurus – Scorpio. Your eclipse in Capricorn, a friendly one (as eclipses go) will arrive on June 24, mainly touching Cancers born on or near the date it falls. Overall, even this eclipse should be beneficial. It's in a happy angle to Uranus, the planet of all things unexpected.

All eclipses indicate a change of status. With eclipses being such wild cards there is always the possibility of a breakup, but this does not appear to be the case.

The message of the eclipse this year is this: If you are so-so about your closest relationship, either make it better or move on. What the eclipse will not allow you to do is to stay on the fence.

The year ends on a very sexy, festive note. Mars will reach the constellation of Scorpio on December 1 and remain in this sign until mid-January 2003. This is a perfect placement for you because Scorpio rules new love and true love. Not only is a rollicking holiday assured, it also could turn out to be outstandingly intimate. If you are ready to commit, talk of exchanging rings and promises could end the year on a very sweet note indeed!

Summary

Lucky you! You find yourself now on the threshold of one of the *best* years of your life. Jupiter, the planet of blessings and luck, is touring your sign until August 2002. Opportunity will blossom. Higher-ups will go out of their way for you, and you will find yourself at exactly the right place at the right time. For the first time in your life, you may get a vivid 360-degree picture of all that is possible for you. Getting this glimpse of your potential may inspire you to think differently. The old fences of your thinking are coming down, dear Cancer, and what remains is a look at the world through new eyes.

The second half of the year should be simply outstanding for consolidating financial gains in a tangible way. If matters involving credit or taxes have been a sore spot (likely, considering your chart) 2002 will allow you to set things back on track.

This year is more about reward for time and effort than about drastic professional change. Career advancement is there for you if you act in the months indicated. It seems likely that you will stay put in your present firm, happy to advance through the ranks. Certainly you are feeling appreciated, and you are going to be looking at your contribution to this firm — and to the world as a whole — in a new way. It is nice to be appreciated, isn't it? From mid-January through February you are able to see just how you can fly, and it's exhilarating.

If you have been out of work, don't let a little bad luck make you lose your confidence. Your skills are highly valued in the marketplace, and you should not lower your sights one bit.

Romantically, if single, this could be the year to meet a soul mate, if not immediately, then by mid-year. Be patient! Remember, you have to circulate more to make this happen. If you are paired with another, you may see a change of status in your relationship near the eclipse on June 24, but any changes you see seem to be highly protective and stabilizing. Here too, something new has been added. While as a Cancer, you are always sure something terrible is about to happen, now you are more confident. This will bode well for the relationship in the future.

If you are attached, watch the period on or near June 24. This may be the time to decide where to take the alliance next. You could be pleasantly surprised with the developments on that front. You want more from your relationship than the status quo, and you can have it. May, June and especially July are so good that you may be a little surprised at your own powers of persuasion and magnetism.

The year ends on a sexy, soft and intimate note. Mars is intent on enlivening the most romantic house of your horoscope, making the 2002 holiday season one for the record books. Your relationship seems more balanced, and you both are getting what you had hoped from it. Get that mistletoe, dear Cancer. By the holidays, you'll have a reason to use it!

LEO

The Big Picture

This year you are going to live on a grand scale, dear Leo. You like to live large and will finally be able to do just that, for the first time in a very long time. Just a little more patience is required of you. The year won't seem so fantastic until around the time of your birthday. Don't be disappointed if life doesn't feel like it's holding that much surprise and promise at the beginning of January. By the time the year is over, you will recognize 2002 as having set the gold standard for success. This will be that magical year against which you judge all others. It's set to be quite a spectacular period, dear Leo — well worth waiting for!

Jupiter, the planet of happiness and gifts, is steadily moving through space to reach Leo by August 1. Once there, Jupiter will remain in your sign until August 27, 2003, nearly thirteen months. It has been almost twelve years since the planet of good fortune last graced your life, and you will definitely notice a turning of the tides to your favor once it returns. The beauty of Jupiter's help is that it won't just enliven one area of your life, it adds zest to all of it, bit by bit!

2002 will emphasize self-expression, increased creativity, social opportunity, romance and commitment. While new contacts will pour into your life in record numbers, you may see one special friendship recede. Your paths are pointed in different directions; you feel highly cognizant of the passing of time, and nostalgic for the past.

The eclipses due this year, thankfully, are fairly mild. They will, as ever, test your resolve to stay with your present lover / spouse. If any adjustments are necessary, you'll make them in order to move forward and continue to share each other's lives. In 2002, you are in no mood to wait for things to happen, nor should you be. It's time for action. For example, if you are ready for children, they can absolutely be part of the picture now.

2002 will also return to you some of the control that was so sorely missing in recent years. Mars' is a particularly swift orbit. Its trajectory will arch over the pinnacle of your chart in the first part of the year, then move across the eastern half until it ends up at your chart's home- and family-oriented foundation in December. Mars' extended trip through the eastern side of your chart will keep you in the driver's seat for much of the year. You will be able to direct the course of everyday affairs with more mastery than before. You will also be able to put yourself first. This is a change for the better if you're one of those Leos who feel that others have gotten the longer end of the stick, i.e. you've given them your time, energy or good nature, and they've taken it. Thanks to Mars' path in 2002, both the public (career) and private (home and family) portions of your chart are energized. The year will be balanced.

This year is not going to be completely free of tension. What else is new? The massive transition that you sense underfoot — mainly in terms of career — won't be visibly apparent until November 19 when a somewhat disruptive full moon lunar eclipse falls in your achievement sector (tenth house). This period is sure to trigger meditations and decisions about what you want to do with your life. Exciting? Yes. Stressful? Of course.

If you are already passionately committed to your present career path, not even this eclipse could lead you to waver. In fact, you will be even more determined to get ahead, no matter what obstacles are strewn in your way. If your present career course is not pleasing you, well, there'll be no love lost if you leave it. You'll be free to move to a position that makes better use of your talents. Keep in mind that by November you will have Jupiter, the planet of good fortune, at your side. This is a wonderful blessing! Jupiter always protects, dear Leo. You will have the strongest Teflon shield of any of the signs by the second half of 2002.

The big outer planets have the power to give form and structure to our lives. They move slowly enough through each constellation to allow real development to take place. Their messages are always clear and indelible, if only because they set up a strong spotlight on very significant stuff. This year, these four planets — Pluto, Neptune, Uranus, and Saturn, will remain in fire or air signs, elements that mix superbly with your own, fire. In August, as Jupiter moves into big, bright, expressive Leo, you will have a fifth powerful planet added to the ones that are already so helpful to you. Have you any idea how lucky that is? Earth will be a very friendly environment for you, dear Leo. Your ideas will be more readily accepted. Let's look at all the trends in detail, and outline some key dates to watch.

The Planet of Cosmic Goodies: Jupiter

As the year takes off, Jupiter continues its cruises through Cancer, which throws a golden light into your twelfth house of behind-the-scenes activities. The plans you are quietly working on are apparently getting the well thought-out, organized and practical approach that will ensure success, dear Leo. You seem intent to polish them until they shine. For whatever reason, you appear to be uncharacteristically reflective and philosophical in this first phase of the year. You also seem more interested in the building blocks of your overall strategy than on any initiation. Right you are! You have time, dear Leo. Don't rush this part of the process. The second half of the year is when you'll want to set them in motion.

Solitude will be soothing and inspirational in the first six months of 2002. Do try to find as much time alone as possible. If you are a writer, designer, musician, artist, in film or entertainment, you may create work of unusual depth and distinction during the first half of the year. The quality of the work you turn out now will be very special.

Do what you can to sneak in some time alone for reflection, even on the job. If that's not an option, set your alarm for an hour earlier or stay up an hour later. You need that quality time, dear Leo. Make room for it. Too many distractions will leave you with too much to do, too little time to do it in, and frustration that you simply can't stop long enough to come up with a game plan.

Your intuition will be ultra-sharp from January through July 2002. If you don't get some time by yourself, you won't be able to hear your heart's whisperings. Time alone to think, pray, walk, reflect, muse, remember or even to sing will bring inspiration for the future.

Medical and psychological matters fall under the governance of this same twelfth house. Should you find you need an operation, treatment or other procedure, get it done; you can't lose. Just about any point this year would be a good time to move forward. Just don't schedule a procedure for a date during the Mercury retrograde periods: January 18 through February 8, May 15 through June 8 and September 14 through October 6.

In the first half of the year you will have Jupiter helping you find the right doctor. After this mighty planet moves on, it will still be in a position to help you heal. If you experience any chronic distress or a substance abuse problem, seek help without delay. No matter what your difficulty, the sooner you become determined to get help, the sooner you'll enjoy relief. The twelfth house is the last house of the zodiac and symbolizes the end of a cycle. You are being asked by the universe to set things straight. You don't want to be burdened with anything extra when you enter your new twelve year phase.

During the first half of 2002, at least one influential individual could become your guardian angel. Jupiter's move thorough your twelfth house suggests you will be blessed with such "fairy godmother" types. This "someone" will work on your behalf so invisibly, you may not even be aware of his or her existence. They will make introductions, help you get plum assignments, and generally be there to catch you if you fall. Bless their hearts, they seem to ask for nothing in return. It is highly unlikely that you would have any secret detractors during 2002 either. It seems all the behind-the-scenes activity is in your favor. Are you lucky, or what?

From a Frog to a Prince or Princess

Once Jupiter moves into Leo on August 1, everything will change for the better. From that point on, doors will open. All those plans and schemes that you thought you'd do "someday" seem to be possible in the near future. Your wonder year will extend from August 1, 2002 - August 27, 2003, a period of almost thirteen months! You will be given many opportunities. Some of these will be vastly new to you, even a bit alien, and represent areas of enormous personal growth. It would behoove you to adopt an open, experimental attitude. As you move through this period, you want to take advantage of the chance to nibble on these choice offerings, no matter how foreign.

Do be choosy about what you take on long-term, however. There will be the dangerous tendency to spread yourself too thin, to handicap your ability to concentrate sufficiently in any one area. Study your offers and decide which hold the greatest potential. Set all your energies on those. Also, with so many people presenting proposals, there is the danger that you'll sit back and allow complacency to get the better of you. If you see yourself getting too laid back (or worse, a little arrogant), give yourself a strong talking to. It's time to keep pushing forward! Don't get lazy or cocky.

Some of the best days of the year will cluster around July 19, when your ruler, the Sun, walks arm in arm with Jupiter. That's a five-star week for sure, Leo! While both the Sun and Jupiter will technically be in Cancer on that day, the mathematical degrees of that conjunction will fall very close to the cusp. If you are a Leo born near the very start of your sign, July 23 or thereabouts, you will benefit two-fold.

Career

This year brings all kinds of news in your career sector, good and bad. You seem to handle all circumstances with your usual grace. The beginning of the year is actually your best time to make a big career move or to highlight successes. March may turn out to be your best career month because Mars, the great energizer planet, will be zooming through the mid-heaven part of your solar chart (tenth house). This is what the ancients referred to as your "house of dignity", the sector where astrologers look to find honors, awards and achievement. Your status should climb skyward.

Mars will help you push forward from March 2 through April 14. This is the most powerful cycle you've seen in two years, since May 2000. If you are restless for a new and better job, now's your time to strike out and find one. By the time the new moon arrives in your professional sector on May 12, you will have built up enough momentum to generate awesome offers in the two weeks that follow.

Just when you thought all the good news that could possibly emanate from your career has come and gone, there is another fabulous point due on June 2, when Jupiter and Venus sing a duet. Under their harmonizing, you seem to be able to hit that ball right out of the ballpark, and the crowd around you will be cheering you on!

Terrific news about money earned, such as a salary increase, should come on or near July 19 when Mercury brushes close to Jupiter. September through mid-October are expensive months, but you don't seem worried. Perhaps this is a much-deserved time to live it up. If so, enjoy it.

A Challenge Arrives Near Thanksgiving

Your career progresses steadily until it hits a sudden snag or shift in direction due to the full moon lunar eclipse on November 19. Eclipses often bring outside conditions over which you have no control to the fore. Yes, that can be frustrating, but even so, often these are the situations that allow you to recognize your true character and rise to the occasion.

On or near this November date, news brewing within your company, your industry or the economy at large could cause seismic tremors in your life. It is very likely that a top honcho will announce a departure, or that your company will initiate a major change in its strategy. You may plan to change jobs but feel torn about which way to go. No matter what it is, it is clear that this time generates stress; those Leo born near August 20 will be most affected. Still, keep in mind that you will have racked up some very impressive career gains earlier in the year. Having them in your pocket will help you a great deal during this period.

Keep in mind that although all this sounds scary, but it isn't. Hard to believe? You will be able to capitalize on the shifting landscape. Eclipses often give us a chance to learn new skills and evolve to a new level of maturity. They make as much massive change possible happen within the very narrowest time frame. The movements of these eclipses may be sudden, but that's because the universe is impatient. The cosmos has a mission for you. The nature of this mission is revealed to you at eclipse time.

One part of your job (or the job itself — hook, line and sinker) may end in late November. At the same time a new chapter will begin. It's just as possible that two phases of your company morph into a bigger unit. If you were bored, or had found yourself at a dead end, you will be able to use this eclipse to hop into a much more interesting spot. Eclipses are catalysts of change. If your boss doesn't appreciate you or if you find yourself in a company that is struggling, the eclipse may urge management to close your division as part of a major consolidation. Keep in mind, this does not mean that you are doomed. You could be hired to play a much more important role in a new division. If worse comes to worse and your boss lays you off in a downsizing effort, let them have their old job. There may be greater opportunities for growth elsewhere. Remember, most of the time, none of this is personal. It's about business, and nothing more. Of course, keep in mind that this eclipse, despite the possible difficulties, may bring positive news.

What can you do to prepare for this eclipse on November 19? Make sure your work is thorough and above reproach. Show an eager, enthusiastic attitude — positive energy attracts more positive energy. Should your boss have to make decisions about which of her staff to cut, you won't want to be the one who she remembers is always struggling with deadlines or zero with new solutions. Keep your wits about you. As said, by November, Jupiter will have had a chance to spin its magic. We have to look at the *whole* chart to get the whole picture, not just month by month or minute to minute. Yours is truly fantastic. It is clear that the latter half of 2002 shows you able to turn *anything* to your favor!

Health Glows

This year you should feel better than ever. With Jupiter in

your twelfth house in the first half of the year, medical, dental or other consultations (trainer, nutritionist, specialist) are favored. You will be able to locate someone who understands your problem. During the second half of the year, Jupiter's presence ensures renewed vitality and strength to a degree you have not felt in a very long time. This is your year to get healthy, Leo!

There is one problem with Jupiter's tour your sign in the second half of 2002 and first half of 2003. Jupiter expands everything in sight, including your waistline. That means you'll have to battle weight gain in a very focused way or pay the price with unwanted pounds. The Pillsbury Dough Boy will creep up so silently that you probably won't even notice the extra padding, at least not until the day you see a photo of yourself and panic. You can counter this trend by getting started early this year with a fitness routine. Astrology is not destiny; it's the study of trends that we do have the power to direct.

Start by integrating more activity into your day. Concentrate on sports and activities that you enjoy. Allow me to make an analogy. The lion in the jungle would much rather sit under a tree and enjoy a snooze than have to hunt for dinner. As king of the jungle, he tends to leave that job to the other animals. However, occasionally the lion is roused to fight a battle that only he can win, and when he does, the rest of the jungle cowers in his presence. In terms of physical strength and endurance, 2002 is the year to show the world what you're made of, Leo. You are no softie! Don't let yourself look like one!

The full moon lunar eclipse in your sixth house of physical well being on June 24 may highlight an area of your body you have neglected. Falling in Capricorn, this suggests that your teeth may need attention, or you may be liable to stress fractures. Bones and teeth should be shored up with a diet rich in calcium. You might want to take up weight training early in the year, in combination with yoga and stretching. Such a balance of weight bearing, aerobic and stretching helps keep your bones and body strong. Check with your doctor to design a program right for your needs. If you start early you may be able to avoid rusty in the first place.

Neptune's opposition to your Sun suggests you should be very careful about taking any drugs, including medicines your doctor gives you, as there could be a negative reaction. Always ask about the side effects of a prescription before you start taking it. Read the indications. Those Leos born in the first week of August are most liable to problems. Uranus' position in opposition to the Sun (especially for Leos born on August 14 – 23) means that nervous tension may be hard to deflect. Schedule in soothing moments to your day: take a long walk to work rather than squeeze on a crowded bus or train, schedule a soothing massage, or put fresh flowers on your desk. Leo is very sensitive to beauty. Having that little touch of luxury in your life will keep your spirits up your on days when nothing seems to go according to plan.

Friendship and Charity

In 2002, Saturn is still touring your eleventh house of hopes, wishes and friendships. The difference is that this year, the taskmaster planet is cordial to just about every other major "outer" planet in the zodiac, including Pluto, Uranus, Neptune and in the second half, Jupiter — every planet except Pluto, in May. (We'll cover that in a moment.)

With Saturn in your eleventh house all year, you may meet an older or more mature friend who teaches you something valuable. Perhaps this person is a mentor; he or she clearly cares enough about you to want to do all they can to help you get through a tough period. At times you may not agree with what this person has to say, but you'll be mighty glad he or she is around. No matter how old, this someone really cares. Their attention to your cares reveals a great deal about the nature of your friendship.

Saturn's position in this eleventh house may also urge you to delay some short-term pleasures in favor of a bigger goal. You may decide to save up for a new house or to work less and give your child more. (These are only two of many possible examples.) There is usually an element of sacrifice or delay with Saturn present — though the word "sacrifice" is not really accurate because it won't feel like you are losing anything. You will gain stability and long-lasting benefits. Saturn is urging you to direct your time, money and energy into something that will stand the test of time.

This year Saturn will be unusually friendly toward Neptune, the planet of compassion in the eleventh house of humanitarian efforts. This suggests you may be moved to take on a leadership role in a volunteer effort. If so, you'll learn new skills that you can to transfer to other areas of your life. Leo is a highly creative sign. You may get involved with an artistic project, such as a screenplay, an important piece of music, or any other body of work. You want to create something that raises the world's consciousness of a concern dear to you. The funds you raise should be impressive — Saturn will make you determined to reach certain goals. Note these great dates for a chance to make a difference: January 23 and April 1, 2002.

Later, Saturn will call on Uranus on August 21 and December 16, 2002, both meetings that could bring lasting positive change.

Romance: Close Relationships Change and Mature

The Long View

This year will not present the wrenching problems of the past. If you suffered through the angry eclipses of 1998, 1999 and early 2000, know that those are over and done. What you do have now is the usual suspects, Uranus and Neptune, exerting the same little gremlin aspects, but by now, having hosted these two powerhouse planets for so many years in your house of true commitment, you know how to handle it. Let's look at each, and what we can learn from them.

Hosting unpredictable Uranus, a big pushy planet, in your seventh house of committed partnerships is never easy. This position suggests an interesting dichotomy: You look to your relationship for excitement, but when you get it, it's too much to handle. You seem drawn to highly creative, idiosyncratic partners who, though wonderful in many ways, are quite independent. Finding enough time with this person could prove hard. It could be that his or her career demands may be keep you apart, or they fear closeness and need space. Whatever it is, it's slightly discomforting. Still, Uranus' position here might have an upside. Since Uranus entered this house in 1995, you may have met (or are about to meet) a new partner who will exert such a strong influence in your life that this person blots out everything else. This person could easily become your overriding force for change and enlightenment. (Ah, this is starting to sound like the power of love, Leo!) Your "partner" might as easily be a business collaborator.

Your vision of relationships and marriage has evolved, for sure. That new vision is rapidly being incorporated into your expectations for the future. Through trial and error you have learned a great deal about the nature of love, and although many people can say this, your experiences have been rockier than most. Ah, we learn little from times of ease, dear Leo. You've lived through those tough times, and have plenty to draw on now. Your expectations are more realistic, less waffled by prevailing winds.

Later-born Leos (specifically those with birthdays from August 14 – August 20) are currently feeling transiting Uranus in opposition to their Sun in the seventh house of relationships. (Leos born *before* August 14 have already felt what I am about to describe. If you are born earlier within the sign, you still may want to check out what I am about to say; it could clarify some things.)

This is a very radical aspect. It will help you realize the depth of your inner strength, and your will to exert independence. The lessons it teaches you will remain with you for the rest of your life. Should you encounter a struggle in matters of the heart, it will be comforting to know that this year your Sun has help from Saturn. Nearly every Leo will benefit in 2002 because Saturn covers so much ground. Uranus will leave this house in 2003 — a big event, as Uranus has been in this house since 1995.

Sometimes it is easier to know what you don't want in your life (whether relationships, work, or any other area), rather than try to figure out what you *do* want. This may well be one of those years when you know you can't continue the along the same old track. This is, indeed, a year of action, not waiting. You may not have all the pieces of your puzzle yet, but you have enough to start. You'll be able to make course corrections as you go along, so don't worry. First things first, dear Leo.

There is no doubt that if you were born from August 14 to August 20 (or close to those dates), you are about to pry yourself free from long-term conditions that were limiting or debilitating. When you make the decision to leave, it will be somewhat sudden. Opportunity barrels your way, and emerging conditions will force you to move decisively. Although you may find all this rattling, the changes you make will be good for you. As much as you'd like to ignore what's happening, you won't be able to. Be philosophical: confronting problems head-on is best. It allows us to move forward, full throttle.

Let's step outside this discussion about relationships for a second so that I can explain something important. The energy that Uranus is propelling at you, especially for Leos born late, is most likely to be felt with your closest relationship, but it may spread to other areas as well. Uranus is famous for tearing down structures it deems of no future value, quite unexpectedly and radically. You may leave a job or a whole industry, leave a city you've lived in all your life to seek opportunity elsewhere — you may even go abroad. You may decide to end a long-term marriage, or choose to marry after decades of bachelorhood. You decide to open a business or shut one down. You get the picture. Your direction in some area will change radically.

All kinds of crazy quilt situations come up, and the experiences could either be welcome or not. There are so many possibilities. You emerge as the unique person you were meant to be. Uranus takes 84 years to circle the Sun.

You won't ever feel this aspect again — it is truly an once-in-a-lifetime configuration. Whatever happens, you seem to have no doubt in your mind that it is necessary. Although you are ready to walk away and not look back, there is something about this situation that leaves a scar. You will feel you simply had to move forward. Good! You will be stronger as a result.

Let's center our attention on your closest, most intimate relationship — which, I will admit, may be a little more complicated than necessary thanks Neptune's presence here since 1998. Neptune will not leave this house until 2012! The problem with Neptune is that this lovely planet can play tricks on us, making us fall in love with the idea of love rather than the real-life person. Neptune also raises one's risk of falling in love with someone who isn't available. Neptune can make us victim to disillusionment. In terms of matters of the heart, it is very important to remain as clear-eyed as possible with Neptune in your seventh house.

Neptune's position here can have a good effect too. It can draw you to someone who is artistic or creative, someone with a remarkable ability to inspire you. If you were born between July 31 and August 5, you are most sensitive to Neptune's influence.

Luckily, all Leos have Pluto making a long trek through their other relationship house, the fifth house of love, children, fun and creativity. In 2002, Pluto reaches its halfway point, 15 degrees, considered the most powerful point. (Signs of the zodiac each have 30 degrees.) With Pluto in such an elegant angle to your Sun, anything is possible!

Pluto may help you become very passionate about your lover. This person seems to have the power to capture your imagination in ways that others have not been able to. Every Leo, of any birthday should partake of this lovely, powerful energy. If you are born in the week that spans from August 5 – August 10, you will receive Pluto's strongest, most beneficial rays.

As you see, you have a lot going on in your relationship houses. With the most powerful planets in the solar system — Pluto, Uranus, and Neptune — pushing and pulling at your heartstrings, relationships will teach you the most about yourself. These planets will also help you clarify what you want in life and give you an understanding of the nature of love. In the end, this experience will help you decide where you want your life to go. If it is true that we are the sum of all our experiences, you are becoming much more mature, reflective and thoughtful about what it is that will make you truly happy. And *that* is wonderful news, dear Leo.

Romance

The Short Term View

Your best period for love will occur in the second half of April and in May, then again when Jupiter enlivens your sign from August through the end of year. Jupiter's move over your Sun (a once-in-twelve-year occurrence) marks the very best time to meet a soul mate. I'm talking about *now*. You will have to circulate, dear Leo. If you do you won't be sorry!

Throughout the year, eclipses will work with Saturn to bring you in contact with more people, and to help clarify your role within both society at large and your day-to-day interactions.

For Leo, ruled by the sun, the solar eclipses are more important than the lunar eclipses. This year, luckily, these eclipses are as not fraught with emotion as those in the recent past. Both solar eclipses in 2002 will fall in relationship areas, in terms of friendship (in Gemini, June 10) and romance, children/ pregnancy, leisure activities and fun, (in Sagittarius, December 4). They are both sweetly angled to your Sun in compatible air and fire signs, so the effect should be fun and bubbly. Your life is spiced with new social events. Single Leos should be flattered with all the attention they receive, while married Leos may now grow closer or think seriously about having a baby. If you have had difficulties with conception, you have reason to be more optimistic now.

The lunar eclipse on May 26, 2002 falls in your fifth house of true love, and brings a romantic matter to fruition. Should you experience unwanted news at that time (remote but possible), the mutable nature of both eclipses suggests a positive outcome. You should have room to give such surprise situations appeal.

Saturn and Pluto: Possible Struggle for Control

In early August and in early November of last year, the world experienced the first two parts of a very rare and difficult aspect, Saturn's opposition to Pluto. These two planets continue their row with a third and final confrontation on May 25, 2002. Unfortunately, this may have played out with subtle power struggle in your closest relationship, a situation likely to continue until this midyear point. An eclipse complicates this aspect the next day on May 26, heightening each side's need to be victorious. You may feel this tug-of-war in terms of one particular friendship or a romance — both polar houses are equally lit. Keep cool, Leo.

At the same time, please don't over-analyze your relationship to such an extent that you never go out dancing, dear Leo. You need to enjoy it. With so many brainy signs at play (in Gemini- Sagittarius) you may have the tendency to view your relationship in purely intellectual terms. With so few water signs dominating, "what I want" will supercede "we both feel". This will be true for you as well as for your partner. Keep the fun alive and much your relationship will take care of itself. If you are not having fun together, almost nothing else matters.

Jupiter to Pay a Happy Visit to Pluto: Your Love Life Benefits

No matter what discussions you have in your closest relationship early in the year, its outlook will brighten magnificently by the last quarter of 2002. Jupiter and Pluto will have a very lyrical, joyous personal discussion (with you as the topic). Whenever these two powerhouses meet, happiness and exciting success follow. Jupiter will be in your sign, beaming rays to Pluto in your house of true love. This is an amazing development at year's end. The last time Jupiter sent Pluto such a cheery hello was on March 29, 1999! This coming year we will have harmonious conversation between these two planets on October 27 and December 18. Put five gold stars next to these days, perfect for love, true, but also for initiating any endeavor dear to your heart.

Whatever occurs at the end of October and December is powerful enough to change your life for the better. For you, Leo, this activity is centered in the area of true love, creativity and matters related to children. These realms all have the power to lift you into a whole new world. Jupiter and Pluto will both be in fire signs, suggesting that when things start to happen, they will happen fast, growing and multiplying with incredible force.

As a fixed sign, you tend to want to keep things "as is". You're not one to upset the apple cart. Yet when Pluto is involved, there is no turning back. Why would you want to, dear Leo? This year, when a door opens, you won't just walk through it. The universe will blow you through it. You will probably have an experience similar to Alice in Wonderland's, falling through the Rabbit Hole to a more curious, interesting place than you've ever been. Your experiences will lead you on a new personal journey. The cosmos is unfurling the red carpet, dear Leo, just for you. Are you ready?

Summary

You've come a long way in the past few years. Life has thrown many obstacles your way. By finding novel ways to overcome them, you've become more savvy and able. With Jupiter's recent move into your twelfth house (where it will stay a year), you are positioned to show off your originality this coming year. Dreams, both in the form of vivid night visions and day muses, may be the source of inspiration. Your intuition will also become sharp in months ahead.

From now until your next birthday you will ready yourself for a far more important cycle, from August 2002 – August 2003. This period could easily make for the best year of your life, thanks to Jupiter's move to your sign. Before that happens, however, you will need to get ready.

This year, try to set aside some time for yourself. Your best ideas will surface in peaceful solitude. Your friends also have a big role to play in the coming year, with one possibly playing the role of advisor /mentor. With eclipses due in your houses of romance, children and new contacts, you can expect a change of status within one of these areas. It will be through self-expression, falling in love and having children that you learn most about life. While relationships can be difficult at times, they are worth it. They offer you the stimulation you need. This year April and May bring social surprises, but the events at year's end, when Jupiter and Pluto meet, that could truly change the course of your life. It is a year filled with force and weight, and one you will not forget.

There is nothing to fear, however. Changes are likely to be surprisingly positive. Indeed, the life that awaits you is far more exciting than the one you're about to leave behind. Get into the spirit, dear Leo! You have one thrilling ride ahead!

VIRGO

The Big Picture

When we begin a New Year, we hope it will be filled with personal success, memorable experiences and personal growth. Along the way, we hope for clearly marked signposts so that when we make life decisions, we won't make a misstep or wander off in the wrong direction. Getting lost and having to backtrack takes up valuable time and energy, something we all would like more of, not less of. The ideal year is full of cosmic events that give us precise directions about which path to take, every step of the way. As you can imagine, that kind of year rarely comes along. After a while, we begin to think that perhaps it is too much to hope for. Not for you, it's not!

Remarkably, dear Virgo, you're headed for such an ideal year. Much of your news and growth will be generated by career, which will become the centerpiece of your life. Everything else will revolve around it. For now, this is how it should be.

Recently the cosmos singled you out for a much more significant professional role. Before that could happen, however, you were asked to prove your mettle. At some point last year, you were thrown into the deep end of the swimming pool to see if you could swim. You proved that indeed, you could, with stamina and style no one would have predicted. Saturn, now positioned at the very highest point in your horoscope, is responsible for these vigorous career tests you have been undergoing. That process of testing and learning will continue in 2OO2.

Your current professional apprenticeship may not make you feel like part of a privileged few, but looking at your chart that seems to be the case. Once you have completed the hard work that Saturn has cut out for you, the world will see you in a new light. More importantly, you will view yourself and your abilities differently.

If you have a career now, you are all set. Finally given some room to move around in, you will grow and develop a specialty. You may be at a job that you didn't take very seriously, one that you have viewed until recently as a mere "gravy train" — a way to pay the rent. Well, you may have been wrong. It seems you are being urged to think twice, to take on more responsibility at work, and could be in the process of moving toward your true vocation.

This is true whether or not you are in a career in the start of 2OO2. By the time this year comes to an end — if not sooner, all Virgos could discover the drive necessary to make work a pleasure. They may realize they actually feel committed to what they're doing. Of course, you have to make an effort. You have to show the universe that you intend to be a success in a given field. The great news is you won't have to scale these great career heights alone. There is a mentor or at least one influential person who will reach out to help you. 2OO2 has all it takes to help you fly to the top, dear Virgo. Again, all you have to do is show the universe that this goal is important to you.

Thankfully, this year won't be about all work and no play. Due to the passage of Jupiter through your eleventh house of hopes and wishes during the first seven months of 2002, you'll meet many interesting people, one or two of whom may play an important role in your future. Your capacity for spirituality and compassion will grow as well. This may be the year when you get involved in an important humanitarian or community effort — one that makes you proud.

Romantically, the year holds promise. If you are single and looking for love, the eclipse in your true love sector on June 24 will lead to romance. If you are married or involved in an ongoing relationship, this eclipse will bring your alliance to the next level. (From what I can see, your relationship appears to be quite stable.) However, due to pressing career demands, you may deliberately choose to slow the pace of your relationship. In 2002, love is to be enjoyed, not rushed. You seem to have enough pressure in other areas of your life. If you choose to go slowly, no one would blame you.

The one exception to the "take it slow and easy" rule comes in for married Virgos; there may be talk about having a baby. While some might think that considering parenthood in a year as busy as yours is sheer madness, it's not. You could actually make it work. Maintaining your personal life will take organization, but you are a master at management, dear Virgo. With an understanding partner, if you work together as a team, you could conquer the world.

A Public Role

A look at Mars' path through your chart over the course of the year reveals quite a bit about what you can expect in the next twelve months. In 2002, Mars will make a huge arch through the upper regions of your horoscope, over all the sectors governing your public life. This is practically proof that although you will certainly have family and domestic issues on your mind, 2002 is a year when public (and most noticeably career-related) matters will take precedence.

Once Mars reaches the constellation of Virgo, where it will stay from August 29 to October 15, you will begin a new, vital two-year cycle. It will be your best time to pursue your most important endeavors. No rush — you'll have all the time you need.

The Year in Detail

Your Career Will Skyrocket

There is no doubt that you have been working hard over the past year (2001). Although the pace will continue straight through 2002, the good news is that what you are doing now will lead to a very significant role — much bigger than anything you would have imagined. Your career will grow and develop exponentially, to bring even *more* opportunity in 2003.

As mentioned earlier, Saturn, the teacher planet, is having quite an influence on your life during its two-and-a-half year (and once-every-29-years) tour through your sign. This year, Saturn is making its way through your tenth house of honors, awards and achievement, found at the very apex of your chart.

It might be comforting to know that you are nearing the halfway-point of Saturn's testing; this difficult phase began quietly in mid-2000. At that time, you may not have noticed any radical changes in your career environment — though, boy, were they there! This probably did not get hammered home until around May 2001, or even a few months after that. Saturn will continue to test and tutor you until it leaves your tenth house of career in June 2003. When it does, your test will not be repeated for nearly three decades. The lessons you learn from Saturn are hard won, and will stay with you forever.

While Saturn rarely brings big rewards during its thirty-month tenure, it will leave a substantial gift at the door upon leaving. That should motivate and reassure you! At that point in 2003, you will start to get pretty appealing job offers. To your delight, you will be courted and wooed by all the right people, and they will want you working on their team.

Saturn, as ruler of the tenth house, is naturally quite comfortable here. Saturn works with ease and fluency from this sector of the horoscope. Still, no matter how much Saturn enjoys tutoring you, chances are you aren't in love with the experience of being his pupil. This great taskmaster planet has been hovering over you like a ballet master with a stick, whipping it against the floor again and again, to emphasize each and every point, making you repeat your moves again and again until your form is polished. It's not easy.

Other signs of the zodiac might whine in exasperation about how demanding Saturn can be, but not you, Virgo. Even though it can be taxing, you actually appreciate having someone show you the ropes and teach you specific ways to improve your output. Your sign is all about excellence and increased productivity. If your direct superior or client seems to be cold, critical or demanding, you can be sure that is Saturn speaking. This person actually wants you to succeed, but has a weird way of showing it! They know you are up to precision and excellence, and they expect you to get there!

All this would be simpler if there was nothing else going on but, of course, it's more complicated than that. For one thing, you have responsibilities back home, to a lover or a spouse and possibly also children — to say nothing of the role you play in the lives of friends and neighbors. Saturn doesn't want to hear that you have a life outside work, for Saturn needs to sense a single-minded devotion to his demands. To gauge your commitment, Saturn will continue to throw work-related obstacles in your path, just to see how you do and if you have the motivation to keep on going.

Saturn doesn't thrust responsibilities on us without warning. Instead, you are usually asked to accept them voluntarily. Still, I'm sure there were times when you looked up from your desk at 3 AM and wondered what you were thinking to accept all these new responsibilities. Ah, dear Virgo, never regret your decision to go down this road — it was wise. The universe has a plan for you, and it's an exciting one. Saturn gives rewards only after victory over hardship. You are coming out with flying colors, so press on!

You seem to be working within a communicative field, as Saturn is in Gemini. You may be working in book and magazine publishing, the Internet, television and radio broadcasting, software, computers or other electronics, telecommunications, public relations, sales, marketing, library science, book retailing, courier services, the post office, transportation or the travel industry. If so, you're on the right track. These areas all hold enormous potential.

This year, Neptune's friendly position to Saturn suggests that creative / artistic or humanitarian (not-for-profit) fields may also be areas of success. For this, watch what develops near January 23 and April 1, 2002.

If you want to start your own business, this would be the time. With these planetary dynamics, you have all the self-discipline needed to get things off the ground. If recent eclipses have forced you out of a job, you should consider going into business for yourself, even if you need a part time job to keep you alive during the start-up stage. If you hesitate to go at it alone, consider partnering with someone you love, even one of your children if you are a more mature Virgo. (This advice is given because the ruler of your fifth house is touring your tenth house.) Think about how you could turn a special skill or hobby into a profitable business.

Uranus's position suggests that emerging technologies play a big part in your efficiency at work. Learn how to use new software or equipment, and stay ahead of the pack.

Finally, before we leave this topic, let me leave you with this. You like to be productive, so you always work hard. As a Virgo, you are hardwired with this work ethic. Yet despite your good attitude and hard work, you've never received the recognition that you deserve. Maddeningly, praise and promotion always went to others. Perhaps they were more aggressive about hogging the spotlight — your modesty may have worked against you. Or, you have not found yourself in the right place at the right time. Maybe you lacked the favor of vips who were willing to help you. No matter what the reason, this is all changing now. Finally, *you* will be the one who makes the news. I am sure you will say happily, "It's about time!"

This begs the question, "Do the circumstances make the man, or does the man make the circumstances?" At the end of 2002, you will be able to answer that. Tell us the answer when you find out! The value of a Saturn experience is usually not in the destination, but in the journey.

You are the hero of your particular quest. No matter how many twists and turns of this particular plot, in the end you will be victorious. Proceed.

Career Breakthroughs

Make a note: Your best, most exciting career period of the year will occur from mid-April through May.

August and December will be marvelous, too, for launching new endeavors, thanks to a rare and very stabilizing aspect between Saturn and Uranus on August 21 and later, on December 16.

Ruler Mercury Retrogrades! Beware!

The planet Mercury rules Virgo, so when Mercury is out of phase (a sleep stage for this energetic planet) you will find it hard to make any lasting agreements or to make any meaningful progress.

Avoid big commitments or initiations during the three 2002 Mercury retrograde periods: January 18 – February 8, May 15 – June 8, and September 14 – October 6.

As you see, the first exciting career period for you, mid-April through May, partially overlaps with a three-week Mercury retrograde span. Therefore, be ready to move assertively in your career at the start when the going is good; get moving right on April 13. Try to get your goals wrapped up by the first week in May. It is not wise to accept new positions too close to the time that Mercury retrogrades on May 15.

Financially, Better Days are Due

While it would be great if you could be well paid during this strenuous Saturn workout period, that's not usually the case. No, Saturn has a kind of perverse pleasure in seeing us all suffer a little — finances included. Maybe it's in order to ascertain that you keep focused on the lesson, not what you can buy with its rewards. Money can be so powerful that having too much during a period of tutorial could confuse your sense of purpose, pulling you one way or another depending on the compensation offered. No wonder Saturn is taking money out of the equation for now. Patience is one of the virtues you will learn this year, for sure.

That's not to say there is no chance of a salary increase in 2002 — there is a strong likelihood of significant gains at three separate points in the year.

Your first arrives near June 2, when Jupiter embraces Venus, ruler of your second house of income. This could easily bring you a handsome raise or news of a business coup.

Watch July 3, too, when Mars and Jupiter meet on your behalf. A cash settlement could result. You may win a small prize.

Finally, your third key moment arrives later in the year, at the new moon on October 6. That new moon ushers in two weeks of strong positive energy that could bring an increase in your cash flow. (Note, like the June 2 date, the cash you see will be cash you earn, not money you receive in other ways.)

Your most costly periods will be during the second half of January and all of February, and from mid-October through November. It might help to know about these periods before they arrive so you can prepare for them.

Throughout this period, remind yourself that the reputation you have built for excellence and integrity is priceless, worth more than any amount of money anyone could ever pay you. While jobs can be won and lost, the core that makes you uniquely "you" is yours for life. It is an awesome bargaining chip that will pay off for you as soon as planets rotate into more favorable positions. No one ever entered a Saturn period and left the poorer for it. Your chart proves true the old adage that if you do what you love the money will come. Keep the faith, dear Virgo.

Romance and Friendship: Jupiter Offers Fun in the First Half

In 2002, whenever you feel a yen for more balance between your personal life and your career, friends will be there to add a little fun to your life. This year, thanks to Jupiter, your friends seem to be very sensitive to your needs. They will be looking out for your welfare, coaxing you out of the office, inviting you to events, and delighting you with introductions, ideas, and their unique perspectives on a variety of issues. They will stimulate you when you're bored, cheer you when you're blue, and pep you up when you need a boost in self-confidence. Bless them, Virgo, they will show you in 2002 the true meaning of friendship. In all they do for you, this message will be clear: You are loved. There is almost nothing your friends wouldn't do for you.

So strong will their help be in 2002 that you'd do well to turn to friends, not professionals, for help with just about any dilemma, from finding a new apartment to getting a new job — or just leading you to a better bargain on that expensive item you're about to buy. You name your need. Your friends will be a big help!

Romance: Hitting Your Stride

The special favor you get from friends will extend to intriguing romantic introductions. If you are single and looking for love, call a friend for that special meeting. Don't waste time prowling the club scene. While your chart suggests that you might meet someone outstanding in your office (after all, you will be spending so much time there) you also have magnificent aspects for finding love through friends.

Your closest relationship, whether dating or married, should remain fairly steady in 2002. You may feel you have reached its foundation, its core. This ease in your interactions will allow you to enjoy one another without the dramatic scenes that may have marked your earlier times together.

If you are single, the January 13 new moon offers you a plethora of dating opportunities, and continues beaming you good energy through the end of the month. You may be tempted to rekindle an old flame or to take a friendship further. Maybe it offers something more.

If attached, the first two weeks of January might be a bit rocky. Mars' placement in Virgo's seventh house may make your partner a little cranky or needy. This appears to be a matter of his or her need to blow off steam. Just remember, your insane career schedule could well have a jarring effect on everyone in your vicinity. Your partner is bound to be effected, and I'm sure is trying to be patient and understanding. Why don't you cut him or her a little slack? It will make things easier for you both.

If you do encounter any sticky moments with your partner in early January, don't panic. Things are due to improve almost immediately, once Venus enters Pisces from February 12 to March 8. This is sure to be a highly romantic period when you are in complete harmony with one another. Pisces is such a romantic sign. So sensitive may you be to one another, you may be able to transmit sweet thoughts to each other without uttering a word. Luckily, this enchanting period arrives just in time for Valentine's Day. (Unlike last year, this is due to be a really glittering Valentine's Day! Help things along, Virgo!)

Later, the middle of the year shows another lovely perk-up period for fun and love. Venus, by then in Virgo, will be a lovely influence, intensifying your magnetism from July 11 to August 6. Just in time for the lazy, crazy days of summer!

Generally, this year you seem to accept yourself and others much more readily. This openness comes without the prerequisite censure that can limit a relationship before it has a chance to begin. You seem less likely to analyze things. This is a good sign. Just relax and enjoy.

The months from April through July will be among your best — that's a nice, long span of good times! Later in the year, the time around your birthday should also bring some magical romantic moments.

With Jupiter in your "hopes and wishes" sector (eleventh house) during the first half of 2002, you may attain something you've always wanted. This new addition or acquisition could be something spiritual (a baby) or material (your first house). In 2002, you know you are working for something bigger in life. That "something" is practically within reach.

Joining Groups is Lucky For You Now

If you are not a member of a club or group, consider joining one early in 2002, for you have much to gain by joining forces with others. The contacts you make will not only help you get ahead professionally, but also may teach you to enjoy life a little more! Jupiter tours your friendship sector from the beginning of your forecast until the end of July, your ideal time to join. Whether you claim the ranks of a group that is professional, political, or creative and social, you will see benefits you would never have imagined — get involved with anything, from your city's block organization to knitting clubs.

The eleventh house, so brilliantly highlighted in 2002, rules charity projects and humanitarian efforts. If you ever hoped to make a big difference to someone who needs help, you have your chance now. Make sure to be realistic when planning your time for this; make a commitment you can keep.

When you join a group, be sure to get active. As we discussed, this is your time to sharpen those leadership skills. There isn't an organization on earth that couldn't use an extra pair of hands. Roll up your sleeves and dig in, dear Virgo. What you learn in the friendly confines of a group can eventually be transferred to your attitude about work life — and to your perspectives on the world, in general.

Your Best Day of the Year

Here's a date to key into your calendar: July 19, one of the best of 2002 for favor from friends and groups. It should be a very gratifying time, when you feel touched by the generosity of friends. It is a five-star day, and its glow will extend to the days surrounding it. So special is the week of July 19, it may stand out later as the very best period of the year.

Remarkably, on the following day, July 20, Mercury will conjoin Jupiter to make this week doubly special. Whenever your ruler is involved in a planetary configuration, it makes waves. Mercury *is* your protective ruler, dear Virgo. Mama Mia! This really will be a week to remember on just about any front. With your ruler involved, personal and professional satisfaction should reach an all-time high.

After August, Expect Inner Growth

Once Jupiter enters Leo on August 1, you will begin a year-long assessment of your future. The second half of 2002 will coax you into the process of deciding what to take into your important twelve-year cycle (to begin in mid-2003) and what to leave behind.

From August on, you'll find a great deal of comfort and rejuvenation in solitude. You'll do exceptionally well when working alone, and may be twice as productive as usual. If you have to do any project that involves concentration (such as writing a book or thesis), this is an ideal time to tackle it.

Your spirituality and awareness will also be heightened. You may want to delve into religious teachings or muse over philosophical matters. With your sensitivity so keen, your dreams may become more vivid, possibly even prophetic. Your intuition will be heightened — a special gift of the cosmos. You must try to listen to it rather than question it, as analytical Virgo is sometimes prone to do.

At this phase in your development, you will also find yourself becoming far more compassionate and less judgmental. Virgo is sometimes thought to be too critical but now, with Jupiter in the twelfth house, your heart will speak first and your words, second. Your participation in charity projects, perhaps ones that started earlier in the year, becomes more significant with Jupiter in Leo. You seem particularly interested in the plight of children, possibly on an international scale.

If you have any fears or self-destructive habits, this would be the time to seek professional help to let them go by. This part of the chart rules your subconscious. Try to direct as much energy as possible to this area. At this point in your life, you don't need to be weighed down by excess worries or people who drain your energy. You need to enter into your new cycle (set to begin in mid-2003) feeling lighter, free of the shackles that held you down in the past. Dear Virgo, it is clear that you are getting ready to become your own person!

Health: Pamper Yourself

Throughout the year, your main health aim should be to reduce tension, especially on the job. While getting a soothing massage now and then may seem like an extravagant luxury, by the looks of your chart, I'd say it's a necessity. You should treat yourself well this year, dear Virgo. You, of any of the signs, can so easily go into overdrive. If you find yourself continually coming down with colds, you are probably doing too much. The cure may be as simple as a package of spa treatments now and then, or concert tickets, a candlelit dinner or a well-deserved vacation. (For starters, why don't you lounge around for an entire Saturday — imagine that!)

Virgo is one of the most health-minded of all the signs, and leans toward alternative remedies. Your sign prefers to use herbs and natural remedies over synthetic

THE YEAR AHEAD 2OO2

medicines. It's a rare Virgo who doesn't get her fair share of fruits and veggies every day. Taking care of your body will put you in good stead in 2002.

If you'd like to kick off a new exercise program or take up lessons in a new sport (or improve on one you already love), there are two excellent dates on which to start.

Your first auspicious moment will arrive at the new moon in your sixth house of health and fitness on February 12. That new moon will set up a positive two-week window in which to act. Start then. You'll be glad you did!

Your second favored time to act would be any time during the month of September — though you might as well start at the month's beginning, and make the most of great vibes for the entire four weeks! You should be in top form, thanks to Mars and to the new moon in Virgo on September 6. Together they offer a strong outlook for increased health and radiant fitness.

Should you need any major dental or medical procedures during the year, schedule them for the second half of 2002, when Jupiter will be in your twelfth house. The twelfth house is the part of the chart that rules what the ancients referred to as "confinement" of any kind, and as such covers hospitals and rehabilitation centers. With Jupiter, a planet known for its healing properties, touring this house, you can now seek and find top-notch professionals who will be sympathetic to your condition, people who can offer advice that is likely to bring relief. This is also your year to get rid of any self-destructive habits, dear Virgo — you don't need them.

It is also possible that you may be looking for medical help for a close relative or friend this year. If so, the same positive outlook would extend to that person during the second half of the year.

Domestic Demands Strong

Along with your amazingly sweet relationship experiences and good times with friends, plus all your professional gains, it is inevitable that tensions will arise. You will be busy trying to juggle family needs (or pressing real estate concerns) with the demands of your career. You've been feeling this push-pull since last year, so in some ways, this is nothing new. Pluto, a powerful planet that orbits slowly on the outer rim of our solar system, is currently visiting your fourth house of home and family until 2008. This planet has lately been stirring up some extra tensions.

The fourth house is the place of the chart that symbolizes the cradle of your life, including your home, your family (especially parents), roommates and any people who help you care for it, such as landlords, decorators or contractors. There may be changes afoot there — a move, or a divorce or marriage — that requires a realignment of family dynamics.

Planetary patterns suggest a tug-of-war between the public and private "you." If you were born around September 8 – 13, you will feel the tension most, as Pluto is in harsh angle to your Sun. However, you have experience with this aspect, as it was already at play the latter half of 2001.

The dynamic I'm talking about is Saturn's opposition to Pluto, a configuration that has happened two out of three times. These two planets have been having a long-running argument since last August (2001); the third and final confrontation will occur on May 25, 2002. Once that confrontation concludes, you should feel pretty relieved. You'll shoulder less internal conflict about which to attend to, the people at home or at work.

THE YEAR AHEAD 2002

This aspect puts Virgo in a bit of a pickle. Your Sun is caught in the middle of this tug-of-war; both Saturn and Pluto challenge you. Saturn is still in a tough angle to your Sun. If you were born around September 13 – 23, you are probably already dealing with the related tensions. Big breath, Virgo.

There will be certain points of the year when this pressure cooker atmosphere will build up. Fortunately, there is a way to deal with them: know your priorities. First, you've got to know when they are.

Pressure Cooker Dates

First, watch early January 2002, which will highlight your partner / lover / spouse. Be prepared to give that person a good deal of attention. Despite other demands on your agenda at work, your relationship really needs to come first at this time.

Second: May and early June. Despite any tugs by family, your career should get your focus.

Third: In September, particularly at mid-month, you may feel pressured. This time is different, however. You will have much more control, and be free to choose where to put your best energies.

Two Wonder Days for Home and Family!

Ah, dear Virgo, just when you thought the universe put you in hot water and left you there, it sends you some of the very best planetary vibrations possible: Jupiter hits a perfect angle to Pluto. The last time this sensational aspect occurred was three years ago, during the last week of March in 1999. Whenever Jupiter and Pluto team up, each works to expand the other: Pluto expands Jupiter's goodness, and Jupiter expands Pluto's passion. Success is guaranteed.

Your magical dates will be October 27 and later, December 18, 2002, with a plus or minus of about four days on either side. Mark them on your calendar! Your wonder days seem to help you most on home and family matters, though these heavy duty planets may spill luck into many other areas. These lucky dates shed a glow on the days immediately surrounding them — count plus or minus four days of luck. This widened time could allow you time to buy or sell property, or find a wonderful solution for a beloved elderly relative. As said, however, Jupiter's conjunction with Pluto can make luck spill beyond the confines of home and family into career, travel, and other parts of your life. The following two days are so vital, you should watch closely what is happening in your life and who you meet at that time. It's all bound to be pretty significant.

The Eclipses

Eclipses are wild cards, comic events that announce surprising new themes and demand a response. In fact, they make us react and deal with news, even if we are preoccupied with other matters.

One of the most important eclipses this year will arrive on June 10. It's a new moon solar eclipse in your tenth house, ruling career. (More highlights on your professional profile!) This eclipse may put in motion several surprising offers. Any agreements you make should work out to be fairly long-lasting, as Saturn glides close by. There seems to be no doubt that whatever happens at this time will add another stripe to your lapel.

There are five eclipses in all in 2002; two others will fall in your sixth house of coworkers, work methods, procedures and skills. Of these two, the first eclipse, a full moon eclipse on May 26, will be the more dramatic of the two. There may be company cutbacks or changes in routine that are initially disconcerting, and require some adjustment. This eclipse is more difficult to deal with because it coincides with another aspect that we've already discussed: Saturn's opposition to Pluto, due one day earlier on May 25. Emotions are running high. It will be hard not to feel a bit strung out as a result.

The second work-related eclipse (which also falls in your sixth house) is a new moon solar eclipse on December 4. While the May 25 eclipse discussed above marks an ending, this second one offers a beginning. It is likely that a new assignment of enormous potential will arrive in December. It could be that you'll be able to hire some extra personnel in your group if you are a manager. There is plenty of news around the office at this time, and in many ways this eclipse will represent a return to normalcy after the disruptions caused by the last eclipse at the end of May. (Yes, that earlier one will require some adjustment!)

There will be an eclipse in your romantic sector on June 24, a full moon in your fifth house of true love, pregnancy and the care of present children. (This eclipse will bring to fullness all these matters, which is why I wrote earlier that I felt a pregnancy could be realistic this year, despite the demanding presence of your career.)

This June 24 eclipse will be the last one to fall in your romantic sector for many years to come. In 2000 and 2001 you had several in this house. This eclipse will help you make a decision about your present partner, or whether you want to start or add to your family. If you are single, you may meet someone new who intrigues you in a way others have not. Saturn is close to that moon, so you seem ready to make a serious, long-term decision at this time. Happily, Uranus, the planet of surprise, is in perfect position to throw in a few sweet surprises.

Finally, later in the year, November 19 brings a rather stubborn eclipse, filled with aspects of many fixed signs. Whatever occurs, just about everyone will dig in his or her heels and refuse to give an inch.

This eclipse falls in your ninth house of long distance travel. You may find yourself dealing with living arrangements abroad, interacting with foreign people, or those based far from you. This same house also rules in-laws and other distant relatives. It would cover university settings certifications. Add too, your relationships with publishers, religious organizations, and the judicial system, including the courts, and your relationship with lawyers. Unfortunately, none of these areas is likely to go completely smoothly. There could be some news that makes you sit up and take notice. Luckily this eclipse falls in Taurus, a fellow earth sign, so if anyone can figure out how to surmount obstacles that come up, it's you.

Extended Outlook:

Mid-2003 to Mid-2004
Your Stars Sparkle Brightly

By time you are finished with Saturn's tour of duty in June 2003, something rather extraordinary and exciting is due to happen in your chart.

Jupiter, the great planet of goodness and growth, will enter Virgo on August 27, 2003 to stay until September

24, 2004. This will mark the advent of one of the happiest periods of your life, a nearly thirteen-month period like none you've seen in recent years. It will, quite simply, be the very best period in the decade. Goodness in your life will extend far beyond career, although it will encompass that too, if you like. Romance, travel and many other parts of life will glitter.

The contrast of having Saturn leave and Jupiter enter your own sign will be like going from the dark into the light. In fact, it will mark the start of a whole new era for you, dear Virgo.

All-important eras begin with preparation, dear Virgo. Now is the time to do yours. As you see, what you are learning now will stay with you and help provide profit and security for you for a decade or more into the future.

It is clear that your gold crown is being forged; the precious jewels to be set into it are being mined. Meanwhile, that lofty professional post is being readied for you. When you want it, your crown will be presented to you, dear Virgo. No one is more deserving of this cosmic favor than you!

Summary

In the past twelve months you've impressed top-level people with your professional abilities. As a result, you were (or soon will be) given a rare, once-in-a-lifetime opportunity to show them that you've got what it takes to handle more responsibility. Your new position will require a great deal of self-discipline and long hours, but stay the course. You are putting in place a firm foundation for your professional future, one that could support successes for decades to come. Your current projects will reap astonishing rewards in mid-to-late 2003.

In the meantime, Jupiter is blessing your house of hopes and wishes, friendships and social groups. You can expect stimulating new people to enter your life soon. Join clubs, and get involved in community / charity efforts; both bring pleasure and will increase your self-confidence.

In mid-year, Jupiter will move into your twelfth house, beginning a year-long meditation about what to take into your new cycle and what to leave behind. Working in solitude will bring marvelous results. Attending to health and fitness matters are favored throughout the year.

Finally, romance should be comfortingly steady and loving. With your career making enough demands on you, if single, it's time to take love slow and easy. This year you seem more at ease with yourself and who you are. As a result, you have room emotionally to be more compassionate of others. Married Virgos may choose to have more children.

In all, it's a year filled with activity, and more productivity than you could possibly imagine. Along the way, it is important to be good to yourself, and pamper yourself where you can.

When you end this year, you will emerge stronger, wiser, and more capable of handling anything life throws your way. As I wrote in the beginning, it will be a year where all the markers along the path of life are clear and well defined. How lucky you are! No more swimming through murky waters!

Enjoy your year, dear Virgo! After this, everything will change, and bring you to a far better place. You wouldn't want the future any other way!

LIBRA

The Big Picture

There's a lot to cheer about in 2002, dear Libra. You will see great progress in not only one area of life, but in at least two! Your most successful endeavors will be career-oriented. A breakthrough seems imminent on that front. By the time you get to the second half of 2002, your attention will shift to social matters. The company of others will prove to be sparklingly stimulating. A community event or charity project may play an important role in this trend, and would help you grow as a person. Libra, you always say you need balance — 2002 brings the elusive mix you yearn for.

Romantically, the coming year will be as vibrant as you want it to be. (This is a big change from last year, when opportunities for love and fun were less abundant.) Venus and Mars will hook up for most of the year — something we didn't see in 2001. When together, these two planets have the power to set off sparks bright enough to ignite new relationships or to rekindle established ones in a sexy, passionate way.

In order for any of us to have a strong outlook for love, Venus and Mars need to establish a stable relationship; when they do, we have the ideal conditions for affection and attraction. Last year, these mythological lovers had very different orbits and agendas. They had precious little time together. When they did meet, it was great, but brief. The opportunities to find or experience romance were too few and far between. As I said, this year, instead of being apart, Venus and Mars will remain cozy much of the time. 2002 offers a much better atmosphere for engendering tender love. Later in this report, we will discuss your best months. As a Libra, you can never have too much love and affection. In 2002, you finally have enough! You finally have a chance to experience the consistent love you've always dreamed of!

Of course, you have to help things along. Get yourself out there! Circulate and make an effort to see and be seen. That is how astrology works best: when we work to enlarge the potential of a positive cycle, rather than sit back and wait for others to take the first step. If you are attached, try to think of ways to perk things up between you and your sweetheart or spouse. If you do, you'll likely get the fine reaction you seek — your relationship could become stronger and more passionate than ever before. Indeed, you need to show the universe your intentions. How else can it give you what you want?

There's more to your life this year than work and love. We'll talk in detail about each and every area in the course of this forecast. I want you to be able to map out your plans to coincide with your best planetary trends for the year.

Mars Takes the High Road

Mars's orbit, and the constellations it visits on its way, gives us a clear indication of what to expect over the course of a year. Each stop it makes in an area of your life presents a snapshot of the *all* you will experience there. Let's start by stating the obvious: You will be focused on more than love. Mars' influence this year is ubiquitous. In 2002, rather than dally in one house of your horoscope for very long, as was the case last year, Mars will spread its energy through many areas. There will be plenty of variety to your life — and consequently, more opportunity. Mars will spend ninety percent of the year in an arch over the upper regions of your chart. This suggests your career will bring the biggest gains. You seem more intent than ever to make progress on this front.

It is also clear by Mars' position that collaboration is the best way to make progress during the first six months of the year. This comes naturally to you. Partnering is never difficult for Libra; you do some of your most brilliant work as part of a team.

You will turn an important corner during the months of May, June, July and August. Mars will be working hard on your behalf by then. Your energy will surge, and your optimism will skyrocket. To supplement this high energy, Jupiter is due to enter friendly-to-your-sign Leo in August (something we'll discuss later). At that point, gather up the reigns of your life and take it where you want to go — even if it means separating from your team.

Libra is a feisty cardinal sign and likes lots of action — this is contrary to your reputation as "laid back". Your charm hides a fierce drive. Make no mistake: when a Libra puts his or her mind to something, that goal is achieved! Although you collaborate superbly, you get a little antsy when you have to wait for others to catch up. Like anyone else, you find it tiresome if people take too long to make up their minds, and occasionally wish you could just forge ahead alone. That's exactly what you'll be able to do in the second half of 2002.

Impressive Advancement

As mentioned, your career could be the area that enjoys the most tremendous growth, propelling you forward in ways you still can't quite imagine. This all comes thanks to Jupiter's position at the very pinnacle of your chart, shining like a brilliant star at the top of your horoscope. Jupiter will make sure you get help from very influential people. You will suddenly find yourself at the right place at the right time, and will finally get credit for years of hard work.

Of course, nothing will happen if you lock yourself in your office and refuse to answer the phone each time the headhunter calls. If you concentrate on your professional situation, the phase you enter now could bring you profit and satisfaction for a decade or more. You are in a cycle that comes once every 12 years and lasts a full year; yours started middle of 2001; you still have six months. You might say, "Wait a second. Can we re-roll the videotape? My career wasn't *that* spectacular in the past six months!" If so, there's a reason. Jupiter was not in a strong position during the last several months. That will change now. It doesn't matter how old you are, or how educated — you can make great professional strides. With some effort, you'll surprise yourself with your accomplishments. You can't know the potential this period holds until you tap into it.

This is a time to clear the decks and focus on career. For once, the whole universe will be behind your every move. You've got to make tracks before Jupiter leaves your tenth house of fame and honors at the end of July 2002. If you work in a creative field, your innovative abilities and the powers of your imagination will reach an all-time high. Take your ideas seriously. There could be substantial profit made from at least one. As a result of the December 30 eclipse, you may have already experienced major career-related news. Because this was a full moon lunar eclipse, it may have marked the end of your role in a certain company or line of work. It could also have helped you crystallize hopes for a large project or negotiation.

Once Jupiter, this mighty planet of good fortune, wakes up on March 1, you must be ready to roll. You will be on a steady upward curve, and your name should come to the attention of high-level people. All key moves require preparation, and this period will be no exception. The more organized you are, the more focused your efforts, the more success you will have to show for your time. Remember: aim to have your promotion or new job by the end of July.

March and April are wonder months, but even better opportunities come in June and July. The year may start out well, but it just keeps getting better. Each month advances your goals.

A lovely, important day comes on June 3, when Venus, your ruler, meets up with Jupiter. Your popularity on the job reaches new heights. You are so golden, there's nothing you can do wrong! On this day, think, "pay raise"!

One of the best days of the year will be July 19 / July 20. Jupiter meets with the Sun, and then with Mercury, bringing excellent news. La-de-da. These are five star days! Please circle them on your calendar; you could be announcing a very important career move!

You do seem to be spend lots of money in July and August — try not to overextend yourself financially.

2002: Part II – Golden

Dear Libra, life will become more social and relaxing once Jupiter enters your eleventh house of hopes and wishes, friends and social groups in July. When positioned in Leo, Jupiter relates exceptionally well to your air sign, and is therefore in an even better position to help you than it was earlier. From this point until August 27, 2003 (thirteen months!), Jupiter will help you attain a long and deeply held wish — perhaps one you've almost given up on.

In the second half of 2002, old and new friends will come out of the woodwork. Your spirit will soar thanks to their genuine good will. In fact, one friend could quietly change the course of your life when he or she goes out on a limb for you. Look to friends for wise recommendations and advice. Let them introduce you to special contacts. No longer will you feel like you are coping with life's stresses alone. What a relief!

The new moon on August 8 will be a great day for all kinds of social activities, whether for giving a grand party or for making future plans that are especially dear to you.

In the second half of the year, you should think seriously about a membership in clubs and organizations. If you have never been a "joiner", you should look into at least one group now. The benefits from your new affiliation could change your life.

If you miss your opportunity to land a new position in the first half of the year, you might still be able to maneuver into something good. Though the first part of the year really is the best time, by far, for career efforts, you are favored even in the second half of the year. However, it will be even more important to network and to cast a wide net. Nothing you can ask of a friend is too much.

Pluto and Jupiter will help you through friendships on two red-letter days: October 21 and December 18. Whenever these two planets team up, happiness, success and celebration are around the corner. In your case, connecting with a pal or participation in a group acts as the catalyst to success. The dynamic created by Pluto and Jupiter may bring outstanding financial news, or even the fruition of a big dream, such as to have a baby, to publish your poems, or to move to Europe. Your desires will be the first priority of the angels at this time, dear Libra. If you are self-employed, this favored eleventh house also represents the rich fruits of past labors. The luck of this configuration could highlight hard work you put in over the past twelve months. Expect to see results on projects you may by now have assumed were shelved — those activities will gain new momentum. You'll be proud to see how beautifully your endeavors blossom. Finally!

This all seems like a miracle. Can so much change so quickly? Yes, dear Libra — you can believe it.

Outer Planets Boost Your Chances

Your bright forecast this year is due to the placement of the large "outer" planets. These planets, which include Pluto, Neptune, Uranus, Saturn and Jupiter, orbit along the outer rim of our solar system. They all have long lasting and long-range potential, especially when positioned in a superb angle to one's Sun. This is the case for you now. (Jupiter will move into its perfect position in August; the others are already in favorable spots.) On their journey through deep space in highly supportive fire and air signs, remarkably, *all* of these outer planets will create the right climate to sprout the seeds of your greatest desires. Under the influence of all their energy, you'll get closer to knowing what will make you truly happy. It's time, dear Libra, to take a risk or two.

First, you stand to benefit from Saturn's perfect angle to your Sun. With Saturn covering so much ground this year, virtually all Libras will partake of this marvelous trend. You may not be aware of it, but you will set up a strong platform on which to build in the future. Saturn will make sure that the decisions you make can stand the test of time. That doesn't mean the world will be a tension-free place — far from it. It does mean that you'll be able to get more control over your own personal universe. That's the most any of us could ever ask.

The cooperative spirit that Saturn will exhibit toward Neptune and Uranus is unusual; in both cases, its favor could extend to many areas of your life. It will be particularly helpful to your romantic affairs. As a cardinal sign, you are willing to take big chances, but your analytical air-sign nature first needs to know that you've covered all the bases. Before you take steps in any direction, especially a new direction, you need to be able to anticipate anything that could crop up in your way. You take calculable risks.

You are right to be prepared. But let's face it: There's a difference between being prepared and being obsessed. Libras have a tendency to get mired in their thoughts — so much so that some end up in a kind of paralysis whenever there's a big spontaneous risk to take. The ability to make decisions in the face of ambiguity or in short time is a skill the planets will teach you this year.

Any decision is better than no decision. If you don't take a position on important issues, others may do so for you. You don't want that! You are less likely to allow that to happen this year. Fear will not keep you from moving forward, not if you can help it. Adopt an assertive attitude. Sometimes all it takes is a shrug and a smile. Remind yourself, "It's now or never!" That's the way, Libra! As I said earlier, unfortunately, tensions will not disappear from the world. If you view pressure as a way to get ahead of the curve, as something that exists to teach us things, you will come out ahead.

Speaking of the tensions in the world... let's discuss Saturn's opposition to Pluto.

The Saturn and Pluto Conflict: Finale in May 2002!

Last year we had to deal with the first two of three angry tiffs in a major planetary configuration between Saturn and Pluto. The first two clashes were in August and November 2001. Being slow-moving planets, this conflict created tension that existed for the entire second half of last year, especially in a global political arena. This is an aspect that comes every twenty-nine years. It is indeed rare.

We feel the effects of this conflict on a personal level, which I will get to in a moment. Astrological scholars have studied these two planets and have come to the conclusion that their effect reaches far beyond the confines of individuals' lives. A struggle for dominance on the world stage breaks out every time these two planets oppose one another. Think: Vietnam, World War II

As 2002 opens, these two power planets are going at each other again. Apparently, they haven't resolved their differences. You will note tension in the air as the year opens. The good news is, you are familiar with this aspect and by now have found the tools to cope with it. Once these two plants resolve their confrontation in late May 2002, tension will begin to subside.

For those of you who were wondering, it is simply out of the question to set your alarm clock for May 2002 in the hopes to sleep through this phase. The universe is betting that you will learn something new from the process, start to finish. This particular exercise has to do with realigning your attitude, perceptions and possibly even your expectations. At the time of this configuration, Saturn and Pluto will be positioned in your third and ninth houses, the areas of the chart that rule intellectual curiosity and your attitudes toward a variety of issues, whether political, philosophical, moral, ethical, spiritual and / or religious.

Assessing New Perspectives

Some of your opinions and principles need updating. Adopt a new position — and feel at peace with it? This is no small task. It may prove to be more difficult than you had ever imagined. Your principles are terribly important to you. Whether you use them like old friends or crutches, these ideas help guide you through life.

As ever, your analytical side wants to look at all angles of every issue until you find the one pure kernel of truth. Proof of absolutes will probably be hard to come by. The cosmos will teach you to be a little more comfortable with making decisions in ambiguous circumstances (never easy for Libra). Although you understand on an intellectual level that things can't always be black and white, you haven't internalized this on an emotional level. You seem frustrated that you can't quite nail everything, you don't have all the facts you need to prove your instincts are correct. Give yourself time to let these factors incubate in your mind. If you don't rush the process, your internal equilibrium will reach the center you seek, even without all the facts.

The importance here is that you take the trouble to go through with this process of assessment in the first place. If you do, you will be able to build your future on a foundation of clarity, based on your inner voice. Rather than blindly follow the attitudes of others, you will know where you stand, and where you want to go. Few people bother to assess why they feel the way they do; you are to be commended for trying. As you proceed through this process in the first half of 2002, you may find yourself considering points of view that you wouldn't have given a tumble about a year or two ago. That's evidence of an open mind — and what could be better than that?

Remember that both Saturn and Pluto are perfectly angled to your Sun sign, making *your* adjustment easier than others'.

Incidentally, if you were born between October 11 and October 22, you have extra special help from Pluto this year. This intense planet will give you a boost in communicative endeavors, such as self-promotion or a web site launch. The third house, so lit up for you, also rules contracts of all kinds. Deals and agreements should go smoothly.

Spotlight on Relations

I should add that the emphasis on these same houses, the third and ninth, could sustain existing tensions with a close relative. This person could be an in-law, aunt or uncle, or sibling, or possibly (but less likely) a neighbor.

The roots of your disagreement appear to go way back. It concerns an issue that was never fully resolved. Saturn and Pluto's configuration will urge you to confront these issues head on and resolve them, once and for all. One of you is trying to dominate the relationship, to win the argument. Think of it this way: Perhaps there is no need for either side to be pronounced "right". If there seems to be no end in sight, and this relationship proves to be impossible to maintain, aim for peaceful and respective co-existence. Unhook, and move on.

These issues will be particularly sensitive around the eclipses on May 26, June 10, and December 4.

Saturn Pushes Education, Travel, Publishing and More

Saturn's location in a horoscope indicates in what area of life one can expect to face challenges, shoulder new responsibilities and strive to reach goals.

What does that mean for Libra? Saturn is still in your ninth house, a holdover from last year, and set to stay until June 2003. The ninth house is where we prepare for the future. From this position, Saturn will encourage you to strive for a higher education, develop interests in people based afar (even abroad), to delve into publishing and legal matters, *and* to reassess the role of morals, ethics, religion and spirituality in your life (which we spoke about earlier). These are areas that will require patience and a prudent, realistic approach this year.

Saturn expects an earnest effort from you, Libra. This taskmaster planet will see that you pay your dues and concentrate with all your might on the areas mentioned above. If you do, you will see handsome rewards in the second half of next year.

You would be better able to guess the specific ways in which Saturn could affect your life this year, especially because its presence in this sector is not new. I'll throw out some possibilities. Saturn's influence may mean that you will carry a particularly heavy schedule, perhaps in school at night and at work during the day. This would be a fine way to use the energies of this transit. Other Libras may be finishing up a complicated thesis, or writing a lengthy, research-heavy book. There's work in your future, dear Libra.

This house also covers aunts, uncles and in-laws. You may be charged with the care of an elderly relative on top of your everyday responsibilities. Your relationship with your mother-in-law could become difficult. If you have a case in the legal system, it appears that the wheels of justice are moving ever so slowly — if so, bide your time. You will benefit from an attitude that allows things to take their natural course.

Remember, whatever your personal circumstances, Saturn has been in this same ninth house since early last year. There's no need to fear that something will jump at your from out of the blue. I don't see any ugly surprises in store. Indeed, the start of 2002 will in many ways seem like a continuum of 2001. You will be able to deal with the unfinished business of this house.

Once Saturn leaves in June 2003, your focus on this area will fade. Though it may feel at times that you are grappling for a hold, take solace. You will benefit from having dealt so nobly with your challenges.

Spring Travel Soars

April, May and June should bring at least one extraordinary long distance trip. If you have no vacation in the works, find a destination and plan one. It would be a shame not to use these wonderful vibrations.

One of the best moments to go away would be when Venus and Mars embrace on May 10 in the house of long distance and foreign travel. Believe me, this would be a terrific time to fly to Paris, Venice or New York. This aspect favors any kind of travel, but especially trips to romantic destinations. Either you'll have a fantastic time with your current main squeeze, or you'll enjoy the ripe opportunities to find love.

If all you can muster during this period is a business trip, go. Substantial profit could result! (Venus has the ability to bring a strong financial boost if. For you, this is doubly true; a Venus is the guardian of your eighth house of joint financial matters.)

Most of the eclipses this year seem to send you away. These are the best times to take short, quick trips: May 26 is favored for the unexpected. June 10 rocks for long trips. December 4 guarantees wonderful results no matter where you go!

I should mention that the June 10 eclipse seems to have more weight. If you go somewhere, because Saturn is close by, you appear to have an objective or a goal to accomplish. Still, this eclipse is in a lovely angle to Uranus. Your journey may be completely spontaneous. Sometimes it's much better not to plan life — for once, just go and see what happens!

Finally, the full moon on December 19 could urge you to fly away for the holidays, whether to a winter ski chalet, where you can curl up in front of a roaring fireplace in the arms of your sweetie, or to a perfect white-sand beach, where you watch the world go by from your chaise lounge. The choice is yours!

Health and Well Being

If you want to get healthier and feel more energetic, this is your year to commit to a new exercise routine. With Saturn in a favorable aspect to the ruler of your house of wellness on January 23 and April 1, you have two ideal initiation dates. Choose these days to make changes in your fitness routine or in your diet, or both. Neptune, ruler of your sixth house, will urge you to look into alternative remedies to common problems, or to find soothing stress release.

In August, Jupiter makes a wide opposition to Neptune; this is a preview of a much tighter opposition due next year. Alcohol, pills (even the kind your doctor prescribes) or the wrong foods (i.e. too rich, processed, or simply too much) could pose a problem. In fact, anything that feels foreign to your body could provoke an uncomfortable reaction. Be good to your body, and be gentle to yourself at this time.

Those Libra whose birthdays fall from October 3 through October 11 will benefit most from Saturn's warming beams to Neptune. If you've lacked the self-discipline to get rid of bad habits, get ready for a new feeling of commitment. You can now replace bad habits with really good ones that have the power to transform your life. You will be able to harness that inner power to work for your well being in 2002.

Romance in 2002: Focus on Stability

As mentioned earlier, romance should be strong and sweet in 2002, without the dramas that so often marred your relationships in the past. Now that Saturn takes such an interest in stability in your fifth house of true love, you seem to be much more serious about long-term relationships. If you are single, you'll be more choosy about who you date. You want your time to count for something. To that end, if you are in an established relationship, you may decide to commit before the end of the year.

For those who are single and looking, you seem to have changed your taste in the type of person you date. While the exciting artist or actor would have turned your head before, you seem to be more impressed by something completely different: people who have a solid job, know how to save and spend money, are good with children, and who you can count on when the chips are down. Friends may tell you that all this is because you are starting to listen to your mother's advice, but it's much more significant than that. In a nutshell, you've become more realistic. At the end of the day, you know it's important to have a mate who will help you navigate life's rough waters. Life's too hard without having to deal with flaky people. You know that too.

Parties and other social gatherings will be the best places to meet someone new this year; the office does not seem to offer much in the way of new faces these days. There is potentially one exception to this: an attraction to a high-level official or client you come across in June, perhaps at a routine conference or meeting.

If you are a female Libra, you may hear your biological clock ticking in 2002, and move up your timetable concerning pregnancy and babies. It would be an ideal time to do so if you feel ready.

If, as a couple, you have experienced difficulties with conception, seek a specialist early in 2002, especially in mid-February when you could finally get the help you need.

Attached? You'll investigate what more is possible together. You want some excitement — that's sure. You'll set bigger goals, ones that may also involve a new baby or plans for children you already have.

Libras born between September 29 and October 5 will get a boost from Neptune. Its shimmering vibrations may bring you the kind of love that takes your breath away. Enjoy that feeling — it really is rare and special.

If your birthday falls between October 11 and October 23, you may find love suddenly — maybe even at first sight. Uranus is cooking up something special for you.

No matter when your birthday, there will be several key moments when you feel the passage of time. At these times, you will do whatever is necessary to bring extra stability to your personal life.

The first two such dates come early in the year, thanks to Saturn's meeting with Neptune: January 23 and April 1. Later, Saturn meets with Uranus, the planet of the unexpected. You may experience some rather spine-tingling moments of bliss. Saturn will help you turn a chance meeting or intriguing introduction into something much more. Key moments to watch: August 21 and December 16.

Mars and Venus' Romance Sparkles

If you're ever interested to know more about romantic prospects, just look at the positions of and relationship between Mars and its cosmic lover, Venus. Whenever this good-looking pair is together, flashbulbs go off — they charge the air with electricity so strong, you can feel it across the room. It's red carpet time, deliciously romantic, glamorous and thrillingly memorable.

Mars and Venus had busy schedules that kept them apart for much of 2001. They hardly had a chance to nod at one another, let alone slink off for some private time. This year is completely different. They are so happy to see one another that they can't bear to be apart, and they do spend the entire year either in each others' arms, looking forward to a speedy reunion, or enjoying the glow of recent dates together.

The second half of January through early February will be bright and beautiful. Venus will travel through your fifth house of true love. On its way, Venus will gaze at surprising Uranus and get inspiration by dreamy Neptune. Your magnetism will be at an all time high.

Not only will Venus be helpful. Mars will be in your opposite sign of Aries from mid-January through February as well. Attracting love should be so easy, you'll be the envy of your friends. If you are attached, your partner will become the center of your attention. You seem to be in a light, airy, happy mood, quite willing to put other parts of your life on hold. You want nothing more than to have time to enjoy one another. This would be a superb time to slip away on a romantic vacation. Mercury will be retrograde from January 18 to February 8 anyway. You won't miss a thing at the office if you're gone for a while. Just make your plans before that period, and stick to an uncomplicated itinerary.

Valentine's Day should be glorious. At that time, Venus sends Jupiter kisses — many Libras will be getting engaged, or simply feel wrapped in a very warm blanket of love. For once, Valentine's Day does not disappoint. No, this year, it takes your breath away with feelings you never knew you had, or never thought you'd feel again.

The new moon on February 12 could be magical for those who are single and looking for love, or for those hoping to see some powerful developments within an existing relationship. All kinds of unusual things happen, none of which you thought would ever occur, let alone now. This new moon brings two solid weeks of luck in matters of the heart.

Venus moves your partnership sector in March, sure to bring some enchanting moments in your closest relationship. If there were any little squabbles or difficulties with your sweetie, this would be the time to talk them over without fear. This is one of the best possible placements for Venus in any established relationship — it brings a kind of full moon effect. Venus will help you find a lot to agree about.

Two Other Days Fill You With Happiness:

June 3 is just beautiful. Venus and Jupiter dance the last dance at sunset. Ah, all days should be this perfect! If you meet someone on this day, the future seems rosy indeed.

Circle July 3 as well. Mars and Jupiter set out to provide you with many happy surprises when it comes to your closest romantic relationship. (This date helps those who are already attached.)

Venus will be in your sign from August 7 to September 7, a perfect month to buy some new clothes, and improve your looks with spa treatments. At this time, you'll generally feel terrific. You'll be at your charismatic best — and your calendar should show it.

The end of August brings a full moon in your fifth house of love. Some sort of big decision is coming up for you!

Venus Retrogrades in the Fall

Venus will retrograde from October 10 to November 21, a time when matters of the heart could hit a snag. When Venus retrogrades it is never a good time to get engaged, married, to schedule beauty treatments. Nor is it a smart to spend large amounts on clothes or jewelry. Having cosmetic surgery would be very risky at this time; don't schedule any procedures during this period.

One thing Venus retrograde does favor is the realm of former flames. You may rekindle a past relationship. See if you can make a go of it the second time 'round. If you still have feelings, and you're both available, there is no harm in trying. Who knows? You've changed, so has your sweetheart. They say timing is everything — of course, that's not quite true, but it does count for a lot. Perhaps things can work this time.

For those Libras in existing relationships, a Venus retrograde period can lead to discussions about sticky issues that need to be addressed. Even if problems haven't shown up on your radar, they may show up at this point.

The fact that Venus rules your eighth house suggests such discussions could center on sex. They could revolve around that other hot topic with couples: money. Talks could center on the power it brings (or denies) in a relationship. You may discover, much to your surprise, that your relationship has gotten off track in one of these areas. If you should discover problems, welcome this chance to air them. It is only the topic that you stop talking about that can never be solved.

Holidays: Glorious for Love

Admittedly, Venus retrograde is especially unappealing for you, as Venus is your main ruler. However, just when you were about to give up, catch your breath and close your eyes! The universe has a wonderful surprise for you.

From the very first day of December, Venus and Mars will come back together in the constellation of Scorpio for the year's finale. Here, these two planets create a thrilling show of unity, grace and beauty, more magical than anything we've seen in years. Mathematically, Venus and Mars will be in perfect step all month, waltzing to a magically romantic tune only they can hear. The dance they create is so perfectly patterned, so magnificent to watch, that December 2002 will find you swept away.

The whole month rates five stars. No other planets try to steal their thunder. December is your holiday gift from the universe: peace, love, and joy.

Finally, A Range of Choices

If you want to make a fresh start, this would be the year to do it. You won't be forced to do anything you don't want to do, and are less likely to be thrown off course or distracted by other cosmic events.

In the past, you were given a limited range of options. This year's buffet will be much broader and more intriguing. Some of the choices before you in 2001 were so dull and inevitable, you probably didn't even consider them to be options. Who could blame you? While last year you had to settle for options you never liked in the first place, now you'll be able to make decisions you can get excited about. With very few difficult aspects on the way this year, you'll feel less "put upon" by events — and more relaxed. You'll feel like the master of your life.

The recent series of eclipses in Cancer — Capricorn was disruptive. These eclipses fell on the top and bottom points of your chart — particularly sensitive spots that rule your career / reputation and your private home / family life.

In the former category, wild changes took place in your company and in your industry. Those shifts made you sit up and take notice. They required a few tough decisions and adjustments.

Chances are, you saw some change in your personal life as well. You may have had to relocate because of job developments, or make other adjustments to your living situation. Or, you may have experienced difficulty getting along with one of your parents this year, or were worried about the health of your Mom or Dad.

Like most eclipses', these changes were not of your own making, but due to external conditions. There is only one more such eclipse, a difficult one falling on June 24 in your house of home and family. This eclipse will have a most pronounced effect on Libras born near September 26. This could indicate a move or other change in your living arrangements or within a family relationship.

This will be the last such Cancer — Capricorn eclipse. Those eclipses will move on and usher in new ones in the kinder, gentler placement of Gemini — Sagittarius. You'll no longer be the cosmic topic of conversation, a relief, I am sure. Your life will begin to stabilize (remember that?) and you'll feel less at the mercy of so much upheaval.

Of course, this will require a new approach and a different attitude. Now that the eclipses won't create that push from the outside, it will be up to you to create all the push from within. You are going to drive the change in your life, just the opposite from what's been happening since mid-2000.

This could be the year where you find the powerful motivation to take a critical step forward. Ask yourself, "What do I have to lose?" Indeed, with such a supportive cosmic climate, you have little to lose and everything to gain, dear Libra! You have a real shot at maneuvering events to fit into your plan. You will not feel forced to fit your feet in someone else's shoes. It is a year that you can make truly your own.

Summary

As you begin the year, you find yourself in a dazzling cycle of career success. It is imperative that you waste no time in landing a prestigious new title. Work to this end from day one of the New Year. This phase is so special, it won't be repeated for over a decade. You will even have help from sympathetic higher-ups, so you won't have to do this all alone. Be ready to roll in a very assertive way from March through July.

While you'll need to give your career almost all your energy in the first half of the year, plan to focus on enriching your social life from August on. You can widen your list of contacts and enjoy a much livelier lifestyle than you have in a long while. If single, you will feel popular, and could meet someone whose background is quite different from yours.

All year, your creativity will soar. It's time to take your talents seriously — put a price tag on them. If you were born from around September 29 through October 5, you will be doubly blessed with Neptune's encouraging vibrations.

You find yourself in your strongest career position in over a decade. Influential people will be sympathetic to your growing impatience to move up the ladder of success. Ask them for advice on how to plan your next move to your best advantage. Expect to reach your professional goal by the end of July.

A residential move, improvement, or property sale / purchase is likely near June 24.

Attached Libras will find their relationships cozy and comfortingly steady all year. Single? You have reason to be optimistic. Your stars will twinkle especially brightly in October, February and July. Your ideal sweetie is intellectually sharp and comically spontaneous.

SCORPIO

The Big Picture

2002 should be all about money, power and increasing your status in the world. This should please you. A typical Scorpio finds these areas fascinating. Money was a sticky topic last year, but 2002 brings trends that should turn things around. Before that occurs, however, you'll need to be your most innovative and resourceful. Certain planetary patterns will test you to make sure you are self-sufficient. It is all very ironic that this should happen to you, of all signs, Scorpio. You understand that making money is a game. Others may claim that it doesn't matter if you win or lose, that it's how you play. You scoff at that attitude — to you, winning is everything.

There is no getting around it: You have a very complex chart in 2002. I see a number of superb planetary patterns and a number of equally difficult ones. This will be a year where the volume is set on high, with lots of drama, twists and turns — some of which you have not anticipated. Other surprises, fortunately, you are quite prepared for.

One thing is sure: your life is improving. 2002 will not be as hard as 1999 and 2000, but there will be times when this year won't exactly be a piece of cake. The stresses and strains that were gathering force in 2001 will come home to roost in 2002. You need to make a financial decision, come up with a plan of action or reach final settlement before you can really move on.

In 2002, Mars' strong, swift orbit takes it along the highest echelons of your chart, and ends the year in your sign, Scorpio. Every month will bring you closer to regaining the control over your life that you've missed lately. The end of the year is sure to be the best.

As you go along, keep in mind that career conditions will improve dramatically once Jupiter moves into Leo on August 1, set to stay until August 27, 2003. That's thirteen months! The work you do then could change the course of your life for a decade or more. It's my experience when one area of life is difficult, every other part seems to be colored the same shade of gray. Life may have seemed this way to you last year, dear Scorpio. Conversely, when one area starts to brighten, the rest turns to Technicolor hues too. These "darkness to light" contrasts will be true for you come August. Luckily, your life should move in the right direction.

Money, Money, Money

For about a year, you've been determined to improve your lifestyle and increase your security. The path to riches has not been straightforward, nor has the game always been fair. It has been more of an obstacle course. Any stress you feel is related to a financial obligation that has you strapped for cash. At times, it makes you feel frantic for greater stability.

This is puzzling because you've worked so hard, and feel you should have more to show for your efforts. You are so savvy about these matters, you should be coming out on top. You are never one to give away the farm without bargaining hard. Scorpio invented the rule, "To give, first you have to get."

The eighth house, so strongly figured in this test, is where we are encouraged to think big. We go to this house for extra funds when we want to make our grandest schemes possible. The financial constriction you feel now may be related to a noble cause, such as an effort to start a new business, buy a new house, or to send your child to college. It's also possible that your financial situation may be very robust, but you feel cash poor because of the influence of this grand planetary scheme. Those Scorpios for whom this is relevant are in the most enviable situation: they have enough money, but they're not liquid — maybe they've just invested. I dare say they may be in the minority, but they are out there.

Other Scorpios may not have watched financial matters as closely as usual, and may be surprised to see how tough things have become when it comes to making money. You probably assumed you would get a raise, that your business would grow, that you'd be able to borrow funds if you needed them, or that your ex-spouse would send child support. Whatever your assumption, it proved to be false, much to your unpleasant surprise.

There is some financial obstacle in your path. As you enter 2002, you may face overwhelming credit card debt or tax worries. Be very careful when you file for taxes, lest you take too many aggressive deductions and trigger an audit.Whenever you loan money or put charges on credit cards, realize that, according to your horoscope, repaying those loans and charges will take a very long time. It won't be easy. Remember, when we deal with bank loans and credit card debt, there is interest involved. The longer it takes for you to settle up, the more it will cost you. There is also a danger that, if you are self-employed, one of your clients may go bankrupt and stiff you for an invoice. To avoid this, be sure to check all credit references, just to be sure. Verify your own credit reports because someone could steal your identity and go to town with unauthorized charges.

Making matters more complicated, bankers who had been so friendly to you in the past are about to become pickier when it comes to loans. Last year they opened doors for you before you knew you needed them, but this year when you stop by their bank, they'll pretend they've never seen you before. Grrr! This, just when you need them! Everyone has had this experience at one time or another, dear Scorpio. It's the way of the world.

Whatever the financial situation you've already faced, you seem to be digging your way out from under it, but progress has been frustratingly slow. You will have to follow a conservative course, as Saturn is not leaving this house until June 2003.

Some of these aspects are due to a difficult configuration we are all dealing with: Saturn's opposition to Pluto. We are two-thirds through this challenging planetary dynamic. The first two clashes occurred in early August 2001 and early November 2001; the third and final one will occur in May 2002. This difficult aspect has asked you to prove a commitment to your current means of making a living or to a particular financial negotiation. Saturn may have asked you to make a choice among several possibilities that you felt were all less-than-ideal. While you may not have liked any of your options, you had to choose one. For someone as bent on excellence as Scorpio, this has to be hard. Nevertheless, the message was, and still is, deal with what "is" rather than what you wish it to be.

Near the end of May 2002 (again, the next and last time these two planets will meet), it seems reasonable to assume you will grapple with this financial issue quite intensely. Looking at your chart, your problem seems to be the 800-pound gorilla (signified by Pluto), notoriously self-absorbed and insistent about getting his own way. There appears to be a struggle for control, but hand-to-hand combat would *not* be the wisest way to go. If this all sounds familiar, please consider the following advice: Back out of the tangle you're in and come at it from a new direction. Try an imaginative, and less direct approach. (The problematic gorilla may be a family member, soon to be ex-spouse, business partner, or other person with whom you share funds now, or used to.)

A series of eclipses is coming to this very same financial area. Although these can be disruptive, eclipses might work to your long-term benefit. They will force you to get to the core of the problem and work through it. They will illuminate hidden snags, and force change where it's needed. For example, a job or endeavor that is simply not working will end if necessary, freeing you to seek better opportunities elsewhere. Eclipses test our strength and resolve; if the endeavor is dear to your heart, you will find an answer. That's how the universe works — it tests our strength over and over. Only those projects that we are most passionate about, those for which we have created the strongest base, will survive.

You seem to be beating yourself up over getting into this financial quagmire to begin with. You shouldn't, dear Scorpio. Your current situation may not be your fault; it may stem from deteriorating conditions in the larger market. It may be due to the state of the economy, or relate to other forces operating in your industry or company. Or, it may be that someone promised to cover certain financial costs and neglected to fulfill that obligation (an ex-spouse, or family member, for example). With Saturn in this house, you'll have to be patient and practical to get through this; you'll need to work slowly but consistently. If you have not faced any of these situations, trust me, your chart shows the possibility that you might. Keep your antenna up.

Unfortunately, the world doesn't work on your timetable. Your past efforts will add up to something big, but maybe not when you want them to. If you concentrate hard and give this question all your effort, Saturn will see to it that you come out of this period a much stronger, wiser, and better money manager. People around you are impressed with your courage and staying power, especially in the face of difficult odds. That counts for more than you can imagine.

As I said, the area of your chart we are discussing is where we think big and broad. It's where we try for big goals that involve large amounts of cash. Whenever the solar eighth house is involved, there could be two parties or entities involved. Certain rules and conditions need to be agreed to. Saturn is making the rules tough. That's why you find the terrain so strewn with rocks lately.

Reflections on Saturn's Teachings

When Saturn first showed up in your eighth house last year, you probably quickly grew to despise his presence. You were shown the importance of keeping records and saving receipts, checking your credit rating now and then, and reading contracts thoroughly.

Luckily, because you have had Saturn in your eighth house since last year, you have developed a few tools to cope with whatever financial challenges come your way. The process should be easier for you in 2002. This planet will give you exactly what you need to learn — no more, no less. What you learn will remain with you for a lifetime. Saturn will never ask more of you than you can handle. Once Saturn leaves your eighth house in June 2003, you will be generously rewarded for your attentiveness. No one ever was left poorer after receiving Saturn's cosmic MBA.

Certain basic economic assumptions that you've held for a long time, perhaps since childhood, may no longer seem relevant. If you should find this to be true, you may need to change your financial habits. This process depends on what you still have to learn. For example, if you never paid much attention to paying bills on time, you may be horrified now to learn that you have been turned down for a mortgage or loan. (Even if you kept up with payments, if you are always late, that will work against you.) Or, if paying taxes was something you considered optional and "forgot" to file in certain years, you may be hit with an audit, and have to deal with the consequences. If you owe child support, you may be forced to pay it now, regardless if you think your spouse "needs" the money or not.

Saturn will see to it that you keep up with obligations, follow rules and take no short cuts. This planet of endurance also teaches us that things of value are won by hard work and hardly ever come for free. Should you experience any difficult financial episodes, you can say to yourself, "I will make plans and put certain procedures in place so that I never have to go through something like this ever again." That's the point of this testing period.

July 20 should be one superb date for financial activities. (Make any moves a couple of days earlier; this date is a Saturday.) Contracts and agreements made at this time should turn out to be solid gold. Jupiter is walking with Mercury, a lovely day for putting your signature on any papers.

A Closer Look: Eclipses

Eclipses are coming in 2002. Three out the five due will fall in your solar financial houses, and will do the same in 2003. This is the beginning of another financially oriented process. Saturn and Pluto are working with these eclipses to amplify their messages, and to move you speedily to a new level of experience. You're going to be going through change much more quickly than usual. Eclipses exist to create as much change as is humanly possible in a very short, compressed period of time.

The advent of these eclipses suggests a whole new chapter is being written. From now on, your income will come from a new source. You may lose one source of income and again another — but not necessarily at the same time.

The three eclipses that will affect your finances are: May 26, June 10, and December 4.

The eclipses listed above will highlight your solar second and eighth houses, both financial houses. This indicates that a great deal of movement is due in this area. It is clear that outside conditions will continue to influence your present situation. You would be smart to read the papers keep up with changes in the world, the marketplace, and in your industry.

As you move through the first half of the year, it is imperative to remember that you have a lot on your side. You must not lose hope or get discouraged. The universe is testing your determination, your resourcefulness and your resolve. You can win. In fact, once Jupiter enters your tenth house of achievement and promotion this summer, you should feel far more in control of your income. Others might even be a bit envious of your fabulous career rise.

Tapping New Resources; Reevaluating Values

Money is, of course, energy in concentrated form. It is what is left at the end of the day. For many people, money is one powerful, tangible proof of achievement. Pluto, your ruler, governs transformational energy, and continues to live in your solar second house of earned income, set to stay until 2008. This means that your determination for a better standard of living is no short-term goal. Scorpio is known to have remarkable endurance — now you prove it.

Pluto is comfortable in your second house. It's one where transformation of energy (Pluto's specialty) is very obvious — you spin work into gold, so to speak, because you get paid for what you do.

Yet with such a bright spotlight on money, it would be easy to think that's all that matters to you right now. Not true. The second house is more about resources, not just cash. Resources include your time and effort. 2002 will be about reevaluating the way you spend your days to make sure you get the satisfaction you need from your job. While you focus on money and improvement in your lifestyle, you may put more emphasis on the quality of your experience. If you have to make less money in order to be happier, so be it.

While you come to grips with your own values, it seems clear that you will have to grapple with someone else's. This is hard. It seems that both *your* values and *his* (or hers) are evolving simultaneously. To find a middle course that you both can agree to is like trying to get two shuttles to dock in space — possible, but very tricky being that they are both moving along at very rapid speeds. Ah, that's what makes this year so interesting.

Good-luck Planet Jupiter, Backs You

Jupiter enjoys being in Cancer, its placement at the beginning of the year — this combination symbolizes the growth of new life forms. Because Cancer is a fellow water sign, it relates perfectly to your Sun sign. Jupiter's presence in your ninth house suggests that this sector will produce some of the very *best* news of the year.

So what can you expect from Jupiter? For one thing, you are likely to be doing *much* more traveling in the months to come. Think about taking a trip to a beautiful city near water, or going on a romantic cruise.

You'll yearn for time to think. Expect to go through a philosophical awakening during this period, one where you reflect upon some of life's deeper issues. You may sense within you a longing to return to your center, to get in touch with your spirituality, whether you want to read more of the Bible, attend religious services, or simply study and compare the religions of the world. This may be a time when you come to terms intellectually with your moral and ethical principles. You'll question your own integrity. Generally, it seems to be a good time to step back to examine the principles that guide your life.

Try to take a trip to a gentle spiritual retreat during the first six months of the year. Find a destination far from the bustling world to get in touch with your spirituality. If you can't get away because of other pressures, you may want to attend lectures, read uplifting and inspirational material, or simply take time out to think in a simple, quiet environment.

In 2002, especially in the first seven months, you may be dealing with people based at a great distance, maybe abroad. Or, you may be dealing with a person at home base who speaks with a foreign accent. No matter how this works out, it will be clear that citizens of other countries could be quite lucky for you. Maybe you are working on a project that involves international trade, or on a publishing project that has application to other cultures or may be translated into other languages.

You will also be fortunate in legal activities or settlements. With so much emphasis on the eighth house, you might be splitting property after the dissolution of a marriage or a business partnership. If that is true for you, with Jupiter in Cancer you might want to try to find a settlement sooner rather than later. Do it before August 1 and you will have a very good chance to find a fair, satisfactory solution.

Some of you will get a book project going, while others will start a large web site. Still other Scorpios will decide to go back to college for a degree. Any of these would be perfect ways to use Jupiter's golden energy. Academia will be a fertile area, whether you tap into it as a teacher or as a student. Any endeavor initiated on an international stage should be lucrative, including e-commerce, research, study, foreign affairs / diplomacy, journalism, and foreign relationships. You may join the Peace Corps,

Americorps, or a similar organizations within your own country.

If you work in law, the justice system, or medicine, your status will be on the rise. If you always hoped for a grant from a foundation, start typing up your application. One could be coming your way.

Take a good look at this list, and "read" it in many different ways — any or all of these areas could bring profit and happiness. For example, if you are an agent, you might decide to represent a foreign artist. If you own a business, you may begin to market your products or services to a more international market. If you are a businessperson, you might investigate the college market now. Free-associate about these areas and try to generate ideas. You should act in one of these areas, and if you do could find yourself to be quite lucky. Consider tapping into fields that are unfamiliar to you; these are the areas where you are likely to find your best profit and a great deal of personal growth.

Now that you know *where* much of your luck lies, let's discuss specifically *when* you might get your big opportunity! Mars will perk up during all of June, so consider an early summer getaway. The new moon on July 1o is also superb, and ushers in two weeks of sensational energy. A friendly eclipse on June 24 may bring a short, quick trip, perhaps to see family.

My favorite day of the whole *year* for you is July 19. Circle it on your calendar as a five star day. The Sun and Jupiter will walk arm in arm, a very lucky cosmic happening! (There is a bit of glow on either side of this date, so circle the days surrounding it.) That is a big day to watch. Whatever happens may relate to any of the activities we have been discussing in this section (all ninth house activities), or to your career, as the Sun happens to rule your career. Jupiter is *always* lucky, so this is probably going to be your brightest standout day of the year.

Jupiter rules your second house of earned income house, so all the areas we have discussed should be super lucky for profit around this time too!

There are so many ways you can use this energy. Don't sit back! Write those letters and make those appointments. You may not have anything going on in these parts of your life *yet*, but this is a long trend — it lasts a year. Think about how you can make these areas work for you. Astrology works best when you use the planetary cycles to your advantage!

Career Begins to Glitter and Glow

After August 2002, Jupiter will move into your tenth house of honors, achievement and fame for the first time in 12 years, set to stay until August 27, 2003 — a period of almost thirteen months. You will have an unprecedented chance to advance your position within your company, industry, community, or the world at large. If you want to become well known, that is very possible, dear Scorpio! You may be written up in the paper now, or given some sort of award. No matter what you experience in your career, you have to do your part. Look eagerly for the opportunities that should start to pop up everywhere. Some Scorpios will choose this year to begin a new business. If that is you, you will have chosen the best year ever! You might as well buy some new clothes, because by the second half of 2002, you'll be seen and heard — and you name will be on everyone's lips!

In next year's report, as we get closer to August 2003, I will tell you Jupiter will move on to another part of your horoscope, not to return to your career sector until July 2014. Between now and August 2003, if you haven't held up your end of the bargain by casting a wide net, sadly, you will be left behind. (I am trying to sound a little dramatic so that you will listen to me, dear Scorpio!)

The energy in your chart shows no ordinary career trend. This is something that can set up a whole decade of profit if you pay attention to what's available to you, starting now. Decide now to be one of the lucky ones who finds a spot in the sun — you have such a great chance to do so! In fact, if you start now, during the coming months you might advance not once but several times, as hard as that might be to believe. Grab your confidence and your courage! You will succeed!

There are two dates that are so positive, so rare they bear special mention and plenty of attention. Pluto and Jupiter will send each other a very positive, ultra-strong communication on two remarkable dates. Whenever these two get involved, success results. Pluto works to intensify Jupiter's considerable goodness. Pluto is posited in your house of earned income, and Jupiter, by then, will be in your house of fame. Please do write these dates into your calendar, for the discussions you have and the agreements you make on these days are as rare and as valuable as diamonds: October 27, 2002 and December 18, 2002. Both are platinum gold!

For an earlier stellar date, add the new moon that falls on August 8. As best dates go, this is a runner-up. This new moon falls in your house of achievement, and sets up two solid weeks of forceful energy.

Word to the wise: Be sure *not* to take a vacation in August. Believe me, you'll be too busy. Let your colleagues and friends go — you will be making huge gains and need to be near home base. It could be your biggest month of the year for exceptional professional progress.

Romance Plays A Supporting Role

With a month so focused on travel, career, education and other activities, you may wonder if you have any time to indulge in romance. Yes, you will. However, this is not a year when love will take first place, dear Scorpio. In fact, if you do meet someone, or if you have a sweetheart or spouse in your life now, that person seems to understand your need to spend long hours at work, and seems happy to support you through this period. Be glad for this. If things weren't this way, the resulting strain would pull you apart.

If you are single, some of your best moments will come in January. Mars is brilliantly lighting your house of true love, a holdover from the holidays of 2001. Mars will move on January 18, but while it lasts, love should be divine.

After that, your next elegant moment arrives at the new moon on March 13; its glow lasts for the two weeks that follow. It is during these early months of the year that you may find a real life lover of your dreams.

If you are attached, here is another group of standout days, also quite enchanting, when Venus sends kisses to Jupiter: June 1 – 3.

Wait, there's more!

If Mars and Venus are in proximity in space, they ignite sexual passions. In 2001 these legendary lovers were hardly ever together. This year, they are almost never apart! For those who have a partner, May will be simply divine, especially near May 10. It is a sexy, powerfully charged month. At this moment and during the following weekend, you can hardly keep your hands off each other.

Venus will retrograde from October 10 to November 21, not a good time to wed, become engaged or even to do plastic surgery. It is a time that favors former flames; you may look back to an earlier relationship to see if you can re-ignite that earlier love.

Amazingly, Venus is going to work very hard on your behalf at the end of the year. Because of its retrograde action, Venus will stay in your sign not for one month (her usual stay), but four solid months, from September though December! This is extraordinary! This will make you your charismatic best. If you're single or looking, this can help you find someone to love. If you are married, Venus happens to *rule* your house of commitment, another signal that things are improving. During this retrograde period, you might spend some time on areas that need to be addressed.

If you are dating or married, expect a litmus test of your closest tie. The full moon eclipse in Taurus on November 19 is due to be a tough one, as most of the planets are in stubborn, fixed signs. This suggests that no one will want to move an inch on his or her position. Less committed relationships may pull apart now. Others will see this eclipse as the right moment to begin listening to a partner. (While most people feel these cosmic events in their personal life, not all do.) This eclipse may not pertain to a romantic partner but a business partner, agent or other collaborator, even a lawyer or other expert you've hired. This won't be the last eclipse in this relationship house, but it will be the only one in 2002. There is nothing to fear, dear Scorpio. If this relationship means a great deal to you, it will survive.

Home and Family

Your residence (or a property you own) has been in flux, and will continue to be. Uranus and Neptune are testing your Sun in this fourth house sector.

If you were born between October 31 and November 5, you are feeling the misty rays of Neptune. It may make you feel creative, but it could also give you foggy vision. Be sure you read all the fine print and check all references if buying, selling or leasing property. This is not a time to make assumptions or presumptions. Get it all in writing. If you are buying a house, check for past or potential water damage.

Note to Scorpios of those birth dates listed above: should you experience any difficulty with family relationships, it could be due to a miscommunication or misconception formed years ago, when you were very young. Neptune's harsh angle to your Sun may help you get to the bottom of it.

If you were born between November 11 and November 21, you are feeling the jarring rays of Uranus. You may have to move or make sudden adjustments to property matters, or you may be called on to help a parent get through a sudden and difficult adjustment. Stay flexible. If you're in the process of buying a house, have an engineer check the electrics. Be sure everything will meet your future needs.

Scorpios born earlier than the birth dates listed here have already felt the strongest influence of Neptune and Uranus challenge their Sun. Uranus will move to Pisces late next year, while Neptune will slowly move through this house over the next many years.

The big news this year is that practical, stabilizing Saturn has taken an interest in helping you in all family matters. This should be very rare and comforting news.

Saturn will send solid signals to Neptune on January 23 and April 1.

Later, Saturn will meet with Uranus on your behalf on August 21 and December 16.

On these dates, you can make surprisingly long-term home and family decisions that will make you feel more secure. You seem to have moved more than usual in the past five years. (If you only moved once, it appears to have been sudden, due to Uranus' presence).

Let's also note the new moon on February 12. This should be outstanding time to make any improvements to your living situation, or to help an elderly relative find the care he or she needs. You don't have many opportunities this year, but the ones you do have are truly outstanding. Try to work with these dates!

July 19 and 20 would also be terrific for buying or selling a house.

That's your year, dear Scorpio! I have laid out all the most important themes for you so that you can be ready. You are one of the strongest, most determined signs of the zodiac.

SCORPIO

Summary

Jupiter is beaming brightly from the apex of your chart, which suggests that foreign travel could be the most exciting part of your year. Journeys could bring emotional, intellectual and spiritual growth. International commerce or relationships with people based afar could be a fertile part of this trend. If you are interested in pursuing an educational degree, your goals will be aided in coming months. Publishing opportunities also glitter. In terms of these activities, make your biggest effort from March through July. While the whole first half of the year is strong, Jupiter is retrograde in the first two months of 2002. The sweetest part of this trend is the chance to travel more — you tend to be a little couch potato, Scorpio, but this year, you'll get up and go!

Your career status scales new heights in the second half of 2002 — it will be simply remarkable! Be sure to note the days that Pluto and Jupiter cooperate, October 27 and December 18. These days may turn out to be major dates in your time line.

One of your best moments of the year may well be July 19 and the dates surrounding it, thanks to jolly Jupiter conjoined with the Sun.

Finances and credit require vigilance all year — avoid impulsive investments and follow a conservative course.

Romantically, your partner will support you in all your career aims. For those who are attached, the November 19 eclipse could test your alliance. If so, welcome the chance to talk things through. Meanwhile, Venus and her cosmic lover, sexy Mars, will cook up some rather spicy sessions throughout the year, especially in early May and throughout December, your very best months for love.

With Venus setting up shop in the constellation of Scorpio from September through December (an unheard of amount of time), you'll be in a wildly enviable position — at your magnetic best, and holding the edge in all matters of the heart.

SAGITTARIUS

The Big Picture

2002 could be a landmark year, one you look back on as a turning point that changed the course of your life. Certain planets and eclipses are ready to push you and test you, and will turn your life upside down and inside out. And you know what? It's just what you've been waiting for!

A year from now, you'll find yourself in a whole new realm, as if a tornado picked you up and carried you far and set you down at the start of a curious yellow brick road. If you follow the path it will bring you to Oz. Like the characters in *The Wizard of Oz*, you might not know exactly why you're on this journey, exactly when you're likely to arrive, or with whom you're supposed to meet if you do find your way — but none of that matters yet. What matters is that you make a start. It's the journey that counts right now, not the destination.

Your chart in 2002 is one of sharp contrasts. On one hand, the eclipses return to your sign and your opposite sign of Gemini; they will do whatever is necessary to get you going. Whether you like it or not, there will be some major changes in your life this year. Some will occur because you know you can't continue with the status quo any longer. Others will occur because of major developments in one alliance. Your biggest challenge will come from Saturn, which will put tremendous pressure on you and your closest relationship. You must learn to be realistic and independent, as well as compassionate and caring. Change is hard, but change is good.

At the same time, Pluto will help to reveal hidden talents. This intense planet will lead you to transmute your abilities into something you can see and use. Across the sky from Pluto, Saturn will demand you be sure of every step you take, and force you to make choices under less than ideal circumstances. Elsewhere in your chart, Uranus and Neptune will open your mind and sharpen your intellect. Your thoughts will move at lightening speed; you could be at your creative best. You will be able to use this energy in a variety of ways, but particularly with writing, teaching, negotiating, and selling or in public speaking.

Virtually all the heavy-duty outer planets will be in friendly air and fire signs (something we'll look closely at later). They will buttress you, and continually remind you that the universe would never turn its back. While you will be challenged at times, they will see to it that you will have the key tools you'll need to cope. In your hardest trials, a ray of light will always shine through. With a little effort you will be able to swing that sliver wide open. It will be, at times, a sweaty, strenuous and noisy process, but with a real chance for victory. All you need is the strength and courage of your conviction.

Try to see this period for what it is: the adventure of your life. Have faith that the universe is pushing you in the right direction. It clearly has a plan for you, and you will have a big hand in how it all turns out. We are rarely completely at the mercy of cosmic events; rather, we are participants in them. Put twelve Sagittarius in the same circumstances, and you will get twelve different reactions and results. Dear Sagittarius, see yourself as the actor, director, screenwriter, and stage manager of your life. To live your life to its full potential, one must live courageously.

As you begin 2002, eclipses will systematically test the strength of your relationships, your goals and values. If there are parts of your life that have become decayed or which the universe deems are no longer of use to your future, they will be discarded and replaced with something better.

Throughout the year you will be asked to choose which of many paths you would like to take. As you move along the path you choose, you will learn much about yourself, and others will learn about you. We most reveal our true nature in times of stress. During those times we have no extra energy to be anything *but* the person we truly are inside.

You might read all this and say: "My life is just fine as it is now, thank you." Apparently, the universe doesn't agree. It is time to do more with it, perhaps more than you ever considered possible. In time, colors and tastes will become sharper as you begin to live in the fullest sense, fighting for what you believe in and letting go of all that you know does not reflect the true you. In the end, the passionate life is the only one that counts. Take the reigns, Sagittarius.

The Nature of Eclipses

Eclipses are among the strongest cosmic events we experience. And this year they change to the axis of Sagittarius and Gemini. Now that they are back in your sign, they will begin a process of remarkable change. They will bring on cosmic labor pangs and initiate a process that will help you give birth to a whole new way of life. This year, the way you see yourself and your closest partner will change. Your career ambitions will become much more focused. You may decide on some key residential and family plans. Even your looks may undergo a radical revision.

Sometimes eclipses bring bold new opportunities so special, for a moment we feel a little afraid to grab what's offered. If you are a typical Sagittarius, you'll do so anyway. Sometimes an eclipse will crystallize years of hard work in a blink of an eye, bringing joy and reason for celebration. Other eclipses bring stiff challenges that strengthen our resolve, change our agenda, and call us into action. Both kinds of experience have value.

Under the influence of the eclipses, changes that world normally take several years to occur will be compressed into a very short amount of time. Eclipses always play with our concept of time — they speed it up. The cosmos knows human nature, its tendency to stick with what's tried and true. Eclipses pull us out of our comfort zone. New experiences require adjustment and a great deal of energy. Most of us say we're just too busy to investigate all our options. To this, the cosmos lets out a deep belly laugh and then unleashes a great wind that pushes us swiftly out of our inertia, and blows us along our destined path.

Throughout 2000 and 2001, all the eclipses were in Cancer and Capricorn. Those eclipses probably changed your financial situation by ending one source of income and ushering in a new one. Or, those eclipses made you view your talents, possessions and overall financial strategy in a new light. You may have set up new goals for earning, saving, spending and investing. (We'll discuss your finances in a little more detail later.) Now the eclipses are moving on to study different parts of your life. Eclipses always come in pairs; one falls on the new moon, and the other on the full moon. The "duo" of eclipses falls in the same pair of signs (Gemini / Sag, for example), two weeks apart; they hit that axis every five-and-a-half-months, for an eighteen-to-twenty-four month span. Then, the eclipses start to focus on the next pair of signs, and on and on, and so it goes.

As you begin 2002, the horoscope wheel has rotated, grinding slowly, creaking as a big heavy wheel is prone to do, and methodically points its arrow on Gemini and Sagittarius. Here, it will remain focused until the end of 2003, with three eclipses on this axis this year, in May, June and December. (Keep reading for exact dates.) It has been a decade since eclipses last highlighted your sign. You are sure to feel their presence once they return. There are five eclipses in 2002, and of those, two will fall in Sagittarius and one in your opposite sign of Gemini, highlighting your relationships. (Of the other two, which are not on your axis, there is a tough one due in November in Taurus, highlighting health; the other one, more mild, comes at the end of June in Capricorn, and is the last eclipse to highlight financial affairs. We'll discuss these in depth later.)

As you might guess, the universe has no patience. Changes will start rolling right at you, just after the first eclipse in the end of May. This is a full moon eclipse that could prove to be rather emotional.

The full moon lunar eclipse set to arrive on June 10 in Gemini may be especially powerful. It's almost exactly opposite Pluto, the planet of transformation. This will almost certainly signal a change in the status of a close relationship. Some Sagittarius may marry under this aspect while others may choose to end their alliance. You know best if your alliance is headed toward commitment or away from it.

The Process Has Begun

Your cosmic soup is already bubbling away on the front burner — you have recently experienced your first eclipse in the series, a new moon solar eclipse, on December 14, 2001. This eclipse may have signaled news immediately, or in the period shortly before or after the 14th. If nothing has happened yet, watch the date that falls exactly one month to the day later, January 14, 2002, plus or minus four days, for important developments.

There is even more likelihood that you will feel the effects of this eclipse on or near May 4, 2002, when Mars flies over the same mathematical degrees and constellations. It is as if the December 14 eclipse burned a little track in the sky and Mars will travel over that same sensitive little rut in early May. Allow a tolerance of a plus or minus four days, and watch to see what occurs, if anything. Those with December 14 birthdays are most likely to hear news. Something you've wanted to do or say to someone may click into place then, and off you go.

A Look to the Past

Astrology is the study of cycles, and we can use it to try to learn from our past. Years ago, from late 1991 to mid-1994, these same eclipses occurred in Sagittarius and Gemini. Think back to see what might have happened then. What were the major themes? It may be more revealing to go back even further (assuming you are old enough), to 1982 – 1984. The early '80s hold some of the clues about what may happen now.

The reason we go back for a look at previous days is that all eclipses return to the same mathematical degrees every nineteen years. If, for example, you had a baby in the early '80s, you apparently learned to be a parent. Now your child may be going off to college, and you enter a new phase of the parenting lesson, that of letting your grown child grow independently. There are so many possible examples. My advice to you now would be to facilitate the process of looking back. It's a good idea to keep a little diary during these eclipses, and to write down what happens. Someday you may want to check back.

Big Life Events and Inner Wisdom

When eclipses call out your name, as they will this year, they push you forward with a gust so strong all you can do is hold on to your hat and let it thrust you where it may. Trying to stand still would be pointless. Sometimes it almost feels as if fate is at play. Eclipses herald big life events. They bring marriage or divorce, a new baby, an educational degree, a promotion or new position, the start of a new business, or the purchase of a house — things like that. They bring both beginnings and endings, and always increase our understanding of our worlds.

Your appearance is likely to change this year — you may arrange your hair differently, start to sport a radically different style of clothing, for example, or, if you need to, you may lose a substantial amount of weight. (Losing weight is favored when Saturn is opposed to the Sun, a configuration you will have this year; the eclipses will only help things along.) Under such aspects, men often shave their beards — or grow one — while women tend to change their hair color, style or makeup. The French, so wise in these matters, have an old saying, "Change your hair, change your life." What is important here is that these outward changes hint at a deep, inner metamorphosis.

Finally, let's remember that eclipses always take us over a Rubicon. There is no turning back. The old door shuts, and a new one appears. Like in the movies, when the hero has no idea what lies beyond that new door but still enters, you will head in an unknown direction, dear Sagittarius. The universe uses eclipses to make us more mature. They bring changes that can't be anticipated and test our reflexes. They introduce factors over which we have no control — and they watch to see how you respond.

This is the schedule of upcoming eclipses that will affect you in a very personal way:

A full moon lunar eclipse lands in Sagittarius on May 25, 2002.

A new moon lunar eclipse happens in Gemini on June 10, 2002.

A new moon total eclipse occurs in Sagittarius on December 4, 2002.

As you see by this list, most of these eclipses will be new moon events. This suggests a crop of many fresh beginnings.

The lunar, full moon eclipse on May 25, 2002, may require the most adjustment. It marks an ending, and will be most noticeable for Sags born near November 27. That May lunar event will coincide with a heavy aspect that involves an opposition of Saturn to Pluto. Again, the focus will be on what you want, and how you deal with one close relationship. You experienced the configuration of Saturn opposed to Pluto last year in early August and early November — once these two planets stop arguing, your life will improve immediately, from the second half of the year on.

Luckily, you have a strong adventuresome spirit, a funny, wacky side which should allow you to fare quite well in 2002. You are already ahead of the game, and you've only just begun.

Add Taskmaster Saturn to the Mix

OK — It is time for me to admit, your life probably has not been easy lately. It never is when you are going through a major transition. This is mainly Saturn's fault. It holds a very demanding position in your horoscope. You have endured about a year of Saturn's challenge to your Sun so far; this testing period will not be over until June 2003. Now in your opposite sign of Gemini, Saturn will place steady pressure on you, mainly in the realm of partnerships. The purpose of this is to teach you what a close relationship requires. Saturn will make sure you hold up your part of the bargain.

Saturn will now encourage you to be an active participant in your relationship, to take your part in the responsibility to make it work. This is true whether your most important present alliance be a romantic one (marriage) or a business partnership. The seventh house, so lit up here, is the house that brings two people together through contract, with clearly defined responsibilities for both parties. It's the house of commitment between two parties. You won't be allowed to get away with neglecting your partner — you'll have to be a real participant in this union.

If you are dating someone special, you may now be in the process of moving a dream relationship into the reality stage. Perhaps it is time to live with your lover on a day-to-day basis. If you sense your partner is not serious about eventual commitment, you may break up, perhaps sooner than you ordinarily would. Married or single, you want your relationship to count for something, now more than ever. Suddenly, you are in no mood to waste time.

The main effect of Saturn's placement in your seventh house is that you learn to deal with partners on a very intense, day to day level. You may think you know your partner well, but as this trend progresses, you will see parts of this person you didn't see before, and you will need to make adjustments. (You may find traits to admire, or those that drive you crazy.) From now on you will know this person in a much more realistic, intimate way.

At times in 2002, you may find that your partner is not able to give you all the time and attention that you want or need. This is Saturn's way of strengthening your independence, something that, fortunately, a typical Sagittarius finds easy. Most members of your sign need a bit of freedom. If too many rules define your relationship, you may find it psychologically confining; you feel caged. How this all goes depends on the kind of relationship you have, and how demanding your partner will be this year.

Still, as part of this trend, you will be encouraged to find compassion for your partner. Your chart suggests that he or she may be under pressure and would appreciate your support. Your partner may be changing jobs, starting a business, battling an illness, or in some other way changing his or her lifestyle. In the meantime, more responsibility for the relationship will fall to you. This is the proper order of things, and would happen no matter who you happened to be with. If you feel needy, try to get emotional satisfaction from your wide circle of friends until this period passes. Your partner will be quite occupied, and may not always be able to give you what you need when you need it. At times your significant other may be physically separated from you, for travel, or because of night school — something like that.

Saturn is now just about exactly opposed to your Sun. The exception comes for Sags born in November. Lucky you, you are done with the sharpest challenges of Saturn, but admittedly some strains remain. This year all the December-born Sagittarius will feel the pressure at some point.

Saturn and Your Health

Having Saturn placed in opposition to your Sun can be, at times, draining to calcium reserves. Protect your teeth and bones. Get exercise and try weight training.

Saturn will bring demands on your time and energy. At times, you may feel like you could use a nap. (If so, go right ahead!) All I say to you now is, "Don't over-do it." Be sure to eat wisely and get plenty of rest, even if you see yourself as a super high-energy type.

If you have confronted a medical problem in the past year, try to follow your doctor's orders to the letter (assuming you trust your doctor and have asked for a second opinion). Be patient while your treatment progresses — you should see solid results just after June 2003, at which time you should feel much better. That date may sound far off, but it is just around the corner!

In the meantime, if you need a date to lift your spirits about a health matter, or if you just want a fitness consultation, choose June 2, when Jupiter conjoins Venus. Your health should glow. Mercury is retrograde during this period, but as long as you aren't having an operation, this date is superb for healing and other health matters.

There is one eclipse falling in your sixth health/work sector on November 19, a date when you should take no chances if you feel something isn't quite right. Get help — that's what the eclipse is there to tell you.

Jupiter Your Ruler: Financial Boost

There is always one area of someone's chart that is glorious and wonderful; that part usually points to Jupiter's location. Jupiter is the planet of great happiness and growth — and just happens to be your planetary ruler.

Last year, for the first time in twelve years, your guardian planet moved into your solar eighth house of joint resources and financial obligations. This marked the beginning of an incredibly fortunate financial period for you — and came at an especially good time. As mentioned earlier, the eighth house is the same sector that's been the focus of the eclipses since July 2000. Admittedly, you may have experienced a few flutters due to fast-moving events. You still have one more eclipse coming in a financial sector before you are done with this series, on June 24, 2002. This could trigger an unexpected new job or a raise. Don't think only negative news happens on eclipses!

The eclipses cause change rooted in external conditions (such as the economy, profits within your company and so forth); these changes are inevitable. Thankfully, Jupiter protects this same part of your chart until the end of July 2002. While Jupiter has been in this sector for the past six months, the good fortune planet went retrograde in early November. He was not operating at top speed, and performance may have been disappointing. He stepped out for a coffee break, and hasn't been back since.

As the year opens, Jupiter remains in retrograde orbit, but not for long. Your dear ruler will have a sweet, caffeinated buzz on March 1, 2002. Hence, you may want to highlight on your calendar the period from March though July 2002 as your best for financial decisions and progress on all deals.

Do note that from May 15 to June 8, Mercury will be retrograde. Within the larger period of luck, you have this window of static where deals should not be made. As you see in astrology, we need to watch *all* the planets, not just one!

If you want to start a new business, for example, you would do best to incorporate from March through July, while cautious of the Mercury retrograde period from mid-May to June 8. Jupiter rules, among other things, all financial profit. You definitely want to initiate business activities when Jupiter is at his strongest.

Some Sagittarius suffered a financial loss during 2000 or 2001. This loss was most likely a result of events brought on by the eclipses, events that were out of your control. If you lost your job or some other main source of financial support, or are worried about your resources because of divorce or the dissolution of a business, you have a key time to act. Look for a job or finalize your division of property in the first half of 2002. The force is with you.

The eighth house, so highlighted in the first half of the year, rules many things, so let's list them: Commissions, taxes, inheritances, royalties, scholarships, gifts, prizes, settlements in a divorce or other dispute, insurance payouts, grants, venture capital funding, loans, credit and financial obligations. As you see, if you work on commission or a royalty basis, you could make a killing in the year's first half.

If any of these areas are important to you, move forward with vigor, for you will do well. For example, if you are having difficulty with a tax matter, Jupiter's placement in this house suggests you will be able to arrive at a favorable settlement with the government at this time. Voice your ideal payment plan — it could be accepted.

No matter what financial dealings you are involved in, be sure to finish off your talks or decisions *before* the last day of July 2002. Here is another instance: suppose you need a scholarship to go to college, or special funding for a business — for best results, fill out your application from January through July 2002.

July 19: Financial Luck

July 19 is an exciting, wildly wonderful, five star date. It could be one of your best periods of the year! On that day, your ruler, Jupiter, walks arm and arm with the brilliant Sun, showering you with radiant luck. This pairing brings a likelihood for good financial news. Refer back to the list of topics covered by the eighth house; all are shining for you now.

If you work in publishing, this week has the potential to bring you extraordinary news. Get those query letters out early! If you are currently dealing with a court dispute, watch for a satisfactory settlement near July 19 — or offer one. You may travel at this time (marvelous idea), or deal with people in foreign countries (also favored). When you circle July 19 on your calendar, be sure to circle some of the days surrounding it, as there will be a little glow on either side. Remember, it is unlikely that the Brinks truck will show up at your door, with the men rolling boxes of money or gold bars into your living room. You have to go out there and look for options. If you do, chances are, you'll be rewarded.

Mercury's Out to Lunch

Let me reiterate: You should avoid Mercury retrograde periods for any important business or financial moves. Mercury rules contracts, leases, and other agreements, as well as letters, documents and proposals, travel and commerce of all kinds. These areas are complicated in Mercury retrograde periods. Be super cautious and avoid signing or agreeing to anything on these days from January 18 through February 8; May 15 to June 8; and September 14 to October 6.

Pay Days

Keep in mind that though we have been discussing financials in many forms, we have not specifically mentioned salary. In astrology, the second house governs salary. The eighth house, which is so sparkling for you this year, rules money that tends to arrive in chunks. As we discussed, this fat chunk could be an insurance payout, a settlement in a court case, a commission or bonus check, or other such things. It is a certain kind of money, involving joint resources between you and another individual, or company / bank/ credit card or even the government. It is not payment for services rendered.

Bottom line: For a salary raise or a new job, check the two weeks that follow the new moon on January 13; the week of January 14 is particularly strong.

At the full moon eclipse on June 24 a new job, second source of income or other chunk of cash could arrive. Your creativity is high, so you may sell an idea or product that you designed.

Career: Your Name in Lights

Finally, mid-year should bring the career results you've been counting on. Take note of offers that arrive on or near July 20 — this is a five star day! Circle the whole week leading up to it!

Late August and September mark your next big period. These months will bring you all the right ingredients for success. When you do score, push the situation for all it's worth. Send out memos, press releases — you name it. Shout your news from the rooftops.

Keep in mind that June 2003 will herald a hugely important time for your career. Everything you do in the meantime will be judged when it comes time to award that big job to someone — make sure your work is letter perfect, and that person could be you.

Jupiter's Move into Leo: A Major Boon

As a Sagittarius, you love to travel. You don't even see it as a luxury; it's a way of life, a staple. Any friend, lover or boss who attempts to hem you in may be successful, but only for a while. Eventually, you always get away — it is that important to you. Luckily, that won't be a problem this year! The house governing travel, study, and relationships with people based afar will become the most blessed part of your life.

From August 1, 2002 to August 27, 2003, a period of thirteen months, opportunities to travel, study, and possibly even to write (a book, a thesis, you name it) should pop up everywhere. There is no doubt that this period will mark the beginning of an enormous year of personal growth and satisfaction.

When Jupiter leaves Cancer and enters fellow-fire-sign Leo, it will be of greater assistance to you than it could be during the first half of the year. Leo relates better to your fire sign Sun of Sagittarius than water-sign Cancer. Leo is a sign that thinks big and bold. It is colorful, playful, and optimistic — just like you, dear Sagittarius.

Jupiter's visit to your ninth house is sure to have a strong influence on your psychology and overall sense of well-being. You'll feel more in tune with the rhythm of life in the second half of 2002. This is the house of long-range plans and preparations for the future; you will start to think on a noticeably larger scale. You will find possibility in endeavors and relationships that would have escaped you in the past. Later, you will remark at how you used to think in such small terms, how limited were your boundaries by your own imagination.

This influence will also lead you to become more reflective and inquisitive, more interested in philosophy and politics. You will, no doubt, find ways to study more. There's even a chance you will be asked to teach in 2002. This is your time for exotic long-term travel, study or living abroad. You could even get a grant for research in a foreign land. Far travel is so favored, it will be easier for you to get half way around the world than to the town next door. Get your passport ready. When luck lands you will need to be ready to roll.

Spiritual development and enlightenment is so strongly favored in the latter part of 2002, you will probably never be the same. You become more complex and far more seasoned than ever before. In short, you are a new and improved version of yourself!

Global trade, commerce and communication will grow in significance. Jupiter will also give you a feeling of manifest destiny; this will help you to rise above any obstacles you might encounter.

If you are a student, teacher or professor and can get an extended amount of time off to travel or do research abroad, this is the year to do it. You must plan a humdinger of a trip, a journey to a place you always dreamed about but have never visited. If you are a college student, look into living abroad in the August-January 2002 semester or the January-June 2003 semester.

If you travel for business, this Jupiter's placement suggests that your best accounts will lie far from home base. It would behoove you to put in some "face time" with your faraway partners or clients. (You, in the flesh, can be so much more convincing than email!) If more training could help you get ahead, call for brochures and choose your classes! Whatever you do, make the most of this trend.

A very important date to watch is the day of the new moon on August 8. Everything will come together for you in these areas. That new moon will light the torch of opportunity, and Mars, by then in Leo, will provide you with the vehicle to take where you need to go. This is an omen of success. Apparently, whatever you are involved in at this time will be of great importance.

Mark These Dates! October 27 and December 18, 2002

An amazing development surfaces at year's end involving a very high-voltage combination: Jupiter and Pluto. Whenever Jupiter and Pluto meet, each enlarges the other's qualities — Jupiter expands Pluto's transformational energies while Pluto allow Jupiter's goodness to multiply to a much larger level.

Pluto will amplify the messages Jupiter sends from this house, intensifying your luck and progress in the areas we've been discussing. As I said, these areas are travel, foreign relationships, endeavors related to learning, publishing projects and legal matters. With a little effort on your part, one or all of these areas is bound to flourish. On the dates that Jupiter and Pluto tango, progress in these areas will skyrocket. Circle two five star dates that are more rare than emeralds: October 27 and December 18.

Va-Voom! These are extra-powerful dates. Remember, Jupiter is your ruler. This is significant — while everyone will benefit from this superb configuration, you will find many more ways to capitalize than most!

The Outer Planets: Supporting You Every Step of the Way

We talked earlier about the amazing coincidence of having virtually all the powerhouse planets of the planetary lineup cruise in air and fire signs, including Pluto, Uranus, Neptune, and Saturn. Because *you* are a fire sign, each of these planets will go out of its way to help you succeed. Fire loves to be near fire, and fire needs air. The universe will bring plenty of both to ensure that your energy burns brightly. When your ruler, Jupiter, moves into another fire sign, Leo, in August, you will be able to add one more heavy-duty planet to your list of perfectly aligned heavenly bodies.

Let's also note that all these outer planets are in mutable signs. This is astrological lingo for flexible, free-spirited, negotiable and adoptable signs. That's more good news. If you encounter unpleasant developments, remind yourself that nothing is quite as fixed and immobile as it looks. Talking, prodding, urging and cajoling might help — you have nothing to lose by trying.

Finally, many of these outer planets remain in the positions they held last year (and for some, several years prior). If you've done your work, you have developed the skills to deal with them.

Those Sagittarius who are born before December 10 will benefit the most from happy-go-lucky Jupiter's position in 2002. Jupiter will rocket straight over the degrees of your Sun. If your birthday is after December 10, you will see the most dramatic affects later, in the first part of 2003. Don't worry, nobody gets left out of this trend!

Pluto visits Sagittarius — A Once-in-a-Lifetime Happening!

On another front, Pluto, the planet of metamorphosis, has for several years been transiting your sign. You are currently undergoing a gradual period of reorientation. Your self-image and where you see yourself in the world is changing, and with it, your perspective on that world. In the process, of course, your outlook on your most romantic relationships, and intimacy in general, will change. You are now in a powerful period of transition, taking everything you learned before and using that knowledge and experience in new ways for the future. This Pluto trend has nothing to do with pride and ambition. Instead, it emphasizes vocation. This planet, in addition to the actions of the eclipses discussed earlier, will urge you to update your appearance. You will assess the work you do. Talents you have managed to suppress won't be so easy to ignore any longer. Those talents need expression, and you are about to give it to them!

You are so fortunate to have Pluto, the power-planet of the galaxy, touring your sign. This is its first visit in 246 years. Some people never feel Pluto in their Sun ever in their lifetime — its visits in each sign of the horoscope are far too few and far between. Thankfully, when Pluto moves into a sign, it does stay long enough to get some real work done, with visits that last between 12 – 25 years, depending on its orbit. In your case, Pluto will be in Sagittarius for thirteen years; it started its tour of your sign in December 1995, and is set to stay until late 2008.

Pluto's presence in your sign will urge you to let go of the childhood preconceptions and phobias that have held you back from achieving greater intimacy. Note that Pluto's changes are not sudden or disruptive. They occur gradually. By the time you get to 2008, you will see a marked difference in yourself. You will look back to where you started in 1995, the date Pluto first entered Sagittarius for the first time in your life, and you will be surprised by the enormity of your progress.

This year, Pluto is moving directly over the Sun of those with birthdays between December 6 and 9. Those Sagittarius will begin to feel the blossoming of potential that earlier Sagittarius have already experienced.

Uranus and Neptune:
Offer a Sterling Gift for Communication

For several years, you have been fortunate to have both Neptune and Uranus in the third house of your mind and communicative style. As said earlier, Pluto's position in your sign is very supportive to these two planets. Let's take a look at each, separately.

Neptune will increase your imagination; hopefully you can direct this into some sort of creative expression. If you are involved in any kind of writing, from journalism and documentary work to screenplay or fiction writing, you will benefit. You will find a compelling way to say what you want to say. You will excel at efforts related to film or photography, advertising, PR or sales. Neptune will remain in your third house of communication until 2012, quite a long time.

The other powerhouse, Uranus, planet of genius, electricity and eccentricity, tours your third house of communication. This enormously creative energy is meant to help you break through old methods and to get your point across in a fresh and convincing way. Your mind is going down new paths, and the methods you use to express yourself will change. You are marching to a different drummer, by now that's vividly apparent. If you are a writer or artist, these aspects could help you create a product that speaks to a generation. Take your ideas seriously, Sagittarius. Never in your life have you had cosmic help on this level! Computers or the Internet may be making a large impact on your life, as these planets are speaking in futuristic, digital Aquarius.

Saturn and the Power of the Pen

This year something very exciting is happening. (Yes, *another* very exciting thing!) Saturn will go out of its way to help both Neptune and Uranus. The ideas you come up with now have a real shot at becoming established in society. Saturn will help the visual (right-brain) creative Neptune January 23 and April 1, and will give a boost to scientific, innovative Uranus on October 27 and December 18. Schedule time to create on these days.

(You can give a plus or minus one week to all these aspects, but the week *prior* will be far stronger than the week after.)

Neptune will reach out and give extra help to Sagittarius born from November 29 to December 2. If your birthday is prior to the date mentioned, you have already had Neptune's strongest rays; if after December 2, Neptune will come round to "speak" to your sun later.

As Uranus moves through your third house, it will reach out to help those Sagittarius with birthdays from December 14 – 21. Sagittarius born before December 14 have already experienced the benefits of Uranus' rays. Remember, however, that all Sagittarius will benefit in some way, even if it is slightly milder.

Uranus will stay in your third house of thought and communication for nearly two more years; Neptune, for ten years; Pluto, for nearly seven. As you see, these heavy hitters of the zodiac aren't leaving anytime soon. You have all the time you need to develop your expressive talents. Don't squander a single day. You have plans to put into action.

Finally, Romance...

We talked a lot about partnerships. Remember, partnership and commitment are not governed by the same house as love and romance. Romance denotes pure fun, covered by still another horoscope sector than commitment. What if you are single and looking for love? Or what if you are married, but the partnership emphasis discussed in this report doesn't really pertain to your spouse but to your business partner? "So, what about fun," you ask?

The universe in its blessings will provide some of that too.

If you are single and hoping to meet someone, Mars' position is a sure-fire indication that you'll enjoy popularity and present certain allure.

Let's start from the beginning. Love will be incredibly bright in February, when Mars is in Aries, in your fifth house of true love.

Later, the new moon on April 10 and the two weeks that follow should spice your life perfectly.

If you are ready to commit, the eclipse on June 10 may bring an exchange of rings and promises. Love is very serious on this date — "forever ever after" is in the forefront of your mind.

A more joyous date — truly a four star day — would be July 3, when Jupiter and Mars create one of the most radiant days of the year for fresh love and for a celebration of established love. Make note of it!

Throughout the first half of the year, Jupiter's tour of your eighth house should make you feel ultra sexy, always in the mood for love. Couples who have faced a lack of desire could find real success from medical advice or counseling now. Others may find that all they need is lots of quiet, private time. This aspect is quite powerful and capable of bringing about the right turn of events.

Finally, astrologers look to the dance of Mars and Venus for indications of whether that magical spark will be present in your life. Last year, Mars and Venus weren't too helpful, frankly. These two lovers were busy doing their own things, as Mars' demanding schedule kept them apart. This year, they make up for lost time. Big time. They are hardly ever far apart.

Mars and Venus will embrace passionately on May 10, sure to be a most enchanting time. These two mythological lovers meet in your solar seventh house of serious commitment, making this a favorite month to get engaged or wed. Mercury turns retrograde on May 15, so the period prior, from the second half of April through the first half of May, would be best for that momentous walk down the aisle.

Later in the year, gentle Venus and macho Mars meet in December. Wowee. This time they meet in Scorpio, the sexiest of signs. They will orbit so close to each other that entire month, it's simply astonishing. They meet in the twelfth house, a house that suggests complete privacy, and sometimes indicates a clandestine affair. Hedonistic Venus likes pleasure, and prefers not to consider the consequences. Avoid scandalous situations if you can — you are a lot smarter than Venus. Use these sparkling aspects to kidnap the one you love, to enjoy him or her in private. Treat each other as passionately as you did when you first met.

You have no idea how special December will be. I see these two planets as ice skaters, enjoying one another alone in the sky for the entire month of December 2002.

Allow me to elaborate on the beauty of their dance: On a frozen pond outdoors, Venus and Mars will skate on the twinkling ice through the deepest hours of night — they have their love to keep them warm. Mars holds Venus high in the air and spins, twirling gracefully and so quickly, they defy the speed of light. Venus jumps, does a triple toe loop, a mid-air split, then a flirtatious spin. She hurls her delicate body through space and Mars catches her in an embrace. Holding her high, he spins away with her.

Together, they are in perfect syncopation to a music so lovely it seems to emanate from far beyond our galaxy. Their dance is intimate, so close that anyone who stumbles across this pair would know something vital is at play. This is no ordinary dance.

Venus, blue eyed and dazzling in her sparkling outfit strewn with a thousand diamonds, and Mars, so strong, stately, sure and confident, together create a beautiful, memorable vision. Embracing, parting, leaping and twirling, the timing of one anticipates the heartbeat of the other. Your passion will echo theirs. Based on the deepest love, the greatest of emotions, this is a dance you will not forget, dear Sagittarius. This will be your December 2002. Dance with the one you love, the person who is always there for you, and who loves you with all his heart. Together, you will create beauty that is otherworldly. That, dear Sagittarius, is what love is all about.

Summary

In the year ahead, your yen for freedom and adventure will intensify. Traveling or living abroad, a publishing project or a fabulous educational opportunity could become a viable option now. Such an experience would change your life in the second half of 2002.

In the first half, however, there is money to be made. Concentrate on fresh revenue streams. If you look hard enough, you will find a sweet stash of cash.

Due to Saturn's position, your marriage or a business partnership may learn some lessons the hard way. (As long as they're learned, it's worth it.) At the same time, there is a strong theme of union and communion, of transformation, both spiritual and practical. You have quite a year in store!

By June 2003, you'll breathe more easily, and will be well on your way to becoming the seasoned spirit you are meant to be. Every day, in every way, your self-esteem and your willingness to give are growing stronger.

CAPRICORN

The Big Picture

You enter 2002 with clear eyes, enthusiasm and optimism. You are in an enviable position. You've come through a difficult patch of planetary challenges over the past few years, including a series of eclipses in Capricorn and Cancer (your opposite sign) in 2000 and 2001. The last one in this series, coming this June, is due to be much gentler. Those eclipses had the power to change your agenda and focus your mind on the people and things that really matter to you; they brought on a major development in a close relationship. Now, confident as you begin your new year, you're open to investigating life's possibilities, and less concerned with keeping things exactly as they have been in the past. Friends tell you that you seem more playful, happy and energetic than they've seen you before, and they are right. You're ready to live life more freely and fully — and you know it's time to have more fun, too.

This family of eclipses on your Capricorn — Cancer axis has come every six months since July 2000, and will move on after one final eclipse in June. Those eclipses tore down outdated parts of your life and opened you up to new experiences. As a Capricorn, you can get a little stuck in routine and can become too attached to what you produce, regardless of whether or not it's good for your future. (You probably never even think to ask if it's outworn its usefulness.) Well, these eclipses changed that tendency in you. They led you to discover strengths you never knew you had, and changed your perspective in appreciable ways. They also gave you a new language to describe your past, and new lenses to envision your future. Now, with a clean slate, what you choose to bring into your future won't be out of habit, it will be from true desire.

Last year, Mars spent an inordinate amount of time in your twelfth house. This urged you to think about what you want for your future. Mars' placement also meant that, before you could put your ideas into action, you had to wait for others to formulate opinions about your ideas. That was frustrating, but valuable. It gave you time to think deeply about things, and brought up long-buried feelings and dreams. You won't have to deal with a slow-as-molasses schedule anymore. 2002 is a year of action, not dreams.

Mars' Call to Attention

Mars' orbit during the course of any year is a reliable indication of which parts of your life will experience a pop of cosmic energy. During its stay in any one house, Mars gives you a dollop of power to use as you please. In January 2002, Mars begins by buzzing through your home and family sector (fourth house) and gradually makes a steady, sure climb to the very pinnacle of your chart by mid-October. It then remains in your career sector for all of November 2002. In those year-end months, the Red Planet will put your name in lights. This is sure to be a high-key time for you. I expect you will have exciting professional news.

At the end of 2002, Mars will hang a lantern in your fairy-tale eleventh house of celebration, friends and social events, Believe me, this is a perfect way to end a year so filled with progress. A tip to making the most of your potential this year: Throughout the coming twelve months, Mars will remain almost entirely on the western side of your chart. This shows just how critical a partner will be. Collaboration will be a key to your success.

As you begin the year, certain personal matters get top billing. Among them: residence or property; pregnancy / present children; creative projects; health / fitness; and family or romantic relationships. While not all of those areas will be big for you, some will be; which ones depend on where you put your energies. Home and family matters that need to be dealt with get settled in January and February, or just after the new moon on April 12.

You may be surprised to hear that your career is not on this list. As a Capricorn, profession is usually a major element in your life. Don't worry, professional concerns will come back into focus in May, and will show up in much bigger form than in the last three months of 2002. Lucky you, this year will give you a little bit of everything.

Key Planets Let It Be

The key outer planets, including Pluto, Uranus, Neptune, and Saturn — heavy-hitters of the cosmos, will remain in fire and air signs all year. These elements do not relate directly to your Capricorn earth sign, so they shouldn't have much effect either way. Don't feel left out. This can be an advantage. Not being the center of cosmic attention means that there will be no planetary cacophony to take you off course. In other words, while you won't get any help from these big planets in 2002, you won't be hurt by them either. Left to your own devices, you'll be able to set your own agenda and follow it. Expect your level of productivity to be high.

I should clarify here that although these big, outer planets won't be helping your Capricorn Sun, they will be supporting one another, and that is big news. For example, your ruler, Saturn will help Uranus and Neptune this year, and Pluto will bolster Jupiter at two points in a big, extraordinary way late in the year. Later in this report, we will discuss how you will be helped by these friendly skies.

While it is true that Saturn, your ruler, continues his long-standing row with Pluto into the first half of 2002, these two planets are due to settle their score and separate by the end of May, not tangle again for years, thank goodness. You dealt with Saturn and Pluto on two occasions last year, in early August and early November. Chances are, you have developed the tools to cope with the third and final episode of this configuration. By mid-year, these two planets' powers, which have been so disruptive to your work, health / vitality, and relationships with coworkers and underlings, will start to fade away. That will certainly spell relief for you. When these two planets squabble, they the stress in life, and wreak havoc especially for you, Capricorn, as Saturn is your ruler.

An important relationship will be on your mind from January to August 2002. The most ready application of this sparkling trend would be, for many Capricorns, to marry. If you have been serious about someone special, indeed, 2002 would be your best year in over a decade to wed. Jupiter's tour of your seventh house of commitment assures this. Should you choose to marry prior to August, your chances for future happiness together will increase exponentially.

If you are trying to choose a date to wed, your absolute best moments will fall between March and July 2002. These would be wonderful months to set in stone any serious partnership, including professional ones. However, do not act during Mercury retrograde periods, which are listed elsewhere in this report, with explanations. Avoid starting anything new from May 15 to June 6.

Through all your experiences, you have learned a great deal about yourself and your partner. The challenges you faced over the past two years haven't dampened your spirit one bit. In fact, you became more determined than ever to reach your goals. As you enter 2002, you are kicking harder, reaching taller, leaping farther than ever before. You've done your deep thinking — now it's time to swing into action!

Let's look at each area of your life in greater detail.

Lucky Two-somes

By now, you have probably figured out that partners will be gems for you in 2002. And as we discussed, on a personal level, this will be your best year for engagement and marriage in over a decade, especially from March through July 2002. Capricorns who get engaged or married at this time do so under wonderful aspects, and will see wonderful results. Jupiter, the planet of good fortune, will send such warm beams to your seventh sector of commitment. If you are already married, you will find that your significant other is likely to do very well during the first half of the year; you have a lot to gain through his or her good luck. This year your partner will encourage you and build your confidence, and might even help you take a risk that just a year or two ago would have been overwhelming. In that respect, your partner is a catalyst of positive change for you. Listen up to what he or she has to say!

Jupiter, planet of happiness and growth, first entered your commitment house in mid-2001, and will stay put until July 31, 2002. If you found that the last six months of 2001 were not as positive for love and partnership as you expected, the problem could be that Jupiter was in retrograde, a weak position, for much of that time. This planet was hampered from making its usual "all out, no-holds-barred" effort for you. The coming year should bring more dramatic results, especially after Jupiter turns direct, from March 1 through July 31, 2002.

Business Partners Favored

Marriage is not the only form of contractual partnership. There are ways you can benefit from this trend in your career. In the course of your work, you might consider hiring an agent, publicist or other specialist to represent or advise you. You may meet with a headhunter, business consultant or coach, Internet specialist, accountant or lawyer. Such people could help you get to the next level. If you do form a business partnership, be sure to contact your lawyer to go over your contract. Spend time to make it clear and comprehensive. The partnership you build now could be in place for years to come. You want it to be the best it can be.

Even on a very personal level, teaming up with others could prove to be fruitful. If you want to learn a new sport, or investigate a new hobby, for example, or if you want to lose weight (a great year to try, as you will see later), grab a friend and talk to him or her. Find someone who has common goals and work toward those goals together. Being part of a two-some will help you accomplish much more this year. Of course, it will turn out to be much more fun.

Doctors or psychologists may be considered "partners" covered by this same seventh house. This sector governs, among other people in your life, the experts and specialists you hire to get something accomplished, and that includes health goals. Do you have a health issue that should be explored? This would be a good time to do it. Choose your advisor carefully and you will have much to gain from your association. On the other hand, if you work as an agent or lawyer, or represent others in any field yourself, you may land a lucrative client this year. As you see, this trend works both ways. Either way, when two combine energies, the result is magnificent.

Best Dates for Partnering

The date you choose to sign your contract, get married, or begin your business is very important. Partnerships, whether for marriage or business, are favored at the new moon on July 10 and during the two weeks that follow.

One outstanding day will be July 19, or the days that surround it. On July 19, the Sun and Jupiter are in perfect step — wow! This is always the one of the best days of the year, bathed in radiant luck. Use it for some sort of partnering effort!

On the following day, July 20, Jupiter meets up with Mercury, making this day a double-header for signing contracts.

If there is only one thing you remember from this section, it is this: Don't try to do everything by yourself in the year ahead. The symbolism representing combined energies keeps coming up in your chart. Whether you see yourself as Batman, Superwoman or cute little Mighty Mouse, realize that everyone could use a bit of help now and then. It is not a weakness to look for collaborators. With the kind of planetary rays you have, it is clear that the total you create will be far greater than the sum of its parts.

Avoid Mercury Retrograde

Mercury rules thinking, perception, research, data, negotiation and all contractual agreements, whether verbal or written. When any planet retrogrades, it seems to "sleep" and withholds its greatest powers. Thus if you act when Mercury is retrograde, you won't have the full picture; details will be obscured and plans, complicated. Avoid big decisions during Mercury retrograde. Do not sign anything. You may grow to regret your involvement with anyone you enter into agreement with at these times:

Mercury will retrograde from January 18 to February 8; then, from May 15 though June 8; finally from September 14 to October 6. As you see, in astrology, we have to look at the whole sky, not just one part of it! While a six-month period may be favored by one planet, another planet can throw a spanner in the works. Like life, astrology benefits from having both a wide perspective, and a narrow one.

The June Eclipse in Capricorn: Clarifying Your Position

As said earlier, you have been experiencing eclipses in Cancer and your sign of Capricorn for months, going back to July 2000. They have put steady pressure on you to decide on goals. You've felt compelled to make serious decisions about whether you want to commit fully to a partner, or to leave without looking back. There seemed to be no option to sit on the fence. That's a hallmark of all eclipses; these cosmic events demand a very black or white response. If you never thought much about these questions before, you will now, for sure.

As you enter this New Year, you might still be in the throes of an episode you experienced at the end of December. An eclipse fell in your partnering sector on December 30, 2001; if you did not hear news then, you may hear news on January 30, 2002, a month to the day later, plus or minus four days. (You might want to note this January date on your calendar to see what discussions come up.) Like the eclipse coming up on June 24, the December 30 eclipse helped you to see a close relationship in a new light.

Another date to circle on your calendar is May 11, 2002, plus or minus four days. This date triggers mathematical degrees that relate to the December 30, 2001 eclipse. All these eclipses help you come to a conscious decision about what you want from life, especially from a close intimate relationship. They teach you to act on your insights.

There is only one more eclipse due in this long-running saga in your sign's axis, and it will arrive on June 24, 2002. This eclipse, a full moon eclipse in Capricorn, will again highlight your dearest personal interests. All members of your sign will be touched, but more so those whose birthdays fall near December 24. Technically, that June event will not be strong; it belongs to a family of eclipses called appulses.

Any final eclipse in a sequence — which is what you will have on June 24, 2002, brings the finale to a drama, usually related to a certain relationship. However, this eclipse seems to be too weak to force you into a decision. A compromise or a mediocre reaction could probably result. That may not be the best way to go.

Try instead for a more enthusiastic or passionate response to your partner, one based on the strength of your convictions. Whenever another person's feelings are at stake — those of a partner, lover or spouse — they deserve more than lukewarm from you. You should honor them with a focused, clear response, no matter what your emotions are. You may be feeling anything from tremendous appreciation and love to distain or anger about something they've done. (Eclipses bring on extremes, for sure.) As a Capricorn, you may assume your partner knows exactly what you are thinking, but that's almost never the case.

Make this year your time to say what you mean and mean what you say. Deliver your opinion in a strong, clear voice; make sure your responses come straight from the heart. Being the practical Capricorn everyone knows you to be, you aren't given to passionate displays of emotion, but it is clear your partner will want one then; you should give it. They deserve no less, and you are capable of delivering exactly what is needed.

Preventative Health

Now that the eclipses in Cancer – Capricorn are ending,

new eclipses will be moving on to Gemini – Sagittarius, signs that relate to your health and well being, both physical and psychological. Saturn's position in your chart, also in Gemini, suggests that you will need more discipline about health and fitness in the coming year. Sometimes it's a shock to discover that we don't get to keep the body we had at 20 without exercise, enough sleep and a proper diet. The good news is we can look fabulous with a little care and energy.

Having hosted hard-to-please Saturn in your sixth house of mind and body for almost a year in 2001, you may have already started putting new health strategies into place, with visits to the gym ever morning or to your dentist more regularly. You may have already figured out that empty calories are not going to get you to the size you should be. Bowls of fruit may have already replaced the processed snacks in your cupboards. If so, good!

If not, you still have time to make those changes — but not much. Time is running out. You won't want to neglect your body with Saturn, the taskmaster planet, in your health sector. Saturn will not tolerate neglect. If this tough-as-nails planet finds something to howl about, you will know it. Saturn may make you wish you had taken the time to address whatever comes up. If you notice any new medical or dental concerns, try to attend to them sooner rather than later. Don't make excuses, either — if the President of the United States can take an hour a day to exercise, you can too.

While you were feeling the effect of the eclipses from July 2000 on, you may have discovered a health problem; eclipses often bring medical deficiencies in order to make you mobilize and get help. In 2002, what's new is that you will have to take a more proactive role in bolstering your overall sense of vitality.

Pay extra attention to your teeth and bones; make sure there's enough calcium in your diet and go for regular check-ups. (Saturn's presence suggests a lowering of your calcium reserves. If you don't tolerate dairy, make sure to eat spinach, kale and almonds daily.) If you are a more mature reader, a bone scan might be useful to make sure you are warding off osteoporosis. Check with your doctor. Remember this: Capricorn is the sign associated with exceptional longevity. You will want to enjoy all your years, now and later!

This year, all readers, of any age, should pay attention to fingers, wrists, hands, shoulders and lungs — all potential problem areas. The eclipses in Gemini and Sagittarius will occur throughout 2003, and Saturn will not leave Gemini until June 2003. You are looking at a fairly long trend here. Be wary, and don't get lazy.

In regard to your hands and fingers, if you work on the computer a lot, regular hand and shoulder massages — even paraffin wax manicure, aren't just luxuries for you. They could well be real necessities. Massage and heat can relax overworked muscles and leave them feeling relaxed and limber again. Be sure you keep your hands in the correct position when you sit at your computer too, lest carpel tunnel syndrome become a problem. (If you don't know the correct positions, ask if your company has an ergonomic specialist under its employ; if not, go check out a bookstore.)

Your aim in 2002 is to prevent problems, not just react to them. The sixth house is where the body squeaks when it needs your attention. Capricorn is a stoic sign that puts up with aches and pains without complaint. Your tolerance for pain is high. While that is an admirable quality, it could work against you. You may ignore early warning signals that would allow you to protect your body. For example, if your foot always hurts after you run on the treadmill, a quick x-ray may tell you whether you should be paying more attention to that ache. Learning to anticipate what could become problematic and to protect those areas is what this year is about. Be your body's best friend.

A Bright Outlook

Your psychological well-being is also a focus this year. With strength and direction, any pressing concerns can be sorted out. This is the year do the work. Gather up your courage and contact a counselor. If you have had any problems with alcohol or other substance abuse, or if you have any habits you know aren't good for you (and most of us do), Saturn will help you find the self-discipline or enlightenment to kick the addiction. You want to begin your new life in a much healthier state.

Later we will speak of the association between Jupiter and Pluto, and how it can help make your financial affairs shine. This same aspect could help you find assistance in overcoming an addiction or bad habit. The best dates for initiating such efforts are October 27 and December 16. You should be able to make incredibly impressive progress on these dates! Pluto is, after all, the planet of complete transformation! Wow, Capricorn!

The eclipse in Sagittarius in December 2002 could signal a need for you to give your body some tender care and a little gentle cleansing. The first step will be to show the universe that you have a genuine desire to improve the state of your well-being — if you do, you will get the help you need.

2002: An Ideal Year to Lose Weight

If your doctor has said that you need to lose weight, this could be an ideal year to do it. Saturn is associated with weight loss because of its constricting influence. In other words, this mighty planet will help you make your body smaller! Wow, you'll have a big edge this year. With just a little concentration, you may be one of those people on TV who, standing next to "before" and "after" photos, looks and feels great.

Best Fitness Dates

There are several good dates to start new diet and exercise routines. The first comes on January 13, a terrific boost to battling the holiday bulge comes with the new moon in Capricorn. This is a sensational date for fresh starts. That moon will embrace Venus — and you'll be a knockout! (Try extra hard to avoid sugar with Venus around. Stick to slow-burning fruit for a while.)

There's another ideal configuration for heath and fitness coming on June 10. Wait for two weeks to cut calories, after the full moon June 24. If you do, you will have the perfect combination for your new good looks program.

There are two dates that will present you with the right time to seek extended psychological help, or to find a relative or religious person to talk over topics or habits that have been holding you back: May 26 and December 4.

Be warned, however, that Saturn, planet of patience, doesn't like quick fixes. You will want to go about your plan in a slow and steady way. Avoid crazy fad diets. Saturn wants to see that you are in this for the long haul. Rather than concentrate on the scale, concentrate on your daily behavior. If you cave in and eat the super size fries whenever you order a hamburger, you might want to try to avoid the hamburger altogether for a while! Why make life hard? Remember, this is your year to have more fun!

Here's something to consider: Saturn only comes once every twenty-nine years for a two-and-a-half-year stay; we only get about two or three of these visits in our lifetime. Make the most of it while you can! (How lucky you are to have these vibes right around the time your are favored for a wedding; committed Capricorns who, like many brides and grooms to-be, want to be in tip-top shape for their photos, can be!)

Career Glitters

As we discussed in the first part of this report, personal matters will demand quite a bit of attention as the year begins, but the cosmos will help deal with them as the year progresses. This will make more room for career focus.

Your first bright spot comes near May 10, when the meeting of Mars and Venus gives you a boost. You may get a juicy assignment, and all month you should find your services very much in demand. If you are self-employed, your phone will ring. That's always comforting!

An even more important date arrives on June 3 when Venus, the ruler of your solar tenth house of prestige and honors, will meet with Jupiter, the great giver of gifts and luck. This is a wonderful date for a new job interview or a talk with your boss about a promotion! An agent or head-hunter may be very helpful to you at this time, as there seems to be a go-between person involved. (you may be that middle person, and can reap the benefits in your position.)

Your momentum gains by the end of the year, with October and November sure to be your biggest, best months for announcing exciting career news. It is a time of reward for all you've done over the past *two* years! You may want to work toward these magical months from the very outset of 2002.

Focus on Work Methods

With Saturn residing in your sixth house, it is clear that you have been working harder than ever. This trend will continue until June 2003. With a smaller, more stream-lined staff in place at your office, you will have much more to do, and less time in which to do it.

It will be more important than ever to get organized and be your most productive. Everything is relative, how-ever. Though under the gun, it doesn't feel like pressure. After all, it is nice to have a job, especially a good job.

Even if you are not part of the work force, Saturn's position in the sixth house results in a long daily "to-do" list. Even if you're not working formally in an office, it's sure you are busy and working hard. Perhaps you are helping others as a homemaker or, if you are in college, in a very worthy volunteer program.

Having Saturn placed in this house is not necessarily a bad thing, however. Saturn can be helpful in that it will sharpen your attention to detail and give you awesome powers of concentration. You will be able to sink your teeth into whatever you train your mind upon, and have the ability to turn out work of impressive value.

This year, investigate new technology. See if additional training can help you do your job in less time, with less effort. Even if your company has been chopping staff ruthlessly, which seems indicated in your chart, management is especially open to increasing productivity. Find out how new equipment, different software or special training could make you more productive. Present your idea to your bosses in early May — your chart suggests they will be open to any ideas you have. You may wind up being lauded for your resourcefulness. While you are at it, you may be able to talk your boss into giving you a new computer! (If *you* are the boss, well, it's time to go shopping — shiny new equipment gives your staff a morale boost, yourself included!)

Finances Brighten

Over the past few years, money has been a maddening topic, very difficult to control. You have had to put up with both Neptune and Uranus in your second house of earned income. Uranus brings surprise (something nobody wants when it comes to money, unless it comes in the form of a prize-winning, which is unlikely here). Neptune brings confusion or deception, whether imposed by others or by you; you could be prone to self-deception ("Oh sure, I can afford this right now", might be something to question.) While either of these planets could have caused a significant upturn of finances, it also brought a likelihood of radical ups and downs, the kinds that would drive a sure and steady Capricorn a little crazy. It is easy to see why money issues have been such a workout.

Until these big heavy-duty planets leave your second house — not for some time — you will have to remain fiscally conservative. Your chart reflects the importance of getting everything in writing — every promise, every suggestion. If your boss won't do it, volunteer to put the contents of any talks into a summary sheet that you sign and your boss initials.

Uranus will leave in 2003 after seven years in your financial house. This will mark the end of a long period of instability. Neptune won't leave until 2012, but its presence could have an upbeat effect. Neptune can make artistic endeavors, such as music, writing or art, profitable.

Great News about Money

Now that I've told you the conservative "down-side", this is fantastically good news! Saturn, your ruler, will go all-out on your behalf to stabilize your financial situation. Saturn will first meet with Neptune on January 23 and April 1, two sterling dates when the possibilities for gains, mainly through artistic or other creative efforts, will soar.

Later, Saturn puts on his hat and coat and goes to meet with Uranus, the planet that has been such a little prankster when it comes to money in your chart. Saturn's meetings will be highly successful (Saturn would stand for no less). That means good news for stabilizing your money matters. Saturn speaks to Uranus on August 21 and December 16, plus or minus about four days on each date.

More Great News About Money!

ok. The *really* really good news about money will come when Jupiter enters your eighth house of joint financial obligations and resources. You will see the first significant upswing in your financial affairs in years.

Jupiter will remain in this house from August 1, 2002 to August 27, 2003, a period of nearly thirteen months. Oh glory be! Capricorn, this will seem like a miracle.

All areas ruled by the eighth house will start to glitter. If you work on commission or royalties, or any performance based plan, you will do very well. If you ask for a raise and can't get it due to cutbacks, be resourceful about other ways to increase your benefits. Investigate the possibility for a bigger slice of the perks your company offers executives. You might be able to get a better health insurance plan, for example, or a key to the executive health club. Ask for an extra paid week of vacation or an expense account. Little extras can add up to real values. Such benefits are clearly possible in the second half of the year.

You will also see upbeat developments in your private life. Bankers will treat you like the valued customer you are. If you need a loan, you will likely get it in the second half of the year. Of course, "reward trends" only relate to what you've accomplished. If you have proved yourself a good credit risk, even if your friends and relatives have a hard time getting money from banks, you will be an exception to the rule (even in a tough economy).

If you are starting a business, necessary funding may appear. If you have been battling an insurance or legal claim, you are likely to be pleased with a final settlement. If you are currently in the process of splitting resources in a divorce or the breakup of a business, you are going to be very fortunate. If the settlement occurs after August 1, you will walk away with quite a generous check. It is also possible that this year, you will be surprised to hear from your beloved aunt over tea that she has decided to include you in her will.

THE YEAR AHEAD 2002

In any and all of these areas, the time near the new moon on August 8 and the week that follows may prove to you just how financially lucky you are. Remember, you have to *do* something to unlock cosmic goodies.

Keep an Eye on Your Balance in November

There is only one really tough day due this year. Watch your budget near November 19 and at the full moon eclipse in Taurus. Expenses are likely to spiral out of control due to a difficult vibration between the moon and unpredictable Uranus in your house of money.

Miracles Due!

It was mentioned earlier in this report that Jupiter will meet with Pluto this year, a *very* exciting prospect. It's been years since this last happened. (The last time these two planets had a similar communication was on March 29, 1999. Perhaps that date stands out in your mind. Even if it does not, it sure might be lucky for you now!) Whenever these two heavy-duty planets link up, it spells exciting success. Jupiter rules good fortune, and Pluto has the power to expand that good fortune.

Your chart shows that Jupiter will tour your eighth house this year. This sector rules the money-related areas I mentioned earlier. At the same time, Pluto is located in your house of secret, behind-the-scenes talks. The eighth house does not represent your salary, rather money that comes to you in other ways, even through inheritance, credit and tax refunds. If you are having a hard time with cash flow (unlikely, but I suppose anything is possible), the going will get easier when Jupiter and Pluto speak.

Let's say you are being audited and the taxman wants you to pay back taxes. With Jupiter (luck) in your eighth house (other people's money, including taxes), speaking to Pluto (the government, among other areas of life), you may be able to negotiate a better settlement, or at the very least, a payment plan you can live with.

Here are your phenomenally lucky dates, when Jupiter and Pluto communicate: October 27 and December 18. (The first date is better, in that both planets have strong orbits; in December, Jupiter is retrograde. I will admit, both are pretty terrific dates, so watch what happens, plus or minus about three days.)

This December 18 date could reverse some of the outcome of the November 19 eclipse, should you experience any drain on your income.

If there was ever a year to get out of debt, this is it. It appears to be very likely that you'll receive a generous chunk of cash sometime in the second half of the year. If so, put all or a good portion of your bounty into clearing debt. There is nothing like the lightness that comes when debt is gone. As a financially savvy Capricorn, you know this better than most. This is the year when you can enjoy such freedom!

Romance is There

As you probably noticed, this year brings lots of emphasis on commitment and marriage. You may be asking, what about if you don't have a steady significant other, and just want to meet someone new? Or, what if you are already married — will there be fun? Yes, yes, and yes again — everyone can expect some enchanting moments this year!

The year starts off with a wonderfully romantic dynamic. In January, from the very first day through January 17, Venus will glide in your sign — a holdover from December 2001. This planet's influence has made you more popular and magnetic than ever. Early January would be the perfect time to update your looks, or to spend some money on new clothes.

Love will also be bright and beautiful in March and early April, thanks to Mars' efforts setting off fireworks in your fifth house. This will be an ideal month to circulate. Be open to meeting new people.

In May, single-and-looking Capricorn will want to clock time at the office. It's one of the best places for single Capricorn to meet someone new. It seems a coworker suddenly catches your eye. There is another good place to meet a cutie — don't laugh: at the gym. (I guess you really will be hanging out there more in the future! Good for you!) If you think I am making this up, believe me, I'm not! In May, Venus and Mars meet in your sixth house, the area that rules all health matters. (I suppose you could meet at the doctor's office too, but the gym sounds much more likely.) One of your best moments to be hit by Cupid's loving arrows in these locations will be May 10.

If you are attached, March will be a favorite month; it will give you much more time off for fun. It would be a lovely time for kidnapping your sweetie for a vacation. If you have children, think of ways to surprise them with special events and treats, like tickets to the circus, or if they are older, to their favorite rock group. If you hope to have a baby, this is the month where you will begin to make this dream a reality.

There is only one spot in 2002 when the course of true love could go either way, and that is at the eclipse I already mentioned, on November 19. Remember, this is a full moon in Taurus, falling in your fifth house of love. Eclipses are wild cards, bringing up unexpected developments, both good and not so good. They do always deliver truth, which is comforting. You seem to make a big decision about a relationship at that time. This will mark a turning point.

I should point out as an aside that the fifth house, so lit by the November 19 eclipse, also rules creative projects. You may be finishing up a big one at this time. The developments regarding this project could also be influenced by the energy of this eclipse. Keep in mind that we talked earlier about how this point, November 19, could turn out to be quite expensive. Do your best. (I know you will, dear Capricorn.)

I would like to address couples who have been together for a long time. If things have grown a bit dull in the bedroom, Jupiter's tour of your eighth house should rev up your attraction for one another. You may notice quite an energetic change in this area. For some of you, it's been too long since you've allowed yourselves a really zesty time together. I often get letters about lack of desire. Now you will have your best moment in years to reverse that trend. Get counseling or medical advice if you think you could benefit from it, or just set aside some private time together. 2002 could be the year when life becomes more colorful and enjoyable, in the most passionate, loving and affectionate way.

I say this because the eighth house also rules gifts — and according to the ancients, the gift of self, passion and sex. Plot a vacation just for two in a lovely spot. Jupiter's placement in Leo suggests favor for a sunny locale. Book a room in a luxurious hotel or even a castle. If you have small children, ask grandma if she wouldn't mind babysitting for a week or long weekend. Even if she usually begs off, you have such superb aspects, this time she is likely to agree. (Try other trusted friends and relatives; someone else around you will say yes). Off you will go, to the vacation of your life. If you thought you couldn't feel like this, guess again. The wonderful thing about life is that it is always filled with surprises, some of them better than anything we allow ourselves to imagine!

The very end of the year will seem like a dream. Mars and his cosmic lover, Venus, the ruler of your house of true love, dance cheek to cheek during the entire month of December. This is the sweetest month of the year for love. These two planets dance in a dance so close and passionate, it's simply remarkable.

It is due to be a holiday time filled with fun, food, friends and festivities, a wonderful way to end the year and welcome the new one, 2003. There is a touch of luxury to everything you do at the time — that great meal in that expensive restaurant, that outfit to wear to the theatre or that special rock concert, that trip to New York or Paris. Everything that catches your imagination will be glamorous, and it's finally there for the taking, not just for dreaming.

In December, go to those parties you get invited to, dear Capricorn. I know you are very conscientious about work, and that year-end will be big for career progress, but your love stars will be twinkling for you, too! You deserve to drink in the sweetness of it all!

Indeed, this is a year of action. By December 2002 you will step back and appreciate all that you've accomplished, and say with conviction, "This is the life I have built, and boy, it is a good one."

Summary

In the next six months, you may plan to wed or to form an exciting new business alliance. Teaming up is clearly lucky for you now; duos bring emotional support and financial gains, the likes of which you never dreamed possible.

While in 2001 you may have been rocked by fast moving events, the New Year will bring far greater stability. With Mars circulating through the bottom of your chart during much of your birthday year, your most impressive gains will occur in your personal life.

Don't fret about where your career is going — it will take off like a rocket in the last quarter of 2002. Money, a sore spot in recent years, becomes one of your biggest areas of growth in the second half of 2002. Romance is bright and beautiful in January, early May and even more so in December. Capricorn, what a year! It looks like this is one of those rare times you can have your cake and eat it too!

AQUARIUS

The Big Picture

This year should be characterized by a certain sense of urgency. The cosmic clout you will have in 2002, dear Aquarius, will be unsurpassed. Make this the year to take that step forward. Make this the year to reach for that big goal you've been yearning for. If you begin now, the cosmic environment will be enormously supportive of your efforts. Time is running out for these favorable vibes. If you assume that the time will always be right, you will let precious moments slip away — and you may grow to regret it. Aquarius, seize the day!

You will experience real excitement when this dawns on you: You can finally live large. You can have the life you have fantasized about for so long. There is a strong theme of hope and optimism for you this year. You will feel confident to think on a larger, more panoramic scale. Soon you will see that 2002 is not about thinking or planning. It is about putting your desires into action. Finally!

I can imagine what you are thinking as you read this. You may *want* to get started, but may not be sure how. As an Aquarius, you can conceptualize the most advanced and futuristic ideas, but have some difficulty when it comes to implementation, bringing theory into practice. You are a leader, an innovator, but you're not a great tactical producer. The production side, the realization of dreams in an organized, practical way, is usually the domain of one the earth signs, Virgo, Taurus or Capricorn. Collaborating with one of those signs or with someone who *seems* like an earth sign will turn the trick for you now.

Whom should you look to collaborate with? Earth signs are pragmatic, steadfast, conscientious and trustworthy. Find people who have those qualities, and work with them. While they are not known to be visionaries like you, they can put the elements of your puzzle into place more quickly and effectively than you ever could. From August and beyond, your seventh house of partners and collaborators will glitter brilliantly, more so than in over a decade. This should assure you, dear independent-minded Aquarius. You don't have to do *everything* alone any more, nor should you try. Your talent is being an objective, analytical conceptualist. Hand the welding of nuts and bolts to others.

This year will bring sizzling opportunities and the solid support to make your dreams happen. They will soon be realized, in real time, not at some fuzzy point in the distant future. It is rare for the planets to take such an outstanding interest in any one sign. Luckily for you, Aquarius just happens to be their area of interest right now. It would be a shame not to take full advantage! If there's something you want to do, and someone you want to do it with, grab your tool kit in one hand, that other person in the other, and go. This is your year, Aquarius.

Let's look closely at the cosmic support you will have this year, starting with the preponderance of planets in the air and fire signs. (You work very well with fire and air signs.) We will also look at Mars' orbit; it tells us a lot about where to focus energy in the coming year. The most important discussion about 2002 will concern the actions of Neptune, Jupiter and your ruling planet, Uranus. Then we will get into the specifics of love, money, career, home and family — and more!

Compatible Air and Fire Signs Reign

As the planets in our solar system orbit in space, they pass through constellations, signs that can be classified as one of four elements: air, fire, earth or water. As an Aquarius, you are an air sign (not a water sign, which is a common misconception). In 2002, remarkably, all the outer planets will be in air and fire signs. (The outer planets travel farthest from the Sun, along the rim of our solar system, and include Saturn, Uranus, Neptune and Pluto.) That's remarkable luck. These planets are inherently more powerful than the ones closer to the Sun. In their slower movement, these outer planets spend enough time in each sign to make their presence known. All of these powerhouse planets get along magnificently with your air-sign element.

At the beginning of the year, Jupiter, another vital heavy-duty planet, is currently cruising in water-sign Cancer. Happily, come August, Jupiter will move into expansive, warm-hearted Leo (a fire sign), adding itself to your list of the compatible planets in positions of power. That means you don't have one or two outer planets on your side in 2002, but all *five!* Wow!

The smaller, so-called personal planets — Mercury, Venus, Mars, the moon and Sun — are the little fidgety heavenly bodies. They continually move about. It's their role to spice things up and make sure our days are each a little different from the other. These personal planets will spend about half their time in air or fire signs this year. As you see, you'll be "in your element" for much of the year. What a help this will be!

Sparkling innovation is the hallmark of fire and air signs. They tend to bring on a plethora of ideas, and encourage strong communication skills — a valuable combination. 2002 will be a year of discussion, negotiation and agreements. There is nothing heavy about this influence — it is light, breezy and, like the wind, continually shifting. Especially from June on, you will love the playful spirit of experimentation and optimism that was lacking last year. (Last year's weighty dynamic was largely due to a dreary dialogue between Saturn and Pluto. These two planets' third and final confrontation will occur in May 2002; after that, you'll fly free. More on this later.)

There will be a strong spirit of practicality mixed in this year as well. This comes as a result of Saturn's blessings to Neptune and Uranus. It will allow you to anchor your ideas with "feet" that can take you where you want to go. What's more, when Pluto and Saturn reside in mutable signs, they give a certain flexibility and mobility to your life. What you do and what you confront aren't as stubborn as usual. If you should run up against a method or idea that you don't like, try to push it, prod it, reshape it or rethink it. Chances are, obstacles will be malleable. Aquarius, this is all so exciting!

Personal Matters Matter

Mars' orbit through the signs and their houses activates specific areas of our lives. We can look at that arc to see where in your life you will get a zing of planetary power.

Mars spends the bulk of the year below the horizon of your chart, indicating that your personal life will be your area of biggest growth, at least initially. This is not to say that career is less important this year, but personal relationships are more pressing. Domestic issues, fitness / health and your love life will get your most focused attention in the early months of the year.

In the middle of the year, however, something rather radical happens. After having circulated in a relatively hidden area of your chart, Jupiter, the planet of happiness and growth, and Mars, planet of action, break through to the surface. From August on, you will undergo a change. Your persona will become much more public. This marks the beginning of a new maturity. You will be able to crystallize much of what you've learned over the past several years, to step forward into new realms, some of which will involve a partner or significant other.

Your career will bring jubilation in December, a month of considerable reward. If you hurry your project, you can assure your place on the top of Mt. Olympus by year's end. Admittedly, it will take some very hard work and a few risks to get there, but you seem willing to do whatever it takes. Dear Aquarius, the cosmic weather is perfect, the crowd is in their seats, the game is beginning — you are the lead player. Go out to greet your public!

The Last of Seven Years

Uranus Champions All That You Do

In 1996, Uranus moved into Aquarius and settled there for a seven-year stay; this is a once in a lifetime event. It marked the start of an era of personal transformation, one that would take you to places you could not quite imagine. A lot has happened since, and you're still not finished! The last time the world saw Uranus in Aquarius was about 84 years ago, 1912 – 1919. Having a powerhouse planet in your own sign is enough to put you right at the cutting edge. This is fairly heady stuff.

As an Aquarius, you are naturally "ahead of the curve", sometimes described as a bit of an oddball. You keep your gaze fixed not on the present, but at a distant point on the horizon. Have you noticed that other people need a little time to catch up? You are the zodiac's futurist. You are accustomed to being misunderstood and perhaps have gotten to a point where you no longer try to explain yourself. "I am what I am," you say to yourself and to the world. "Take me as such or leave me alone." That kind of self-acceptance is characteristic of Aquarius. You are an independent and somewhat idiosyncratic sign known to use its own yardstick to measure success. Aquarius moves to the beat of a different drummer.

Since 1996, your hunches have all proved correct. Every fashion you've adopted, every opinion you've voiced and every idea you've copy-written has become the new "big thing". This has been rather bewildering, I'm sure — albeit easy enough to get used to. What a relief it is not to have to defend yourself at every turn.

I am sorry to report, this period will soon come to a close, and you'll go back to your normal life. (Well, "normal" for you, I should point out, is a far cry from normal for the rest of the world!) Make the most of this year. Once Uranus, your ruler, pulls out of Aquarius in 2003, a very different climate will move in. You will no longer be the center of the galaxy, arbiter of all that is chic and fashionable. With the sand running down in your hourglass, now is the time. Grab a chance to shine while you have such cosmic support. You can still establish yourself as the leader you were meant to be.

Were you born between February 11 and February 19? Uranus will touch you directly in 2002. This could turn out to be a powerful year, perhaps the most important of your whole life. Remember, Uranus' visits are once-in-a-lifetime events. You may make a discovery in the sciences or technology, or you may have a psychic experience. You will tap into a realm that is above and beyond the concerns of everyday life. Use what you learn. Certain lucky opportunities will land in your lap. You will be incredibly creative. Embark on a project to see just how high you can fly! Literally every area of your life will become lyrical. You'll find it so much easier to put your stamp on all that you do. You'll get the approval and acceptance you need for success.

All Aquarius should watch February 12, 13, and 22; April 7, 8, and 18; May 26, June 10, August 22, November 23, and December 19 — each of these dates should be particularly fruitful and fortunate.

Neptune Gives You Depth

As if it's not good enough to have Uranus in your sign, Neptune followed Uranus into Aquarius in 1998, set to stay until 2012! This is an incredibly long time to have big-planet favor. This inspirational planet's stay will surely change you in a gradual but appreciable way.

Neptune incites compassion, heightens powers of creativity and intuition, and adds depth to your character. Neptune's waters gradually, almost invisibly, bring keen insights. (This planet will never use a megaphone when it can whisper.) When Neptune first arrived, you probably thought nothing of the dreams or hunches it brought with it. All the while, your intuition was being honed and sensitized. Neptune's work has barely begun. Its teachings will balance you in a way no other planet possibly could.

Neptune's goals are too numerous to count, but they include fine-tuning your sensitivity to others. Under Neptune's guidance, you've begun to direct your inner ear to the needs of your loved ones, and extend your empathy to others. Yours is the sign of the humanitarian and philanthropist. Now more than ever you see the faces of those people benefiting from charity. You recognize them not as a faceless crowd but as flesh and blood individuals who happen to be united in a single need. That is a subtle but powerful shift.

If your birthday falls between January 28 and February 1, Neptune is in a perfect angle to your Sun. This is another once-in-a-lifetime cosmic event. Your compassion will intensify, and your ability to forgive others' transgressions will expand. You may become more involved in charitable projects, or with artistic or cultural endeavors. If so, you would do so with great success.

The right hemisphere of your brain — the visual, creative side — is stimulated under this aspect. Music, dance, art, poetry, photography or film (pick one or more!) may become hobbies or serious interests. You will feel an inclination toward such artistic expressions. You may also investigate philosophy and religion. This amazing trend will last throughout this decade and touch every Aquarian birthday, especially those mentioned.

All Aquarius can expect heightened emotional sensitivity. Some people in other signs will never experience such an influence. Neptune's orbit takes 214 years to revolve around the Sun; it cannot visit every sign in one lifetime. Some people never experience this. Be grateful that you are alive at the right time to get this extra cosmic gift.

You have certain golden days this year to benefit from Neptune's gifts of sensitivity, creativity and artistic growth. Mark down January 30, February 2, March 28 and March 29, April 29, July 24, October 28, and December 3 and 4.

A Defining Moment

Uranus spends seven years in a sign, and Neptune, fourteen. Both just happen to be in Aquarius. As you can see, these are long trends, capable of wielding a vital, permanently uplifting effect. Sometimes all we need is a lucky break. That's exactly what is about to happen this year. You just have to put yourself "out there" so that the universe can help you.

The confluence of these two planets adds up to a defining moment for all Aquarius. Working together, these planets will help you find your true life's purpose and direction. I do not say this lightly, so it bears repeating: At this time in your life, you can now find your true life's purpose and direction.

All you need to do is begin. The universe will take you the rest of the way.

Saturn's Gift of Stability

Saturn, the planet of permanence, will assist Uranus to blend the old elements of your life with the new. This is a rare and enormously stabilizing development. It will allow you to tear down certain areas of your life and to build them anew. Saturn will see to it that the resulting structures or relationships have strength and longevity. This is an aspect that comes every four years or so. Count your blessings! Not only will you learn your true contribution to the world, you will get the cosmic support to make your changes last. Circle outstanding dates to act for this energy: October 27 and December 16.

Though these aspects exist in the heavens, you have to do something in order for them to have any effect. It's important to be assertive, and to go after your dreams! You have good vibes, trust me. It is as if you came upon someone on the street handing out bags of cosmic money; of all the people who held out their hands, you got the lion's share. Your hefty portion of legal tender will be worthless unless you actually *use* it, dear Aquarius. Once you start to spend it, you will see just how much cosmic muscle you can exercise!

Love and Romance: Sturdy and Sure

As an Aquarius, you know how to make yourself happy, and you usually don't ask for much in return. Most of the time, all you need is your computer, a few CDs, speakers and maybe your telescope. You tend to land sunny-side-up no matter what obstacles fall in your path.

Recently, however, Saturn, on a visit in your love house, put a cramp in your style. Saturn believes in hard work and delayed gratification. Having the planet of hard work in the house of pure fun is something of an astrological oxymoron. When Saturn tours the "pleasure zone", life can become all work and no play. Saturn isn't in your love house just to be cantankerous — he is trying to teach you patience and responsibility for your romantic attachment. Relationships forged under Saturn's influence have a strong chance of lasting success.

Saturn's placement here can have many possible outcomes. Single Aquarians may meet people who live in other cities, when of course they'd rather date someone close to home. Don't be too quick to decline the date — this person may still be quite special. The relationship could have potential. Other Aquarians may find that the people they meet seem to be too busy, either because they are studying for a degree at night while holding a job during the day, or traveling a great deal for work. Sometimes life is that way. Be patient if something like this applies to you.

Saturn is notorious for bringing physical separation in the house it visits. When it comes to the love house, this does not imply a breakup, but more often the other factors listed above. No doubt, no matter what the reason, it's frustrating not to able to spend more time with your sweetheart / love interest. Long distance romances can work — it all depends on the situation and the people involved. Keep an open mind. This aspect will not last past mid-2003.

There is another reading I should warn you about. Saturn's influence could mislead you to a person who says he or she is available, but who in truth is not. A married lover may try to convince you that he or she will leave the spouse with no intention of doing so. Be careful of new involvements.

(While we are on the subject of difficulties from Saturn, we need to address the area of upsetting gossip, indicated by Saturn's position in Gemini. Indeed, whether true or not, nobody wants to be talked about, especially when it comes to our private lives. Guard your secrets, Aquarius. Watch, too, whom you send email to — accidentally.)

Other Aquarians may gravitate toward prospects who are older, more settled or more mature. If you date someone your own age, this person will definitely seem wiser than his or her years.

The fifth house rules pregnancy and birth. Saturn's position here advises us to delay having children, whether to wait for a time of greater stability or for any other reason. You may be trying to conceive or adopt a child, and may find the endless medical tests or red tape hard to cope with. Keep going, dear Aquarius — Saturn won't deny you a child, but this stickler planet will try your patience. Saturn is testing your resolve, that's all. You are up to the challenge. Remember, Saturn will reward you when it exits this house after June 2003.

Aquarians who are new parents probably found the adjustment to parenthood more difficult than they expected. I remember those years so well! Tiny babies certainly need attention! Most people would agree that a child is the most glorious part of life. Luckily, Saturn is an air sign, and reaches a supportive angle to your Sun. This suggests you are dealing admirably with your new role. Of course you are — Aquarius is a quick study!

If you already have a child, this aspect may impact your relationship with him or her; your child may become uncommunicative. Try not to come off as too distant, cold or stern. This is not a time for "tough love". Your child wants you to be a buddy, even if he or she won't admit it. Allow Neptune's gifts of compassion and intuition to guide you. Saturn brings lessons learned, and in this case it is not the child who is to learn something new, but you. In the cosmic order of things, you are the pupil and Saturn the teacher. The child is serving as Saturn's example, to test your maturity and determination. It is also a test to show your love under any circumstances, even less than ideal. Approach your child with grace and warmth.

Saturn has been positioned in your fifth house of love since last year. Luckily, since this is a continuation of last year, you have some experience and have already begun to cope with this planet's constrictive influence. While it is never easy having taskmaster Saturn in the house that rules fun and love, your Sun sign relates well to Saturn in Gemini. The lessons learned will be more easily assimilated.

Creativity Gets a Turbo Charge

The fifth house rules not only love and children; it also rules creativity. Under Saturn's tutelage, your artistic side should blossom. You will give projects your utmost concentration and enviable "stick-to-it-iveness". This will pay off. If you become stuck over some obstacle, you will work through it until you find the answer. There is almost no chance that you'll give up.

Saturn will go out of its way to be helpful to your creative efforts, especially if your birthday falls anytime from February 8 to February 18.

Is your birthday listed? This is your year to bring your talents to the marketplace. Write that book, make that film or create that website. You will also find relationships less volatile and more stable. (They will definitely be less given to dramatic outbursts and arguments that end with smashed glasses and slammed doors. That will help your nerves, I am sure!)

Saturn's Conflict With Pluto Drags On:

In Relationships a Play for Dominance

The past year was complicated by a long-standing argument between Saturn and Pluto; this confrontation began in August 2001, flared up in early November 2001 and will end in late May 2002, with a third and final flare-up at a full moon eclipse. Saturn is a difficult influence here, and its position suggests that you may engage in a struggle for dominance within a social or romantic relationship. On more than one occasion, you've come close to throwing in the towel due to frustration. Let this play itself out — by the end of May, you will know which direction to take.

Eclipses On Love, Romance, Children

There is so much going on in your love life! It's like a cosmic Grand Central Station, bustling with planets coming and going. Three out of the year's five eclipses will fall in your fifth and eleventh houses, the houses that relate to love, children, friendship, social events and groups. Here are the dates of the eclipses, each considered an ignition switch of change:

May 25 brings a full moon lunar eclipse in your friendship sector, suggesting participation in a group activity.

June 10 brings a new moon solar eclipse in your house of love! Single Aquarians may meet someone new. June brings everything you wouldn't expect. Attached Aquarians enter a new chapter of their relationships. Will you get engaged? Married? The moon is conjoined to Saturn, so a momentous decision seems to be at hand. Your choice will be one that lasts forever and a day.

December 4 brings a new moon solar eclipse, suggesting a vital new friendship or community activity, or a fresh beginning in your closest relationship.

Keep in mind that the fifth and eleventh houses are opposite one another on the same axis; when one is emphasized, the other is too, with energy ricocheting between the two. Both love and friendship will see some rather unexpected developments, most probably within four days of the dates noted. (Keep in mind that an eclipse can take longer to deliver its message.)

Eclipses often act as catalysts. They activate conditions that exist in the outside world, and kick off events whose origins have nothing to do with you — but which, of course, effect you once they occur. These events often test your commitment to a certain individual or endeavor. Eclipses revitalize relationships with an opportunity, rival, or ultimatum — you name it. As the winds blow through your life, anything not securely fastened will quickly fly away.

Keep in mind that the houses we are discussing rule pregnancy. If you are not ready to deal with that, take precautions.

Venus and Mars, That Delicious Pair

Any time we want to know what to expect from love in the year ahead, we look to the paths of Venus and Mars. These two planets, if in close proximity, can guarantee sparkling romantic opportunities for all. In 2001, they were hardly ever together, bringing (by comparison with this year) rather dismal aspects for romance. This year, they will always either be together or about to reunite. They will dazzle you with love.

You have an extra special bonus in this area. Venus will tour your sign from January 18 to February 8. This is sure to be a lovely time for love and popularity. At the same time, Mercury will be retrograde in Aquarius (your sign!), suggesting that people from your past will re-enter your life. This person could be an old friend or possibly even an old flame. Is there a spark left? You decide!

A simply remarkable time comes near May 10, when Mars meets up with Venus in your house of true love. He holds her so closely, it's like he won't ever let her go. These mythological lovers will dance a breathtaking waltz of love all month. May is the perfect month for a romantic vacation. It need not be expensive, but it must be private. Let the world fade away while you enjoy your sweetie, dear Aquarius. It doesn't matter if you are single or married — the month of May is just made for love!

To add more oomph to June (I already mentioned the new moon eclipse on June 10), we have Venus gliding through your opposite sign of Leo, a rather sweet phase for relationships. Mark your calendar: Venus will be in Leo from June 14 – July 10.

2002: The Year to Wed!

There is no doubt about it. Your personal relationships will take a big stride in 2002. It would be a glorious year to wed, especially after Jupiter, the planet of gifts and luck, enters your solar seventh house of commitment on August 1. You will have this favorable placement until August 27, 2003 — a period of nearly thirteen months. Wow, Aquarius!

If you are already married, you and your spouse will grow ever closer. You could even benefit from your partner during this phase. This wonder planet of growth and happiness will show you how to make your alliance greater, deeper and more meaningful. Your spouse will be lucky for you this year, and will also do well in his or her own right. Life will treat you both more kindly. A joy to be around, your partner will encourage you to lighten up. If you get too cocky, your other will give you a little kick in the pants. Listen to your lover, dear Aquarius. This person has your dearest interests at heart!

A great, heart-stopping moment, thrilling for love, could well occur near July 19 and 20, when Jupiter conjoins the Sun and Mercury. This is just perfect for a wedding. It will also be a great time to take a vacation with your partner. A getaway could recapture the joy you once had, and will now experience again.

From late November through early December, the Sun and Jupiter will be in what is called a mutual reception, where the Sun and Jupiter work to make one another stronger. The effect will create a simply gorgeous environment for your closest relationship. In this, the month of giving, you might just show your appreciation. Save up to give your partner a special gift, perhaps jewelry — something he or she can keep forever as a token of your love.

Fitness and Health Rocket Upwards in 2002

This could be your single best moment ever to kick off a fitness program. If you have avoided the gym lately, and along the way had a few too many nibbles from the hotel mini bar or spent too many hours playing computer games, you may be ready for a new exercise routine.

Jupiter first entered your sixth house in June 2001, so you may have initiated your new regime then. If you did, you are probably well on your way to becoming very fit. Jupiter's placement is a good dynamic under which to change your habits, and still is. When a fixed sign like Aquarius *finally* decides to do something, watch out! Nothing short of a bulldozer would get you to stop! Good! You will look like a million dollars!

If you want to know another auspicious date on which to begin an ironclad health project, circle the new moon on July 10, 2002 — with five planets in your sixth house, this point is just fabulous for such goals.

Jupiter has so far spent six months in the part of your chart related to health and fitness. However, if you still haven't seen much improvement (and you've been trying), it is probably because Jupiter has been retrograde. Come March 1, Jupiter will turn to direct orbit. You should start to see a wonderful change for the better.

There is one downfall. Having Jupiter, the ho-ho-ho jolly planet, in the sixth house could give you a sudden lust for fats and sweets. Try extra hard to replace snacks with fresh fruits, or you may find it difficult to manage your weight.

If you have any medical or dental problems, even chronic ones, this would be an ideal moment to address them. Jupiter will move into your health sector for a full year on August 1, 2002, bringing you great reasons to hope. Jupiter is associated with healing and medicine and just happens to be touring a medical sector of your horoscope. Its powers in this area will take on special emphasis.

If you need help with health matters, the first half of the year, from January through July 2002, is the time to look for a specialist. You have great chances of finding a doctor who understands you. You haven't had Jupiter's help in this part of your chart in over a decade!

There is a specific date favored for medical appointments or procedures. July 19 would be a terrific time to schedule anything health-related, from scheduling that all-important medical procedure to taking your first session with a new fitness trainer.

Finally, on two days this year, Jupiter will send a beam to powerful, rejuvenating Pluto, on October 27 and December 18. These days could be extremely powerful for you. If you are not well, your chart indicates that the doctor you are working with at this time knows how to help you in a way others have not. (You be the judge. Second opinions are also favored at this time.) Thanks to Pluto, your powers of rejuvenation will be at an all time high.

One way or another, if you put your mind to it, you can leave 2002 in a far healthier state than when you entered it! The force is with you, Aquarius!

Money Matters Calm Down

For years, you've hosted two of the most difficult planets in your house of earned income, Neptune and Uranus. Neptune brings confusion, Uranus surprise — neither of which we want when it comes to money. This year, however, will be different. Saturn will stabilize both Neptune and Uranus. You do have some outstanding dates for making key financial decisions and agreements.

January 23 and April 1 will both be especially sweet for money gleaned from artistic endeavors. August 21 and December 16 are fine dates for presentations, and electric meetings with clients.

A word of caution: With Saturn in the fifth house, this year would not be a good time to take any undue risks in

THE YEAR AHEAD 2002

stocks or bonds. The fifth house rules speculation of all kinds. Saturn will bring about a rather depressing influence in this area.

A terrific day for a bonus or to make a commission will come on July 20, when Jupiter and the Sun walk arm in arm — a five star, solid gold day!

A Home and Family Boost

Early in the year, you may consider moving or fixing up your residence. These thoughts would be especially relevant and favored during March or the first half of April. The dynamics surrounding these dates could also indicate that a family member needs you. Be prepared to clear your calendar for that person.

Happy news about a house or apartment could light you up near the new moon on May 12. Be critical about any news you receive, and double-check all the facts. Mercury will retrograde soon after (May 15 – June 6). Things may not be as stable as you suppose.

Another superb day for making home or family decisions will be June 3. Venus and Jupiter get together, making it a headliner in anyone's book.

There also seems to be some news about home and family near the full moon lunar eclipse on November 19. You have a mixed outlook for such matters. It is not an ideal time for closing on a house, or signing a promise of sale agreement.

Mercury Retrograde

Mercury rules all communication, including thought, speech, editing, research, negotiation, and agreements.

When Mercury is retrograde, its functions tend to scramble. It's not a reliable time to plan detailed itineraries or to sign contracts.

Mercury will retrograde from January 18 to February 8; from May 15 through June 8; and from September 14 to October 6.

Career Opportunities Shine

Your work environment should be quite cheerful in the first half of the year, with cooperative coworkers, some sleek new computer equipment and other new additions at the office. With Jupiter in Cancer, there may be a kitchen for the employees. (If not — there's a perfect suggestion to slip into the suggestion box!)

This placement would be ideal for finding a part time job, perhaps to save for something special, such as a dream vacation or a new house. If you are in college, you'll be able to pick up some fun and profitable after-school jobs. Your best options and earnings would surface in Cancer-ruled areas, which include food, shelter or child-related industries. Babysitting, restaurant work, a gourmet store, the hotel industry, or a maternity shop would prove to be profitable.

Those of you who are self-employed will be happy to know that the phone will ring and ring with interested customers or clients, particularly between March and July 2002. These are your very best months to pick up interesting new assignments. All this is true because Jupiter, the benefic planet, is "happy" in Cancer — the ancients wrote that this placement in Cancer is symbolic of the embryo, and is one of the best expressions of Jupiter's ability to provide growth.

Should you need to hire some new full or part time employees, Jupiter will help you find the right individuals, people with a terrific attitude and the right qualifications. In fact, they will make *you* look good. Small firms usually have a harder time finding good employees. This year, small firms are so favored, they will see response will be so strong, they'll be turning people away.

On a more general level, use Jupiter's presence to sharpen everyday skills. This is the perfect time to learn how to get more from the software you use, and to improve the look and efficiency of your workspace. Take a look with a critical eye — are things arranged neatly? Do you have a good filing system? If you could use a little advice, you would benefit from a visit with a consultant to help you get organized. The first half of the year would also be an ideal time to register in courses.

Jupiter's placement in Cancer may give you the impetus to work for a non-profit organization, even the Peace Corps or some other valuable global cause. You may choose to work within a religious mission or group. Having Jupiter in the sixth house (a service-oriented sector) is associated with international religious organizations.

There are some magical moments near the full moon in Scorpio April 26 — whatever you expect won't happen, and what you don't expect, will!

Serious Career Advancement

If you've been dreaming about that big promotion or a write-up in the press, this could be your year. Jupiter conjoins Mars on July 3 at the pinnacle point of your solar chart. Your name may suddenly be in lights!

Partnerships shine from August 1–August 27, 2003 — a full year. A business partner, a publicist, agent, representative, or even an attorney could be extraordinarily lucky. Your significant other will be a gem, and will introduce you to people you would never meet on your own. When you have Jupiter in this house, the other person is often the initiator, bringing a plethora of ideas. Here's when you can finally kick those dreams into action, dear Aquarius.

Two high-wattage planets, Jupiter and Pluto, will meet on October 27 and December 18. Their impact will be so positive, the results could transform your career for years to come. (There is about a three-day glow around these dates, with the stronger day coming *prior* to the date listed.)

Undoubtedly, the time near October 27 and December 18 will be incredibly important days in your timeline, ideal for a new business, a product launch, key presentations, or an exchange of business documents. An influential friend or contact seems to be responsible for your success, although a middle person, such as a representative (or headhunter?) may be part of the picture. The developments on these two days prove how highly regarded you are in the marketplace!

The new moon in Scorpio on November 4 will bring another wonder moment for professional matters. This is a truly fantastic vibration that sets up two weeks of marvelous energy to help you get ahead. That new moon happens to coincide with Uranus' turn to direct speed. This is a hugely important day! (Uranus will retrograde from early June through early November. These would be months to meditate on current projects, not to start new ones.)

Finally, Mars, that marvelous energizer, moves into your tenth house from December 1, 2002 until January 16, 2003. This ends the year with fireworks in your house of honors, awards, achievement and fame. You haven't seen anything like this in two years. As we discussed in the beginning of this report, December should be a time of enormous career gratification. Mars' partner, Venus, comes along too, and they will be in perfect step. Not only can you get that big promotion, you seem to be surrounded by enormous good will and applause. Aquarius, in this important year, you seem to have it all!

Summary

With, Uranus (your ruler) in your sign, you are in a superb position. As the zodiac's rabble-rouser, you have become accustomed to being misunderstood. These days, everyone seems to agree with you — an initially bewildering development. If you feel like you've fallen into a parallel universe, one that is more forgiving and supportive than usual, you're right. This remarkable set of circumstances won't last forever. By the end of 2003 these once-in-a-lifetime shimmering vibrations will fade. Make the most of the coming year while you still wear the crown.

In the meantime, Jupiter, the planet of good fortune, will warm your sector of committed relationships (including marriage). This aspect will last from mid-August into the next twelve months. This is one of your most ideal times ever to say, "I do." With Saturn sitting in your pregnancy sector, you may feel ready for a little addition to the family as well. In all, this will be a productive year, but only if you decide to get on the stick and make it happen.

PISCES

The Big Picture

2002 will be a year of extremes, with both high-level tension and unexpected joys. Concerning the former — well, dear Pisces, you have to admit, you work very well under pressure. With several planets and eclipses due to push and prod you, there's no way you'll be able to ignore the changes coming your way. Through it all, your indomitable spirit will keep your enthusiasm high. You'll be eager to explore ways to turn unexpected events to your favor. With no room for deliberation or procrastination, you'll be on a very fast track and will have to rely on instinct. No problem there — as a Pisces that's your sweet spot.

As a fish, nature didn't give you arms or legs, or even horns, with which to defend yourself. Instead, nature blessed you with an uncanny instinct. This sixth sense works as your steady protection. You are able to detect the subtlest ripples in the waters around you; by the time danger arrives, you will have vanished to safer waters. You are also a bit of a shape shifter, so getting in and out of tight spots is something you do with remarkable ease. This talent will come in handy this year.

2002 will *not* be a year to sit back and let things follow their own course. This year will demand passion, hard work, and a set of sharply delineated goals — especially for March-born Pisces (more on that later). Recently you've realized that you have what it takes — now you need to prove it to higher ups. They are considering you for a role in a larger arena. Show them that you are right for the job. You will have to convince those VIPs that you have the depth, experience, maturity and the vision to take it on. One crucial person is not yet convinced.

To make him or her come around, you'll have to reinvent yourself and redefine your role — like it or not. While at times the year's challenges will require a strenuous effort, in the process you will find your true purpose and will rise to a place of authority. As the axiom goes, necessity is the mother of invention; this year you prove this true, in spades. Your efforts will count for something; by the time 2002 is over, you'll look back and be able to say you would never go back.

You won't be left to fight these difficult planetary forces alone. Benefic Jupiter will cheer you on from the sidelines, and will work to see that you are in the right place at the right time. Just when you get to the point of capitulation, just when you think this whole thing is just a silly dream, Jupiter will race in with the encouragement and luck you need to keep going.

Pisces has a tremendous survival streak. You can move mountains if necessary, a trait that surprises those who know only your gentle, nurturing side. It amazes some people that such different qualities can co-exist in someone. Those people (who obviously don't know you well) often underestimate you. Though this is maddening, it does allow you to work quietly under their radar, undisturbed, until you are ready to unveil your achievements to the world.

In the end, this will be one of those landmark years where much of what needs to get settled does. It will allow you to set the foundation for a much bigger personal era due. Dear Pisces, with so much significant development in store, you can welcome 2002 with open arms.

Pluto and Saturn: The Roots of Your Current Situation

During the last few months of 2001, you may have felt you were walking a tightrope between exquisite success and total disaster. Those kinds of high profile, risk-filled situations often occur during a Pluto transit. Something you've worked hard to create may seem threatened; unless you come up with answers, you could have a lot to lose. Focus on the problem and stay calm. You can make difficult situations work to your favor, as Pisces often do. All you have to do is show a strong, honest effort and plenty of concentration.

First of all, don't worry about falling over. Everyone makes mistakes. If you do, just get right back up again — chances are any mistakes you make at this time won't be too terrible. This transit is more about persistence and patience than about being correct all the time. At least you'll know what doesn't work-that could be as valuable as knowing what does work. The key to 2002 is to make creative yet practical decisions, all the while keeping your nerves under control.

The reason that Pluto's a bit of a problem here is that this planet has a tendency to pick on the one area in our lives that we think we can't live without. Saturn, now in a difficult aspect to Pluto, tests structures of all kinds. Looking at your horoscope, the current tension appears to be centered on your profession, but it could relate to just about any part of your life.

What's necessary now is to reinvent and re-launch your-self on several fronts. If you feel there is a part of life that has become moot, you can dismantle it. However, the year's main focus is about standing up and fighting for what you believe in. You must revive the structures and relationships you built that have stood the test of time, and remodel them to be more in tune with your present goals. Don't think you can make a half-hearted effort; Pluto will tolerate nothing less than total, all-out commitment.

What makes this a bit harder than usual is that Saturn has been in a confrontation with Pluto since August 2001; their long-standing row will continue into the first half of this year. After Saturn and Pluto tangle with each other a third and final time on May 25, 2002, tensions will fade. Life should start to feel lighter, and less intense.

Pluto does have one sterling quality that you might want to keep in mind as you struggle along. Just when we think we can't swim against the current any longer, just at the eleventh hour, Pluto will bring a powerful surge of energy. Pluto will always give you the chance to stage a startling comeback. Pluto, symbolized by the Phoenix rising from the ashes, is a master at transformation — they don't call this planet the planet of rebirth for nothing. This planet's powers can change a situation radically, even ones that we describe as "against all odds." When Pluto reaches 15 degrees of any sign, as he is now, he reaches the height of his power. To get the process of change started, you need to show the universe your intention to surmount the odds. It's funny how courage and determination attracts all the right energy.

The Golden Nuggets In Your Chart

There are always a few golden nuggets of outstanding luck tucked into a horoscope. Your chart is no exception.

While you have two of the toughest possible planetary aspects (with both Pluto and Saturn in angry angles to your Sun) you also have two of the most beautifully benefic aspects. Jupiter, the good fortune planet, reaches a perfect angle to your natal Sun, and in the third quarter of 2002 sends two special beams to transiting Pluto, sure to light your tenth house of career honors. (We will go into detail about that lucky energy later.)

Let's continue our discussion about the vital balance you need to strike between innovation / imagination / creativity and stability/practicality / financial prudence. These areas come under the domain of two special VIP planets, Neptune, the planet of inspiration (and your ruler), and Saturn, planet of success achieved through patience, hard work and practical applications. Interestingly, Neptune and Saturn will have a conversation on your behalf, a rare event to occur on two occasions this year.

Saturn and Neptune have very different functions. Saturn creates structure, organization, stability and control. This planet represents the antithesis of chaos. It has a constricting influence, but one that allows us to focus on the topic at hand. Neptune, a highly conceptual, creative planet, does not like barriers and will erode them with its waters. Neptune's instinct is to merge everything it touches into one, large universal form. The problem is that Neptune's penchant for lack of structure can make life chaotic and almost too filled with possibility. That's why Saturn's visit to Neptune in 2002 will be so useful – you will get the best of both planets' qualities. In effect, Saturn will provide Neptune with standards and disciplined creativity. Watch two dates when this should be evident: January 23 and April 1.

Later Saturn will meet with Uranus and increase your already legendary intuition. As mentioned earlier, these will act as a great protection to you this year. Check August 21 and December 16.

Looking Ahead to 2003

To understand how pivotal a year 2002 will be, you need to see it in the context of what's coming down the pike in the next eight years. These are exciting, massive never-before-seen changes, set to start in 2003 when Uranus, (ruling innovation and change) moves into your sign for the first time in your life, set to stay for seven years. Uranus takes 84 years to circle the Sun, and has not been in Pisces since you were born (unless you are a grandma, but you would have been very little when this happened).

Uranus will put you in the center of all that is cutting edge in society-in the humanities, the arts, fashion, literature, journalism, politics, science and technology. You may soon be cast in a leadership role in one of these areas. During these seven years, you may become very well known in your field — even famous, world-wide.

2002 should be the year to lay the foundation and create a framework for your future. Once Uranus settles into Pisces, from 2003 − 2010, it will usher in a period like none you have ever experienced — quite a noisy one, with plenty of people and commotion. Plot your course now, while you have a quiet chance to think. Later, you will barely have time to catch your breath!

Mars Activates Your Personal Life

Let's return to *this* year, 2002. A study of Mars' path over the next twelve months can reveal a great deal about where your energy will go.

Mars will start the year in your sign, Pisces, giving you a wonderful jumpstart. This will allow you to act decisively from day one. Projects started prior to January 18 will develop beautifully, and show a far greater chance of success than normal. The progress you make during this critical period will light the way to your future.

You might want to jot down the key projects, relationships and decisions you were involved with from December 2001 through first three weeks of January 2002, and track your progress in those areas. Even you will be impressed! Of course, you have to apply yourself to see the benefits of any astrologic cycle. If you do so as this year begins, you'll be glad!

After that, Mars will spend months moving through the lower quadrants of your horoscope. This suggests that your personal life will get much-needed attention. Watch these areas for opportunities and growth: personal finances, relationships with relatives, pregnancy, and children. Also, there will be emphasis on your residence (with possibly a move or renovation in the works) and very strong concentration on rejuvenating your health and fitness. Finally, you will also find more time for creative hobbies and expressions.

You may look at this list and laugh — when have you had time to focus on any of these areas? You worked extremely hard on your career or in some community effort in 2001, and probably sorely neglected your personal life. In 2002, you will be able to restore balance to your life. Mars will move with exceptional swiftness, and will only briefly touch each area before moving on. When opportunity strikes, be ready to grab it!

Expect Sudden Shifts in Career and Home

For any number of reasons, your career and / or your home area have demanded a great deal of energy of late. This trend continues into 2002. You have had to concentrate to keep your wits about you; it's been tempting to cave in to the many obstacles that challenge you. This will continue to be a big part of the learning process underway now. There is a difference over last year, however, in that you are accustomed to the kinds of challenges you will face. You have developed effective coping mechanisms, and will begin to see some progress.

If your birthday falls the middle of your sign, from March 3 – March 9, you really feel the stresses and strains of Pluto's opposition to Saturn — but you will also have the most to show for your efforts. Those lucky Pisces with February birthdays have already done their main tour of duty. Some transitions have already taken place, and this year should turn out to be much easier. Saturn is moving unusually rapidly this year, and will touch every March-born Pisces.

Career Aim: Develop Authority

This year, you will need to establish yourself. Prove that you are on top of your game. Show higher-ups how serious you are about reaching your potential. Although Pluto is applying so much pressure, he will also bring you influential people. They will become mentors and advocates, and will go out of their way to help you.

During the course of the year, you will also need to reconfigure your lifestyle. It's time to reassess whether you want stay in your current hometown. If so, you will need to decide how to establish more stability there, perhaps by buying your apartment (as one of many possibilities). If your current residence or locale does not offer enough opportunity (or the right opportunity), you may toy with the idea of relocation. (We will talk more about your don estic situation in a second, after I discuss your career outlook.)

Concerning your work life, one higher up (symbolized by Pluto) doesn't seem convinced that you would be able to handle a job you are up for. This will take a bit of an image overhaul. You may have to re-gauge your thinking and approach. Maybe it's time to take the advice of an expert who can help you accomplish these ends.

The biggest change you need to make is mental. It's time to think bigger and broader than you are now. Think back to what you were doing last year, between February and September 2001, and the events that flowed from the eclipse on December 14, 2001. If you worked hard to get ahead, by the time that recent December 14 eclipse came, you had already forged the path. Your future began to take shape.

December 2002: Career Accolades

As mentioned earlier, your chart is one of extremes. On one hand, you have some of the stiffest pressures imaginable; on the other, you are likely to get the most fortunate breaks possible. The sweet news will come due to a rare meeting of Jupiter to Pluto in the last quarter of the year, as mentioned.

A meeting between Jupiter and Pluto always spells success. Jupiter is the planet of good fortune and Pluto is the planet of transformation. When together, Pluto expands Jupiter's goodness to an umpteenth degree. These two planets' fantastic vibration works for business matters.

Your chart almost guarantees it. Circle these dates: October 27 and December 18.

Use these dates to start a new business, to re-launch an old one, to sign important papers or make key presentations. October 27 is a Sunday; if you can't use the exact date, use the few dates leading to it. The dynamic created on October 27 is slightly stronger than on December 18, as Jupiter is retrograde by then. I am splitting hairs here-both are rare, fantastic, five star days!

Eclipses in Your Career Houses: May 25 and December 4

An eclipse is like an ignition switch for change. We keep an eye on them for major, sometimes out-of-the-blue developments. There are two more eclipses due in your tenth house of fame and honors in 2002.

The first will arrive as a full moon lunar eclipse on May 25, 2002. This eclipse coincides with the third a final clash between Saturn and Pluto, so emotions will be running high. It could be a trying time.

What seems to be difficult at this late May eclipse is not your job — you seem to be doing fine there. Rather, home-related responsibilities seem to weigh on you this time. With both areas of your life on fire, you will wonder which to attend to first. I am exaggerating, of course, to make a point-but you see the picture. Both family and your adoring public / client / boss want your full attention. They key is to figure out how to divide your attention, and to satisfy both. This won't be easy. Keep your schedule clear and light. Your situation will be further complicated by the surprise departure of a female executive.

A more upbeat development in your career is due to arrive on December 4, 2002, with the new moon solar eclipse. This suggests the likelihood of a fresh start, and interesting new opportunities.

In many ways, December will be a key month that will light the way well into your next new year. On another level, both the Sun and Jupiter will be in what astrologers call "mutual reception." This is an uncommon, sparkling configuration where both heavenly bodies work to support one another's powers in a very keen, giving way — much as the meeting of Jupiter and Pluto did for you. It looks like your work will be so superb, your good reputation will forever precede you! The helium balloon is lifting you still higher. How gratifying! What a way to end 2002, dear Pisces!

Need a Raise?

There are two perfect times of the year to gather up your courage, march into your boss' office, and ask for a raise. (Or, to take that call from a headhunter.) Remember, the following dates are beneficial for raising earned income — not winning a prize. Won't it feel great to have such a tangible show of appreciation?

The first moment to strike will be at the new moon in your second house, due April 12, and during the work week that follows (April 15 – 19). If you are alert, you can leave the month of April a lot richer than when you entered it!

Another fabulous day for financial news should be when Jupiter aligns with Mars on July 2 – 3. You will be golden, so speak up and ask for more than you think you can ever get!

Jupiter On The Job

This year would be a superb year to update career skills. The scope of your job description will apparently expand. You will also probably see improved conditions in the work place, perhaps with brighter quarters or new equipment.

The part of the chart influenced here, the sixth house, describes day-to-day work experiences, organization skills / methods, and relationships with coworkers and underlings. All should improve.

Jupiter's move into this house suggests that business is about to be very good, indeed. If you are self-employed, the phone should ring with orders, and the "ca-ching!" of cash registers will be music to your ears. Even if you work for someone else, you will see an increase in activity the likes of which you haven't seen in a long while. You will need to keep track of details if you want to keep up.

In the latter regard, you will finally be able to hire temporary help or even some full time workers. If you are a manager, ask your boss when you will be authorized to add staff — you may be surprised with the answer you receive (sooner than you thought!). Jupiter's placement in the sixth house will create a superb dynamic for this. Applicants will be well qualified and new hires will be compatible to the existing team. This same trend will help you in a personal realm too, and may answer a need for a responsible babysitter or housekeeper.

With phones ringing off the hook, and business due for an upturn, there is only one danger — you will be tempted to go into overdrive. So, from August on, pace yourself, or you may find yourself practically living at the office! Don't overdo it!

In closing, the actual day-to-day job process won't be nearly as arduous as it was last year. This may be an unexpected gain-and a welcome one at that!

Do you want to launch a self-promotion or advertising / publicity campaign, or a new website? Do so in the two weeks that follow the new moon on May 12. Another special date: communication efforts sparkle on June 3.

Want a Pet?

One area of your chart that will glow, from August 2002 – August 2003, is the area that rules domestic pets. Have you been thinking of getting a little creature for the family? Recently on TV, an expert on life goals said that many families will make it their aim to find the right pet in 2002. If that is relevant to you, you could not wish for a better time to go to look for a new pet.

Start with a trip to the pet store; talk to the owner. Read up on various pedigrees of dogs and cats. Ask friends about their experiences with particular animals. Pets teach children responsibility, the value of routine, and the importance of nurturing another creature. They offer to owners of all ages physical and psychological health benefits too numerous to list.

If you already have a pet, you may find ways to enjoy him more. If ever there were a "Year of the Pet" for you, it's 2002. Just remember, your nearly thirteen-month period highlighting this trend begins on August 1.

A Closer Look at Home and Hearth

All Pisces will reassess their domestic arrangements this year, not only because of the presence of Saturn in

Gemini, but also due to a series of eclipses in Gemini and Sagittarius later in the year — May and June — big months — will bring more energy to the very same sector.

Currently, with Saturn in your fourth house of the home until June 2003, your space will seem too small, too dark, or sorely lacking in closet space. Your home may feel like a burden; perhaps there are too many projects to be done, or the mortgage payments are too high. In short, there is something frustrating about where you live, or what you need to do there.

Saturn does add a serious element of strenuous effort. You might have to work hard to afford your new space; your chart suggests that to do so will be well worth the effort. This planet's position suggests you may be setting up a situation that will become more stable, where you will live for twenty years or more.

If you are unhappy with your current quarters, 2002 will be the year you begin to look at options. It is not likely you will find answers immediately — not until June 2003 or beyond. You might as well start gathering information. You never know.

Perhaps you *already* made a big decision about your residence last year, when there was so much planetary energy encouraging you to do so. Perhaps you chose to lease your first apartment or to buy your first house or condo. If not, you will be able to accomplish that goal, but you will need to exercise a bit more patience this year. Saturn's presence suggests slower-than-usual progress.

The spring (in northern latitudes) will mark your best moment of the year to act on home-related matters. To that end, watch April 13 through May 19, when you should hear news and be able to make decisions, prompted by Mars' visit to your home sector.

Speaking of home, maybe you should invite people over! A party would be special indeed if thrown on Friday, May 10. We'll discuss that further under the section on romance. Alternatively, May 10 would also be a terrific day to buy an elegant piece of furniture or some other addition. It's a four-star day.

Domestic issues or real estate transactions may become a focus at or around the eclipse on June 10. (Check the two weeks that follow for activity.) Eclipses bring opportunities and surprises — not all pleasant. Be ready to give this area all the time it needs. Keep your schedule light.

Finally, a wonderful date — perhaps the best of the year — for buying or selling a home would be when Jupiter sends chocolates to both the Sun and Mercury, on July 20.

The fact that these planets will converse in Gemini indicates situations that arise now will allow for flexibility and negotiation. Don't view anything as dyed in the wool. There could be some way to mold the situation to fit your needs.

One young Pisces who lives in a new building in one of Manhattan's most desirable neighborhoods reported last week that she was able to convince her landlord to lower her rent by $300 a month. (She is quite persuasive.) She explained to him that she was trying to get her roommates to stay put, and that they were still showing signs of resistance. They seemed determined to move. A bit taken back by her moxie, her landlord pointed out that she wasn't even on the lease. She smiled and said, "Ah, now you are getting to see how savvy I am in business matters! Do you think I am crazy enough to sign a lease with my friends? Obviously you see they aren't very reliable! But if they go, I go." Charmed by her sense of humor and the glint in her eye, her landlord caved to her plea for rent reduction. This is unheard of in New York City! Dear Pisces, as you see, no domestic issue is set in stone with Saturn in a mutable sign like Gemini!

Gemini is the sign of twins (a "twosome" sign), so let's look at other manifestations of this aspect. Some Pisces readers may consider a second residence or a summer-house rental this year. Others may face a decision between two equally satisfactory options for a property sale or rental agreement. This is an exciting trend, meant to help you set down roots and sleep with the comfort of knowing your living situation will soon be more secure.

It could also be that the people with whom you share your space will drive you a little nuts. Whatever happens, patience is required. Unfortunately, I don't see a major change for the better on the residential front until June 2003. Try to deal with your present situation as it is, even if not ideal. Something infinitely better will present itself in the second half of the year. These conditions will be more easily sorted out when Saturn takes its leave from your fourth house.

Helping An Elderly Relative? Bless You!

For some Pisces, this aspect will not bring about a focus on property. Instead, there may be a concern about an elderly relative, perhaps a parent. This may be the year that you go out of your way to help someone get special care. The fourth house not only rules your residence, but your relationship with family members, too — particularly parents. Although it may be a big responsibility, there would be so many positive outcomes if you lend a hand. Know that this person will be grateful, even though he or she may be a little cranky at times. (That's Saturn's influence.) Even if you don't hear it from him or her, your relative will love you ten times over for taking the time.

Love Glitters

Lucky you. Jupiter, the planet of good fortune, will soon be firmly ensconced in your fifth house of true love, pregnancy / children, and self-expression / creativity. You are in for an outstanding period of love and leisure. This is the happy part of your outlook, sure to give you a boost in 2002. This comes as proof positive that the cosmos wants you to enjoy life to the fullest. No one expects only work and responsibility from you!

If you are single, perhaps you met your soul mate last year, and are well on your way to a more established relationship. With Jupiter, the planet of exceptional growth and happiness, due to pass through your fifth house, it's possible that a love interest may be on the fast track. A relationship could move rapidly through all the traditional stages, from courtship to engagement, marriage and even pregnancy, in record time — for those who are ready. If you are in love, there seems to be no reason to delay an exchange of rings.

Jupiter first entered this house in July 2001. If you felt that the past six months promised much but delivered little, you may be right. Jupiter's power was hampered by other planetary movements, and then went retrograde on November 2001. (It's as if, after a valiant attempt to help you despite currents working against your favor, Jupiter got all tuckered out, gave up and went to sleep.)

Well, fortunate Jupiter will jump out of bed with a start on March 1. When this happens — watch out! The dazzling romantic and social phase that was promised last year (so close and yet so far!) will roll your way. Jupiter has the power to lift your spirits like never before!

All Pisces, of any status and of every age, will be included in a seven-month period of stellar social and romantic activity. This is a huge trend, and one you will enjoy to the hilt. If you are single, love may tip toe up to you and bite you when you aren't looking. When love bites, everything changes!

From March 1 through July 31, 2002 all the activities ruled by your fifth house — romance, creativity, children, and fun — should take on a wonderful vitality.

For one thing, you should be able to find more quality time for yourself. You may even begin indulge in a few of life's luxuries. Buy new clothes, book a spa treatment, or get tickets to a show. You may get invited to a sparkling A-list party — why not have one yourself! Your favorite hobbies should get a boost — maybe it's even time to find some new ones. These months are there to take advantage of all that life has to offer. If you have always wanted to live life large (and can afford to), this would be the time to indulge, dear Pisces.

If you are married, you may decide to get pregnant. If you already have children, you'll find a way to spend more fun time together; maybe you'll plan a memorable family vacation. You may make some other special plans for kids — perhaps a fun camp or special lessons. Doing so would make you so happy right now. If you have older children, you will be able to get especially close. A child may make you very proud indeed. An older child may get into his college of choice.

These are very encouraging vibrations. If you in the middle of a divorce and worry about your children's

welfare, your chart suggests that they are supremely protected. Perhaps you don't have to worry quite so much.

If you have had difficulty conceiving a baby, you may
be comforted to know that the ancients wrote that Jupiter
is "exalted" in Cancer (where it is in the beginning of the
year), meaning it is especially "happy" in this sign. Should
you redouble your efforts to find a specialist during the first
seven months of the year, you would have strong chances to
get pregnant. Those who have been frustrated with the red
tape of adoption should find that easier now, too.

There is no doubt that the universe will be on a sympathetic mission to bring balance to your life, and will
reward you with gentle pleasures. Expect your magical
period to begin almost immediately. Jupiter remains in
this fifth sector for seven months in 2002, but you will see
changes only if you help things along. That's how
astrology works best — when you show that you *want* these
things to happen and that you are *ready* to welcome them
into your life. If you are, show your intention, and the
cosmos will take care of the rest.

Romance!

Here are your best days of the year for fun, love, creativity
and pregnancy / birth or enjoyment of children:

June will be a big month. Mars will set off a display of
fabulous fireworks in your house of true love. Pisces is a
romantic sign — this month should surely please you!

For one of your best, most romantic dates of the year,
the award would have to go to July 19, when happy-go-
lucky Jupiter meets with the Sun. Mercury glides with
Jupiter the following day, July 20, suggesting the third
week in July would be superb for a romantic vacation or

cruise. Single Pisces may just meet that special someone. These are the best of the year. Nothing beats them! Circle July 19 and 20!

My favorite runner-up date to the above comes with the new moon on July 10, which sets off two weeks of lively romantic activity. As you see, things won't be dull in July.

For friendship and festive affairs, watch the time near the full moon lunar eclipse, June 24. (It may occur just a little sooner, over the weekend of June 22 – 23 or the following weekend.) An event you attend might be one that combines friends and family — a double-decker of fun.

Earlier in the year, Venus will glide into your sign from February 11 to March 6. This is sure to mark four weeks when your personal magnetism will be at an all time high. This is a great time to buy new clothes or try a new hairstyle — you'll love the results!

When Venus tours your relationship house, interactions with significant others go smoothly. Pisces of any status: Check out the period from May 20 – June 13 for pure fun and romance.

Venus will enliven your committed relationship sector from July 10 to August 6, and will bring on a wonderful phase for those who are attached. It will be hard to beat the incredible heights you reach in July, which rates five stars, hands down.

Giving a Big Party? Mark Friday May 10

Speaking of Venus, she is at her most romantic when in the company of Mars; Mars – Venus contacts are always ultra sexy and filled with passion. These cosmic lovers first meet on May 10, a Friday, in your fourth house of domestic spaces. (The following date is almost as special.) This would be a perfect date for a party or a candlelit dinner for two. The planetary vibrations on this night will be enchanting, with the caveat that you entertain at home, not in a restaurant.

Romantic Travel: Anytime in December

Last year, Mars and Venus were almost never together. Now they can't bear to be apart! This is *very* good news for you. When these two planets link in the midnight sky, they will set off some serious fireworks.

In December these two magical lovers will glide together in the sexy and romantic sign of compatible, water-sign Scorpio, which will bring abundant joy to your love life. If only you could see their step-by-step progress. (Gosh, with all your success at the office, and all the excitement at home, you're going to be on cloud nine all month!)

There's more. Also in December, Venus will communicate with her lover Mars. A glance, a wink, a look is all that is necessary to speak volumes. To say they will be operating on the same wavelength is to put it mildly! They will create beauty that will take your breath away.

Venus and Mars will share this kiss in your long distance travel house. Ring in your next New Year (2003) in a sparkling locale, wrapped in the arms of the one you love. Start planning your dazzling and memorable year-end getaway now, dear Pisces — the 2002 holiday period will turn out so enticing, it could seem like a dream.

Creativity Piques

If you are a Pisces, you know how much you look forward to your creative various projects. Friends say you always seem to have one that's ongoing, albeit a special piece of music or poem, silk-screen art, photography or simply new recipes. You name it, Pisces. You are one of the most creative signs of the zodiac. As the one sign that rules the subconscious, you are able to draw on your emotions and dreams, and apply them masterfully to your self-expressions. You are able to move others with your work.

With Jupiter in your fifth house from January through July, whether you are interested in art, theater or film, music, fiction, photography, sculpture, or dance (again — you name it!), you should consider some focused experimentation. You could forge into new territories of self-expression during the first half of the year.

This is a year to take your creativity seriously. Jupiter's presence suggests that your ideas will have strong profit potential. Many artists hold themselves back from their true passions because they fear penury. No one succeeds without risks. And now Jupiter, as the ruler of your tenth house of fame, may bring your ideas to the attention of many influential people. You certainly seem to have the ability to reach out to masses — there is no reason to hold back.

Radiant Health

So far in this report, we've discussed the vital shifts that will take place, particularly in the areas of career and home. There is a strong chance that the changes that occur within you will be reflected by a change in your appearance.

I am not just referring to a change in hairstyle or a new clothing style, although those are certainly possible. Instead, the changes I am speaking about will go deeper. You may change the foods you eat (or don't eat), the exercise you get, and what you do to relax. The changes you will be manifest won't be cosmetic but structural, yielding far more substantial and long-lasting result than any quick fix could do.

The Year for Medical Solutions

If you suffer from chronic pain or a health problem that needs treatment, you couldn't wish for a better time to seek help. Jupiter will move into your house of health for nearly thirteen months, from August 1, 2002 to August 27, 2003. This is a positive sign that you can finally find a doctor who understands your condition. Jupiter hasn't assisted this part of your chart in over a decade. You have every reason to expect an improvement.

Perhaps you already feel good. None of us would mind increased vitality, peace of mind, and a sleeker look. The week following the new moon on August 8 will be particularly lucky for a first appointment with a medial specialist or fitness professional, or for registration in a weight control group. If you always wanted to lose weight and get fit — and your doctor thinks you should, begin your intensive program either near the new moon on March 13, or near the new moon on August 8.

For best results, start the exercise portion of your program first, right on August 8. Then begin a change in dietary habits two and a half weeks after that new moon, or a day or two after the full moon.

This year, with your two rulers in houses that rule mind, body and spirit, you'll have an optimum year to experience total well-being. (Jupiter will be in your sixth house, and Neptune will remain in your twelfth house.) If peace of mind is your goal, it is within reach. Bless your heart, Pisces, in the end, isn't this what we all want most? As the zodiac's most nurturing sign, you certainly deserve it.

Summary

For pure romance and pleasure, sunny days are ahead. Lucky you, your golden period will last from January until mid-summer. This is a very powerful trend. You should notice substantial changes. If single, vow to make a bigger effort to meet people and to be open to different types than you've dated in the past. You have a rare opportunity to find a true soul mate, and your magnetism will be high in the first quarter. If married, a baby could arrive soon.

Pisces enjoy creative projects. This year such pursuits will exceptionally gratifying and profitable.

In the second half, you will begin to take your physical health more seriously. You will do whatever it takes to increase your fitness and strength.

Finally, complex residential questions seem to defy solutions — but not for long. Keep searching for options. Career is another pressure point, but will bring such success (especially in the year's last three months), all your efforts will prove worthwhile.

Are you ready, dear Pisces? It is a year to make your mark, and moreover to build your launching pad to the years that will change and improve your life forever, when Uranus resides in your signs from 2003 – 2010. 2002 brings on a big task, but no one is more qualified to take it than you!

COSMIC TOOLS

THE PLANETS, THE SUN AND MOON

The Sun

As seen from Earth, the Sun is the brightest star in the universe. It is the center of our solar system, and the vital heart in any horoscope. Without the Sun, there would be no life. The Sun rules your will, your pride, your determination, your heart, health and vitality, the recognition you receive for work well done, your sense of purpose, and motivation for future goals. The Sun is your ego, governing how you see yourself, your self-esteem. This planet also determines how others view you. An essentially masculine force, the Sun also wields influence over the significant men in your life, especially those in positions of authority. This may be your father, your current boyfriend or your husband, a guy-friend, or a male boss or client.

The Sun rules all daylight. In the same way it rules public recognition and self-image by illuminating who we are, the Sun also clarifies the characteristics any planet it touches and reveals truths about that planet. For example, if the Sun and Jupiter communicate in a special configuration, Jupiter's goodness would be illuminated and made even more brilliant by the Sun. Under the nurturing light of the Sun, Jupiter's strengths intensify, as do the benefits it bestows upon us.

The Sun takes one year to move through all twelve constellations (signs) of the zodiac. The Sun guards the heart. It is the ruler of the sign of Leo.

The Moon

The moon drives your deepest feelings, the fine-tuning of your character, your instinct and intuition, your emotions, and your reactions. The moon also rules your private life, especially your home. Since the moon is feminine in nature, it rules your mother and how you perceive her, and does the same for any other important females in your life, including your wife, girlfriend, or a female boss, your grandmother, girlfriend or wife.

If the Sun represents where you are going, the Moon signifies where you've been. More specifically, the moon rules your history, your background, emotional development, and your roots. Your ability to get in touch with your feelings is dictated by planetary aspects to the Moon.

The dynamics surrounding the moon can also indicate the state of your health, especially if you are female. The moon rules the sign of Cancer, the stomach and breasts, and the light of night (obviously, moonlight). The moon, which takes approximately 28 days to orbit the zodiac, spends two to three days in each sign every month.

Every month there is a new moon. Depending where it falls in your horoscope, it shows which areas would be favored for new beginnings. A full moon arrives two weeks after the new moon; depending on where that moon falls in the chart, it could be time to reap the benefits or consequences of earlier actions.

Mercury

This little guy is the mythological messenger, communicating information to one and all. Mercury represents non-emotional, highly rational, objective thought. Its placement in a sign determines that sign's intellectual style. As a quickly moving planet, Mercury is flexible, responsive and adaptable. A big part of Mercury's job is to disburse information; as such it rules perception, language, writing, editing, research, speaking, all kinds of learning experiences and learning styles and the assessment of data. It rules telecommunications, computing, software, electronic gadgets, the postal service, shipping, couriers, and all forms of transportation. This planet has a *lot* of responsibility.

When Mercury retrogrades (something you will read about often on my website, *Astrology Zone*, at www.astrologyzone.com), it scrambles information, causes static and confusion. Its effects are felt universally. Mercury retrograde episodes are highly unreliable to sign contracts, complete important transactions, access accurate information or make big decisions.

The sign and house in which Mercury resides in one's chart reveals a great deal about that person's natural style of gathering and giving out information. Mercury also rules sibling relationships, maps, letters, travel plans, appointments, roadways, vehicles, advertising, publishing, sales, and public relations.

Mercury rules both Gemini and Virgo. Mercury spends about two-three weeks in each sign, but when it retrogrades, which it does three to four times a year, it can stay in one sign as long as ten weeks. Never far from the Sun, it takes about one year to circle the zodiac.

Venus

Venus rules your affections, your heart, love life, and your pleasures, including gifts. This feminine planet also rules beauty, fashion, adornment, and art. The planet of grace makes the world more attractive and fun. There is another thing about Venus that not many people know about: Venus' placement in a chart can also bring strong financial favor and material gain.

Venus is the governess of all that is beautiful. Venus can bring to us opportunities to hear music, eat good food, enjoy a beautiful perfume, appreciate a good wine, or be motivated to see a great art exhibit. Venus can even help you seduce your lover. What a dreary world it would be without Venus!

Venus is alluring, magnetic and receptive. This is one planet that is never aggressive. (Assertiveness would be left to Mars, her cosmic lover; they make a great pair!) Venus is able to get her way by using charm instead of force. Some see this planet as a bit hedonistic; it's true Venus tends not to be deeply thoughtful, ethical or moral. Thinking about consequences is a job left to Saturn. Deciding what is just is left to Jupiter. Cold hard analysis of facts and data is Mercury's job. (The information you get from Mercury is usually quite reliable, because its observations are completely unemotional.)

Like Mercury, Venus stays close to the Sun. It remains in a sign for two to three lovely weeks — unless it retrogrades, in which case it can stay in a sign for as long as five months. This planet typically takes from ten to twelve months to tour all twelve signs, though it can take longer if it retrogrades. Venus is the natural ruler of Taurus and Libra.

Mars

Mars is the planet that energizes other planets or houses of the zodiac. This is an aggressive, assertive, forceful, energetic, courageous, competitive, and daring planet.

This Red Planet governs the whole spectrum of masculine elements, from sex to war. Known as the Warrior planet, Mars is known for its courage, passion, pure strength and stamina. As such, Mars is also famous for its ability (when in harmony) to help you outlast and outdistance adversaries.

Mars governs all sharp instruments, fire, and anything combustible. Mars must be in a harmonious placement to be of help for any endeavor that requires endurance and determination. When its rays are positive, Mars has an ability to lend survival instincts to any situation.

Mars allows you to keep progressing even when the going gets rough. If Mars is too energetic, an emotional outburst could erupt, or there may be danger of a physical accident. If you are looking for a sense of spirit or gusto in just about any endeavor, Mars could provide that.

Mars takes two years to go around the zodiac, and stays in each sign for six or seven weeks. If it retrogrades back and forth in a sign, it can settle in for as many as seven or eight months. It is the natural ruler of Aries, and the co-ruler of Scorpio.

Jupiter

Jupiter is known as the planet of good fortune. It expands opportunity and the benefits within the house it is visiting. This fortunate planet also rules wealth and solid, financial and material gain.

Additionally, Jupiter brings vision, faith, optimism, loyalty, justice, confidence and wisdom. Jupiter paints a broad picture and makes you want to think big.

Think about this: take all the planets in the solar system except the Sun, which is really a star, and put them together. Jupiter is physically larger than all those other planets put together. That's why we call Jupiter the expansive planet. This is the Great Benefactor.

Jupiter allows us to philosophize and find a higher meaning or purpose in the sector it visits. It encourages reflection, study, and the attainment of higher education. Since long-distance travel is a factor of the education sector, having Jupiter in your sign may inspire you to travel far and wide, or much more frequently than usual.

Jupiter is the natural ruler of Sagittarius. This happy planet takes twelve years to circle the zodiac. Each sign gets its blessings for one full year.

Saturn

Saturn is the planet of concentration, permanence, tangible rewards, tenacity, ambition, and productivity. This taskmaster planet also rules caution, delay, constriction, limitation, responsibility, rules and regulations, pain, fear, authority, discipline, control and denial.

Before you say, "Ugh!", consider this: Without Saturn, we would see little or no progress. We live in a tangible world, and Saturn urges us to deal with reality. Without Saturn we would have no gumption, no standards, or controls, no structure — just chaos.

Saturn grabs us by the collar and forces us to confront reality. When Saturn touches a specific area in your chart, that area experiences a kind of slow-down, or freeze.

Saturn is cold and icy. This planet is also considered heavy or leaden.

Saturn, the Great Teacher planet, brings maturity and teaches us the value of patience and sacrifice.

Saturn is the ruler of Capricorn. It rules the base structure of everything, from teeth and bones to the organizational hierarchy of a company. It governs historical, artistic, or archeological artifacts. It takes 29 years to circle the zodiac, and stays in each sign for two and a half years.

Uranus

Uranus rules surprise and all things unexpected. It also rules the future and new technology, including all that is newly invented and all that is unimagined and yet to come. Uranus is the father of electricity.

Innovative, unpredictable, resourceful, imaginative, idiosyncratic and experimental, Uranus also rules creativity and scientific genius. Uranus' job is to break rules and demolish established patterns or structures, creating sudden — even radical — change. Uranus always works in sudden ways, and is called the Great Awakener.

Uranus gives a strong impulse for rebellion, independence, and even shock. Exciting and liberating, Uranus will overturn anything traditional, conventional or orthodox that it deems has outlived its usefulness.

This planet produces quick, liberating results, blending fact with intuition in its quest to discover universal truths. Uranus is considered the higher octave of intellectual Mercury, and is strongly objective and brainy, with no emotional side. Those people with strong Uranian influences in their charts are trailblazers and forerunners in their communities.

Since Uranus also holds sway over social change, it also regulates the global brotherhood of man and all humanitarian concerns, including environmental issues. Uranus rules the Aquarius. Finally, Uranus rules astrology.

This planet stays in a sign for seven years and therefore takes 84 years to circle the zodiac.

Neptune

Neptune is the planet of inspiration. The higher octave of Venus, Neptune brings beauty to a higher, more spiritual level. It also holds sway over dreams, the subconscious, illusions, fantasies and all things magical and enchanting.

Neptune intensifies intuition and teaches us to be deeply compassionate. Neptune often asks us to sacrifice for the greater good or for love of another.

Neptune refines, purifies, and cleanses. Any planet visiting Neptune will come away purer. This planet cannot bear coarseness. Highly sensitive Neptune gets us more in tune with subtlety, and therefore increases the artistic side of one's personality. Neptune rules all visual communication, whether with symbols or gestures, such as photography, film, ballet and other dance arts, music, painting and poetry.

Neptune also rules the sea and all other bodies of water. It governs rain, ice, and liquids of all kinds — including beverages and alcohol. Neptune also rules drugs — both the bad ones, which make us suffer, and the good ones, which make us well.

Neptune is known as the Planet of Mist. It makes us want to escape mundane, everyday reality and to enter a more ideal, heavenly state. It urges us to excel and to exceed boundaries, to reject any and all limitations.

But since Neptune alters reality and clouds our perceptions of it, there are times that Neptune complicates issues and makes it hard to decipher facts. Neptune can make us deceive ourselves (or be deceived by others), or just make us misunderstand or be misunderstood. It rules all that is glamorous and sparkling. Bear in mind that Neptune's visions are not always real. (It's Saturn's job to give us the cold, hard truth.) We need a planet to inspire us. That is Neptune's province.

Neptune is the ruler of Pisces. It takes 146 years to circle the zodiac, with a stay of about fourteen years in each sign.

Pluto

Pluto rules transformation. It is the father of the phoenix as it rises from the ashes, the symbol of rebirth. Pluto governs the act of ultimate survival in the never-ending cycle of beginnings and endings. Pluto's quality as a catalyst for change and metamorphosis cannot be overemphasized.

If its cycle is active in a chart, this planet can aid an individual in triumph over the odds. Pluto intensifies and strengthens any sector or planet it touches. It also rules obsessive behavior, taboos and compulsions, even crisis.

This planet covers many fundamental issues, including life and death, the ultimate transformation of energy. Pluto rules all that is hidden, unseen or buried, including secrets, undercover work (such as detective or spy work), strategic planning, and even the roots of plants or vegetables. It also drives the unearthing or unmasking of whatever has remained concealed.

Pluto takes 246 years to circle the zodiac, with a stay ranging from eleven years to thirty-two years in a sign! The sign of Scorpio is under Pluto's domain.

THE HOUSES:
THE BUILDING BLOCKS OF YOUR LIFE

As each planet works its way through the twelve constellations (which make up the twelve signs of the zodiac), it passes through one of the twelve houses of each of those signs. Each house governs a different area of life, from relationships, marriage, and children, to your career, co-workers, study, travel, and the home — one of them even rules your identity and appearance. At the moment of your birth, the planets were spread out in a specific formation, each one located in a specific house. This pattern made by the planets and their locations, called the "natal horoscope," is nearly as individual to you as your fingerprint.

On your natal horoscope, some houses may have been full, and others empty. (There are eight planets plus the Sun and moon and, as I said, twelve houses, so there are not enough planets to go around.) It makes no difference if you have a few empty ones. Everyone does — at least an empty house doesn't have any difficult planetary energy in it!

Keep in mind that the planets continually move through these houses as they orbit the Sun. A house that is empty in your natal horoscope could be very full today! To know where the planets are at all times, check your forecast on my free website, www.astrologyzone.com.

First House

The first house determines a lot about what makes you unique… what you look like, your personality, your drive, your goals, and your priorities. It covers your ego, natural tendencies, the way you present yourself to the world, your energy, vitality and your deepest desires.

The first house, when viewed along with conditions in the sixth house (more on that one later) also reflects the state of your health and your vitality.

We look to the first house for any new, important trends and cycles. The first house is the hardest house for an astrologer to read, because your desires are so personal! It also rules your strength of will, your individuality and determination.

The first house reveals the sign rising on the horizon at your birth, also called the ascendant sign. The only way you can find out your rising sign is if you cast a natal horoscope chart for the exact date, time and place of your birth. (All charts are converted to Greenwich Mean Time. Astrology is very concerned with mathematical measurements; we convert everyone to the same birth city to create a common denominator.)

The sign on your ascendant is the sign whose characteristics you express naturally. This explains why all those born under the same sun sign are not alike; most of us are actually a combination of the sun sign and the ascendant.

Once you know your ascendant, you should read both your Sun sign and your ascendant sign, whether in forecasts or personality outlines; reading both will give you a more accurate picture.

The first house is ruled by feisty, entrepreneurial, energetic Mars and by the first sign of the zodiac, individualistic Aries.

Second House

The second house rules your earned income, financial obligations and material possessions. Material gains and losses are dictated by this house. You may be interested to learn that it also presides over your sense of security and overall self-confidence.

This house is ruled by the planet of love and finances, Venus, and by the practical and stability-minded Taurus.

Third House

The third house rules your mind and intellect. It reveals how you approach and analyze problems, and how you perceive information. Basically, it drives your overall learning and communicative processes. For example, this house administers skills in writing, editing, speaking, thinking, reading, and conducting research. It covers your ability and desire to learn, and brings study opportunities your way. Under the influence of this house, someone would decide to learn languages or become a teacher. Other endeavors covered here are the drafting of contracts and agreements, presentation of ideas and proposals, and commerce, including sales, marketing, public relations and self-promotion.

This house covers your neighborhood, short-distance trips, and all means of local transportation and shipping.

The third house also regulates fundamental education (nursery school through high school), drives your relationships with siblings, cousins and neighbors and, finally, covers your perception of childhood experiences.

This house is ruled by the intellectual, communicative planet, Mercury, and by the versatile Gemini.

Fourth House

The fourth house covers your home — what it looks like, where it is located, and with whom you share your space. This includes any houseguests or visitors who stop by to visit or to help you with home-improvement projects or for babysitting. It also rules individuals who challenge domestic harmony.

Family life comes under this fourth house, as would all property matters such as the real estate — buying or selling houses, condos, co-operatives, or the leasing of an apartment. This house also rules your parents and your relationship with them, the foundations of your life. Finally, the fourth house indicates the lifestyle you will have much later in life, for the fourth house is a metaphor for the end of the day.

The fourth house is ruled by the sentimental sign of Cancer, and its nurturing Moon.

Fifth House

Your love life, romance, fun, and pleasure are covered in the fifth house, as are your present children, pregnancies, and the birth of new children. This house also rules creativity, new ideas, hobbies and sports. Any leisure activity, from attendance to social events to rest and relaxation come under this house. So do games of chance and finance, from gambling to investment in the stock market.

This house is ruled by creative Leo and our fun-loving, life-creating Sun.

Sixth House

The state of the sixth house indicates your daily routine and the methods you use to get your work done. The cusp of this house describes the nature of your work and the general environment of your workplace. This house also rules people you employ, whether at home or at work.

This house rules the conscious mind and the proactive measures we take to keep our bodies healthy. (Remember, the first house of the horoscope rules health in terms of overall energy level and vitality, so both have to be considered.) Diet, fitness, and exercise are covered in this sixth house, as are checkups and visits to the dentist.

Finally, all domestic pets and small animals come under this house, too.

The sixth house is ruled by intellectual, news-gathering Mercury and by the meticulous and service-oriented sign, Virgo.

Seventh House

The seventh house rules marriage, business partnerships and any serious contractual agreement between two people or entities.

This house holds both the possibility of completion of an agreement or of conflict. Your open enemies and detractors would be covered here, as would your staunchest allies.

This house also manages experts you hire: attorneys, agents or others who represent or collaborate with you.

For most people, the seventh house is most significant as an indication of the status of a marriage partner. This house describes what you need most from your significant other, and the rapport that develops between you.

Please note that romantic love is reflected in the fifth house, but once a commitment is made, that promise moves the relationship to the seventh house. The "contract" made between two people, or two entities, may be written or verbal.

The seventh house is ruled by gentle, refined Venus and by the partnering sign of Libra.

Eighth House

This house is about rebirth, regeneration and the transformation of energy. Joint financial matters also come under the eighth house. (To the ancients, money is a form of concentrated energy.) The financial dealings in this house do not include earned income (that would be covered by the second house), but do cover money you lend and also owe others. Prizes, gifts, inheritances, tax payments and refunds, bonuses, commissions, royalties, child support, alimony, mortgages, credit, loans and venture capitol are the kinds of transactions ruled by the eighth house.

Any time you need money to fund a big idea, your chances for success would all come under this house. This house also would indicate the state of your partner's prosperity.

Gifts and transactions of all kinds are included in this house, and physical love — sex and reproduction — is also included here. (Note that in astrology, the fifth house is love, the seventh house is marriage and the eighth house is sex, all different houses.) Spiritual and highly intuitive or even psychic experiences are often found in this house too (along with the twelfth house). Finally, this house rules endings and things to be discarded. As such, surgery is covered here.

This house is ruled by Mars and co-ruled by catalyst Pluto and by the intense sign Scorpio.

Ninth House

This is the house that encourages us to think big and bold, and to consider the future in the broadest terms. There always seems to be a certain amount of preparation required before one can take full advantage of all that the ninth house has to offer. Long distance travel, international communication, interactions and relationships with foreigners, distant relatives and in-laws, and higher education are the key areas covered by this important house.

It also rules your attitudes and viewpoints on all topics, and your efforts to understand complex issues, including morals and ethics. This house drives discussions on philosophy, religion, publishing, legal and academic matters. It emphasizes the higher mind and mental exploration.

The ninth house is ruled by fortunate Jupiter and by the philosophical and scholarly sign of Sagittarius.

Tenth House

Fame, promotion, honors, career awards and professional opportunities, reputation, kudos from your company and your status in the community are covered by this high-powered house. Located at the Mid-heaven (tip top) point of the horoscope, the cusp of this house (and the first house) indicates your profession and where you excel.

The eighth house also dictates your professional image. This house covers judges, high-level VIPs, and government officials. It is here where such figures are preordained to help you.

The tenth house is ruled by hard-working, serious Saturn and by the hard-working, focused Capricorn.

Eleventh House

Friendships and all your platonic relationships fall in this house, as do memberships in any kind of group or club. Even attendance at a trade show or a theme park — presence in any congregation of people sharing an interest — would constitute an eleventh house activity. In that regard, even casual contacts, associations and networking efforts come in here.

The action in this house can reveal clues about your employer's financial reality. It can show you where you are most likely to make profits. This house governs humanitarian causes and any efforts to correct social ills and injustices.

Finally, this is the magical house of hopes and wishes, where higher aspirations and dreams come true. While that might sound over-blown, just you wait and see when you have an important aspect occur in this house — you may be pleasantly surprised!

The eleventh house is ruled by creative and scientific Uranus and by idiosyncratic Aquarius.

Twelfth House

The twelfth house rules the subconscious mind, dreams, intuition, instinct, and secrets. In fact, it dominates all that's hidden, including activities going on behind the scenes and confidential engagements.

Psychotherapy and psychic phenomena both fall under this house as part of its rule over the subconscious mind. Dynamics acting on this house can heighten our hunches and intuition.

The ancients wrote that "self-undoing," meaning anything we do to undermine ourselves, also comes under this house. It governs of rest, reaching the end of long cycles — and the termination of any and all confinement, such as hospital stays, nursing home residences or even jail sentences.

This is the house we go to to heal ourselves. It also rules self-sacrifice, inner suffering, limitations and secret enemies. Lastly, this house rules charity, especially on a one-on-one basis.

A little known fact is that all large animals come under the domain of the twelfth house.

The twelfth house is ruled by spiritual and self-sacrificing Neptune and by compassionate Pisces.

ABOUT SUSAN MILLER

Susan Miller is an internationally known accredited astrologer, author, and columnist with twenty-five years of experience. She is known especially for her private work to business clients. Her award-winning website, *Astrology Zone* (www.astrologyzone.com) originated in December 1995, and has since become the most loved comprehensive and detailed monthly forecast available in any media. Her site has garnered eight million page views and over one million unique users a month. *Astrology Zone* has also won many awards for content from such respected sources as the *New York Times, Newsweek* and *Yahoo Internet Life*.

Miller writes a monthly horoscope for *Self* and *Teen* magazines and has written countless cover stories for other consumer magazines, both in America and for publications abroad.

She is the author of the critically acclaimed book, *Planets and Possibilities* (Warner Books, 2001), available in hardcover and paperback, which reached #9 on the Barnes & Noble.com best seller book list. She now teaches a free, eight-lesson course on astrology at the Barnes & Noble University online (www.barnesand nobleuniversity.com). Thousands of students have enthusiastically signed up since the recurring course was first introduced in June 2001.

The success of both her website and her book has made Susan Miller a regular television guest. Miller has been on "20/20" with John Stossel, "The View" with Barbara Walters and has made frequent appearances on "CBS Early Show" with Bryant Gumbel.

Susan Miller lives in the city of her birth, New York City, and is the mother of two daughters, Christiane and Diana, who, she says, are the light of her life.

OTHER BOOKS BY SUSAN MILLER

Planets and Possibilities:
Explore the Worlds Beyond Your Sun Sign

The Astrology Book of Days:
An Illustrated Perpetual Calendar